Critical Reflection in Health and Social Care

Critical Reflection in Health and Social Care

Sue White, Jan Fook and Fiona Gardner

Open University Press

Open University Press
McGraw-Hill Education
McGraw-Hill House
Shoppenhangers Road
Maidenhead
Berkshire
England
SL6 2QL

email: enquiries@openup.co.uk
world wide web: www.openup.co.uk

and Two Penn Plaza, New York, NY 10121-2289, USA

First published 2006

A catalogue record of this book is available from the British Library

ISBN-10: 0 335 21878 4 (pb) 0 335 21879 2 (hb)
ISBN-13: 978 0 335 21878 3 (pb) 978 0 335 21879 0 (hb)

Library of Congress Cataloging-in-Publication Data
CIP data applied for

Typeset by RefineCatch Limited, Bungay, Suffolk

Printed and bound by CPI Group (UK) Ltd, Croydon, CR0 4YY

Contents

Contributors

The editors

Sue White is Professor of Health and Social Care at the University of Huddersfield. She has worked as a practitioner, manager, educator and researcher in child health and welfare for over 20 years. Her primary research interest is in ethnographic and discourse-analytic studies of clinical and professional decision-making, and particularly the moral and emotional dimensions of those domains. Her work spans a range of health and social care settings. She has published numerous books and papers in this area. She is the author, with Carolyn Taylor, of *Practising Reflexivity in Health and Welfare: Making Knowledge* (2000). Her last book (with John Stancombe), published in 2003, *Clinical Judgement in the Health and Welfare Professions: Extending the Evidence Base*, is informed by detailed empirical work and focuses on how evidence and formal knowledge are juxtaposed with emotional and moral discourses in practice by clinicians and practitioners in health and welfare.

Jan Fook is Professor in Social Work Studies at the University of Southampton. Until recently she was Professor and Director of the Centre for Professional Development, Faculty of Health Sciences, La Trobe University, Australia. In this role she provides short-course and postgraduate education in critical reflection nationally and internationally. She has over 20 years of experience teaching in social work and welfare programmes. She has published widely in the areas of critical social work, critical reflection and professional practice. Some of her books include: *Radical Casework* (1993); *The Reflective Researcher* (1996); *Breakthroughs in Practice: Social Workers Theorise Critical Moments* (edited with Lindsey Napier (2000); *Social Work: Critical Theory and Practice* (2002).

Fiona Gardner is an established researcher and evaluator in Victoria, Australia. She has published a wide range of evaluation and research reports for such organizations as Arthritis Victoria, St. Luke's, a major human service agency and for a number of government departments. She has also published more than 12 articles and book chapters in both local and international journals, including *Social Work* (United States), *Canadian Journal of Program Evaluation* and *Reflective Practice* (UK). Fiona has a long-term commitment to the provision of accessible education and training and has provided both formal training and short courses for a wide range of health and welfare professionals, including management, supervision, mediation and counselling skills. In her current role at the Centre for Professional Development, she is running workshops primarily on critical reflection for government and non-government agencies as well as contributing to relevant research in the field.

Other contributors

Gurid Aga Askeland is an associate professor at Diakonhjemmet University College, Department of Social Work, Oslo, Norway. She has broad teaching experience, and developed the first programme for distance education in social work in Norway. She has published and co-authored books and articles, some on teaching social work. Over the years she has held several national and international posts and offices, has made a lot of international work contacts and been involved in international projects.

Andy Bilson is Professor of Social Work at the University of Central Lancashire. He is a specialist in systems approaches to organizational change and has an international reputation for the evaluation of children's services. He has carried out numerous projects in the UK, Australia, Europe and central Asia. He has been a senior manager in social services across the UK. He was responsible for research in two local authorities, and Director of the Council of Europe's information centre for children's rights, the Centre for Europe's Children at Glasgow University. Andy is author of a wide range of publications on social care management, policy and research, including editing *Evidence-Based Practice in Social Work*.

Fran Crawford is an Associate Professor at the Department of Social Work and Social Policy at Curtin University in Western Australia. She is a practitioner, teacher and scholar who has published in the areas of cross-cultural work, interpretive research and narrative practice/research. She joined the Curtin faculty in 1982 having worked for ten years in the state welfare service, primarily in the remote Kimberley region. Currently on study leave in the United States and the United Kingdom, she is working on a research project entitled 'Cross-cultural Learning: Negotiating Differences in the Classroom'.

Lynn Froggett is Reader in Psychosocial Welfare at the University of Central Lancashire. She has a social work practice and management background in both mental health and children and families and co-edits the *Journal of Social Work Practice*. Her empirical and theoretical work focuses on psychosocial and psychodynamic approaches to welfare ethics, practice, policy and institutions, and her publications all reflect this interest, particularly *Love, Hate and Welfare: Psychosocial Approaches to Policy and Practice* (2002). Her current research focus is on the role of arts-based community work in health and welfare and on the development of psychosocial and psychosocietal research and evaluation methodologies.

Sue Frost is Pro Vice-Chancellor (Academic Affairs) at the University of Huddersfield. She has a professional background in health visiting and professional leadership. She has also been the National Director of Adult Nursing Education and led a range of work to improve the research and evidence base of professional education. She has a particular interest in narrative approaches, particularly in their role in offering greater understanding of professional practice. Sue has a continued research interest in professional education and is currently conducting inquiry into the career narratives of nurses.

Jennifer Lehmann lectures in Social Work at the Faculty for Regional Development, La Trobe University, Bendigo, Victoria. She has some 30 years' experience as a social work practitioner, manager, consultant and, more recently, as a teacher. Her practice has focused on the delivery of services, predominantly in the field of child and family welfare, and she has been a committed member of rural communities in both South Australia and Victoria. Her interests include the study of organizations and narrative approaches

Marceline Naudi is a social worker by profession. Her practice (in England, Ireland and Malta) has included work with children and young people in care and their families, ex-offenders, homeless people, persons with mental health support needs and survivors of domestic violence. She lectures in Social Work at the University of Malta, having responsibility for anti-oppressive social work practice teaching as well as student placements. She is also active in the issues of women's rights, domestic violence and lesbian and gay rights. Her publications include a contribution on women in Malta for the United Nations Malta Human Development Report (1996), and a contribution on gender and disability as part of the proceedings for a workshop held in 1998.

Bairbre Redmond worked as a senior social worker in the services for those with intellectual disability; she is currently Director of Social Work Training at University College Dublin. Her research interests include an exploration of the issues for families of caring for a disabled child and also the development of better relationships between health service professionals and such families. She has a particular interest in developing new, innovative teaching approaches to professional training and development at university level and she is the author of *Reflection in Action: Reflective Teaching and Learning for Professional Practice* (2004).

Gerhard Riemann is a sociologist and professor of social work at the

University of Bamberg in Germany. His main fields of interest are narrative analyses, biographical research, ethnography, and studies of professional work. He has done research on topics such as mental patients' biographies (based on autobiographical narrative interviews) and the work of social workers in family counselling.

Colin Stuart manages a community-based action-research project in Ottawa. The focus of the research is on the introduction of information technology to marginalized households in the inner city. Prior to this Colin co-taught, with Elizabeth Whitmore, the graduate research methods course at Carleton University School of Social Work as well as a graduate course in evaluation methods for the School of Public Policy and Administration. He has extensive experience internationally, particularly in Africa and Asia, in programme evaluation and management for small and medium-sized non-governmental organizations (NGOs) and cooperatives. Before teaching at Carleton he taught at the Coady International Institute at St Francis Xavier University in Nova Scotia. His publications include numerous handbooks for particular research and evaluation needs of NGOs. He also maintains an active interest in the development of international and local peace teams.

Pauline Sung-Chan is an Associate Professor in Social Work in the Department of Applied Social Sciences at the Hong Kong Polytechnic University, and the Scheme Leader of the Social Work postgraduate programmes. Her major contribution in professional education is to introduce a philosophy of educating reflective practitioners with the vision of pursuing scholarship in practice in Chinese societies. Since the early 1990s, she and her team have endeavoured to educate practical scholars in China through consultancy projects, research studies and establishment of a master's programme in Social Work with Peking University, the first of its kind. With Professor Donald Schon of MIT, Pauline developed a theory in 2000 to explain how experienced social work practitioners acquire new knowledge. Her long-term research interest is to promote partnership between academics and non-profit-making organizations to pioneer the use of collaborative-action research to promote organizational change and generate actionable knowledge. Pauline's academic and recent research interests include organizational learning and change, collaborative-action research, systemic family therapy, practical knowledge development, and educating reflective practitioners.

Carolyn Taylor is Senior Lecturer in the School of Community, Health Sciences and Social Care, University of Salford, UK. She has long experience of teaching on qualifying and post-qualifying social work programmes as well as interdisciplinary master's programmes. She is co-author with Sue White of *Practising Reflexivity in Health and Welfare: Making* Knowledge (2000) and has published various articles on knowledge and reflective practice in health and welfare.

Elizabeth Whitmore is a Professor Emerita at Carleton University, Ottawa, Canada. She taught at Dalhousie University (Nova Scotia) for many years before joining the School of Social Work at Carleton in 1991. She redesigned the graduate research course, using community-based research as a framework, and draws her reflections primarily from that experience, and her research interest in participatory research and evaluation methodology. Her publications include *Understanding and Practicing Participatory Evaluation* (1989) and two co-authored books, *Seeds of fire: Social Development in an Era of Globalism* (2000) and *Globalisation, Social Work and Social Justice* (2005).

Angelina Yuen-Tsang is Professor and Head of the Department of Applied Social Sciences at the Hong Kong Polytechnic University. She has been involved in the development of social work education in the Chinese mainland since the late 1980s. In 1999/2000, the department developed an MA (Social Work in China) programme in collaboration with the Peking University, which was the first 'training of the trainers' programme tailor-made for social work educators in China. The programme is now admitting its forth cohort of students and is instrumental in nurturing a core group of dedicated and competent social work educators who are committed to the furtherance and indigenization of social work education in China. Her research interests are mainly in social support networks and community care, social work education, social work practice in China, and occupational social work. In recent years, her research focus is on the indigenization of social work education and practice in the Chinese mainland. She has been actively involved as a board member of numerous local and international non-governmental organizations, government advisory committees, and professional bodies in Hong Kong, the Chinese mainland and the Asia-Pacific region.

Preface

> [M]ost of our mental and active life is of the immediate coping variety, which is transparent, stable, and grounded in our personal histories. Because it is so immediate, not only do we not see it, we do not see that we do not see it, and this is why so few people have paid any intention to it.
>
> (Varela 1992: 19)

This book is aimed at providing practitioners, educators and researchers in health and welfare with concepts and methods to help them to 'see what they do not see'. There is a growing interest in the improvement of professional practice in health and welfare settings. The policy climate in the Western world during the last decade has fostered an outcome-oriented 'what works?' approach. Codified knowledge in various forms has come to be defined as a safe and secure base for decision-making. Such knowledge is ostensibly insulated from, and uncontaminated by, the contingencies and errors of everyday practice. The efficacy of interventions is clearly crucially important, but an exclusive focus on narrow outcome indicators can lead to a conspicuous neglect of other areas of professional activity. The complex processes by which professionals formulate their understandings have remained seriously underexplored in policy initiatives.

In contrast, the use of critical reflection is becoming increasingly promoted across the professions as one way of ensuring ongoing scrutiny and improved practice skills in the 'swampy lowlands' (Schön 1987: 3) where cookbook knowledge is difficult to apply. This book arises out of the editors' teaching and research experience in professional education, and in particular their experience in the use of critical reflection with a variety of disciplines and professional groups in the health, social care and social work fields. The aim is to present a range of approaches to interrogating practice in such a way that the hidden, tacit, or taken-for-granted aspects may be properly understood and debated. The tacit dimension has tended to be constructed as in some way unknowable. But, it is essential that we consider how it may be opened up for investigation and how professionals may be assisted to develop a critical perspective upon it.

Our aim as editors has been to showcase work, currently taking place internationally, which explores methods through which professionals may be helped to become intrigued by what is known already – that is, by those thoughts and actions that have become so familiar and taken for granted in their everyday practice that they are no longer aware of them. This requires an examination of the qualitative aspects of judgement, and how they sit alongside and invoke 'knowledge' in its traditionally understood, objective and stable sense.

We have left our overview of the various contributions until the end of the book, concentrating instead in the introductory chapter on providing a review of the extensive literature on critical reflection and its antecedents. We hope this will enable readers to follow through their particular interests. We have divided the book into four parts, but wish to note that this classification is somewhat arbitrary and many chapters could be categorized in a number of ways. A defining feature of the field is its capacity to render meaningless tired distinctions between practice, education and research. All are acts of meaning-making in complex domains.

Interdisciplinarity is a key feature of the book. In the contemporary workplace traditional professional boundaries are eroding. Professionals increasingly need to develop skills in working with other disciplines, and to emphasize shared goals within an organization. Most of the contributors to this volume are from a social work or nursing background, where possibly the majority of the current literature is located. However, there is strong editorial commitment to underscore and illustrate the essentially moral and ethical domains of health and welfare practice across a range of professional groups.

The book is targeted at professionals who may believe they already know about or practise critical reflection, but wish to update their knowledge and skills, and also learn new and more complex ways of working with critical reflection. It provides an opportunity for educators to design better curricula, and for professionals to hone their understanding of critical reflection more systematically and rigorously.

We have endeavoured to be critical about critical reflection and to fight off attempts to turn it into another technology of professional surveillance, or reduce it to a set of outcome indicators or learning objectives. Instead we have selected approaches that encourage disciplined self-surveillance. Critical reflection is not an innocent practice; it has transformative potential. By offering the chance to reflect, rethink and re-experience our professional lives as a struggle over competing values, practices and social relations, it goes beyond 'benign introspection' (Woolgar 1988: 22). We have aimed to hold up the promise of transformation, hope and creativity. Critical reflection matters because:

Each agent, wittingly or unwittingly, willy nilly, is a producer and reproducer of objective meaning. Because his actions and works are the product of a modus operandi of which he is not the producer and has no conscious mastery, they contain an 'objective intention' . . . *It is because subjects do not, strictly speaking, know what they are doing that what they do has more meaning than they know.*

(Bourdieu 1977: 79; emphasis added)

Acknowledgements

The editors would like to thank Geraldene Mackay for her painstaking search of the critical reflection literature and Alison Holmes of the Centre for Health and Social Care Research, University of Huddersfield, for her invaluable administrative support throughout the final stages of the preparation of this book.

PART I
Frameworks for Understanding Critical Reflection

1 Critical reflection: a review of contemporary literature and understandings

Jan Fook, Sue White and Fiona Gardner

There has been a burgeoning interest in the ideas of reflective practice and critical reflection over the last few decades (Gould 2004: 13–14). The interest has grown in a number of different professional fields as well as in a number of different countries. This makes for possibly very diverse understandings of what are also complex processes and approaches to learning and research. Moreover, the increasing popularity of reflection and critical reflection places them in danger of being used thoughtlessly and in an undiscerning manner (Loughran 2002). It is therefore important to try to map and make sense of just what critical reflection is, what is involved, how it may be used, what its effects are and how we may 'unsettle' the tendency for it to become formulaic and taken for granted.

In addition, because of the explosion of interest and therefore literature on critical reflection, it is difficult to track developments in the field across different disciplines and professions. This means that although there is increasing tendency for interprofessional work, it may be difficult to develop further critical reflection models, which are actually relevant across professional boundaries (Huotari 2003), and are in addition based on 'state of the art' levels of practice.

This book has been compiled in this spirit. We recognize the current diversity in the field and so we have tried to be inclusive in our understanding of critical reflection. By including contributors from a range of disciplinary and professional backgrounds, it will assist in documenting some of the current uses of critical reflection, and also showcase some of the newer ways it is being used, as well as some of the newer contributions to thinking about it. We thus hope to begin to provide a basis from which continuing interprofessional work and education may develop.

This chapter begins by attempting to review our understandings of critical reflection from literature drawn from different disciplines and professions, and from a range of countries as well. After a review of the types of literature and of the emerging understandings of the idea of critical reflection, the chapter also explores associated terms and ideas. In the last part of the chapter criticisms of critical reflection are reviewed, key issues outlined and suggestions for further directions are made.

A review of current literature

In this section we give an overview of the types of literature in which the ideas of reflective practice and critical reflection may be found. This section also serves as a guide to the parameters of the literature reviewed for this chapter.

The extent of the literature

As stated earlier, there has been an increasing interest in reflective practice and critical reflection over the last few decades. We recognize at the outset that there may be a difference between the idea of reflective practice and critical reflection, and we will discuss this in more detail later in this chapter. Initially, however, we will review the literature concerning both, as they tend to be linked in most discussions. The sheer volume of the literature available attests to the popularity of these ideas. Part of the reason for this is perhaps the variety of fields in which it occurs, among them nursing (e.g Ghaye and Lillyman 2000a), medicine (e.g. Mamede and Schmidt 2004), allied health (e.g. Roberts 2002), social work (e.g. Fook 1996; Gould and Baldwin 2004a; Gould and Taylor 1996; Napier and Fook 2000), law (e.g. Kenny 2004), management and human resources (e.g. Marsick 1987; Reynolds and Vince 2004; Seibert and Daudelin 1999) and of course education and adult education (e.g. Brookfield 1995; Mezirow and associates 1990). Some of this literature attempts to span relevance to health and helping professions more broadly (e.g. Johns 2002; Rolfe *et al.* 2001; Taylor and White 2000). There is also an extensive range of related areas, such as transformative learning (Mezirow 1991) and action research (Reason and Bradbury, 2001), which also utilize the concept of critical reflection as part of a broader process. In the field of social theory, the idea of critical reflection occurs as a feature of 'reflexive modernity' (Beck 1992; Giddens 1991, 1992). Indeed, conducting a literature review has been extraordinarily difficult in what appears to be a messy and complex field in which traditional disciplinary boundaries and shared criteria for academic rigour do not always apply.

The literature falls into at least three different categories based on three broadly different purposes: it may be primarily educational in its focus (as with the bulk of professional practice literature); it may be located in the body of literature on research methodology; or it may be concerned with the development of theoretical frameworks to understand the nature of social life and/or the application of these in education or professional practice (e.g. Kemmis

1998; Quicke 1997). Obviously some literature spans several purposes so this further complicates matters. The literature reviewed in more depth in this chapter is primarily from the educational and professional practice learning traditions, although other relevant literature is referred to where it is needed to make sense of some different usages.

Related literature and popular usages

Conducting a comprehensive and meaningful review is further compounded by the fact that reflection and critical reflection are sometimes conflated with other terms such as 'reflexivity' or 'critical thinking', so that although similar issues may be discussed, this will be done with reference to different literature and different theoretical traditions. This makes comparison and cross-referencing difficult. We will review the more detailed meanings of these terms and their relation to critical reflection further on.

Further compounding the area is that sometimes, perhaps because the terms are so popular, it may be assumed that their meaning is understood and that there is no need to define or articulate a particular usage of them. Indeed, there is a tendency in some literature to tack 'reflections' onto the end of an article or book and in this sense the meaning appears to be simply referring to a further level of thinking about what has occurred before (e.g. Loreman *et al.* 2005). Another feature of this type of usage is when 'reflection' is referred to but there is no explanation of what it means in detail and no reference to other literature on the topic (e.g. McDermott 2002: 205). In line with this practice, many higher education programmes that require students to undertake reflection, or to display reflective ability in their assignments, may not clarify what this means and may not provide students with relevant reference literature. As Issitt (2000) notes from her own study with women practitioners, very few who claimed to be engaged in reflection had actually read anything recently about it. Stark *et al.* (1999) also notes that many individuals may not know what reflective practice is, and in fact reflective practice may even be scarce amongst its advocates!

Popular usages can confuse meanings in other ways. For example, there is a sense in which the 'critical' in critical reflection is taken as meaning 'scoring negative points'. Lovelock and Powell (2004: 189) refer to this as a 'vulgar' usage of the term. Other authors note the tendency to equate reflection with thinking (Brockbank and McGill 1998: 84–5; Parker 1997: 8, 30).

It is interesting that popular and perhaps relatively uninformed understandings of reflective practice and critical reflection have such sway in the field. Perhaps this points to an underlying construction of them as essentially practices which are developed in the 'doing' of them rather than their more formal theorization. Such thinking would of course be consistent in some ways with the approaches themselves, but to privilege 'practical theory' over that derived from other means is not necessarily consistent with all con-ceptualizations of reflective practice and critical reflection.

Types of literature

A great proportion of the literature on reflective practice and critical reflection appears to be geared to use in teaching. Books or articles of this type may be used either by students who are learning about critical reflection or are required to be critically reflective, or by teachers (at school or higher or con-tinuing education levels). These include textbooks for use in a variety of levels of courses (and of course for different professional groups) and articles which are relatively introductory in nature. The content tends to describe the theory and method of reflective practice or critical reflection, presumably for direct application by students or teachers.

Textbooks range from those that might be used by a first-year cohort in a degree or diploma course (e.g. Ghaye and Lillyman 2000a), to advanced undergraduate and continuing education and postgraduate levels. They tend to give a brief overview of reflective practice or critical reflection (this may or may not include a coverage of relevant theories); an outline of a structure or process which may be used (this may include principles regarding the nature of reflection and the contextual requirements for it to be effective); an outline of other methods which may be used; some discussion of different issues which may arise; and often some examples of usage in different settings or experiences of different participants in the learning process. Johns (2002) is a relatively good example of a text which includes most of these.

It is of course necessary to have a range of material to be used at different levels and for different audiences. We do not wish to imply or argue that some books are therefore inherently better than others. And of course it may be possible to use the one set of materials for a range of audiences (depending of course on how it is used). However, these teaching materials do tend to vary in the extent of theorizing and explicit connection with more formal theories of learning, the extent of discussion of issues involved (contextual, social, polit-ical, emotional, cultural), and the depth to which the usage of specific methods is explored. Brookfield (1995) is a good example of a work which explores both practical and theoretical aspects in some depth.

Introductory articles tend quickly to define the idea of reflective practice or critical reflection, include some arguments as to why the approach and process may be useful, and then give a run-down on the chief principles involved (e.g. Kinsella 2001; Roberts 2002).

A second major type of literature is primarily about teaching and learning from critical reflection or reflective practice, written more for the experienced reflector or teacher. This type tends to include edited books with contri-butions on many different aspects and which may be focused on theorizing understandings of critical reflection in more depth. Topics may include different approaches to and models of reflection; different tools and techniques; the use of critical reflection in different settings and for different purposes (e.g. supervision). Sometimes they also include case studies of the use of critical reflection programmes in different settings (e.g. Cross *et al.* 2004), and/or the reporting of experiences in undertaking reflective practice programmes or using reflective practice tools (e.g. Shepherd 2004). Many of the articles in the journal *Reflective Practice* are of these types. Examples of edited books of the above type include Mezirow and associates (1990), Brockbank *et al.* (2002), Reynolds and Vince (2004) and Gould and Baldwin (2004a).

An area that appears to be severely lacking in the literature is empirical research and/or studies which demonstrate an evidence base supporting the practice of reflection (Hargreaves 2004; Ixer 2000; Mamede and Schmidt 2004; Stein 2000). Although we recognize that the idea of what constitutes research is contested in reflective circles, in this section we are characterizing empirical research (for the purposes of this chapter only) as that which is not conducted primarily by the researcher on the researcher's own experience. This therefore excludes research conducted using methods such as personal reflections, authoethnographical or self-study methods. We do not wish to suggest that these types of research are inferior, but, in terms of learning more about the outcomes of reflection, we take the position that empirical methods (including both qualitative and quantitative approaches) are also required. We have also excluded those studies primarily conducted as an evaluation of a particular teaching programme, and articles which document the use of reflection or critical reflection as a research method. So for the purposes of this review, we are confining our attention to studies that seek to establish the nature of reflection, reflective changes, and the outcomes of the reflective learning process by non-self-study methods.

We found 37 articles or book chapters which appeared to fit this category, that is, claimed to report the results of empirical research studies on reflection or critical reflection. Most of these did not appear to build on the work of each other, and were in the main qualitative studies of a small group of students (usually the students from the classes which the researcher(s) taught). There were three studies which claimed to be experimental in design (Leung and Kember 2003; Lowe and Kerr 1998; Rees *et al.* 2005). Broadly, the qualitative studies tended to fall into two main categories: those which analysed interviews with participants (e.g. Antonacopoulou 2004; Issitt 2000; Lee and Loughran 2000; O'Connor *et al.* 2003); and those which analysed students' reflective written textual material obtained from a formal programme of study, for example, assignments and journals (Jennings 1992; Tsang 2003), email discussions (Bean and Stevens 2002; Whipp 2003) and critical incidents (Griffen 2003; Smith 1998). Some studies of course combine a variety of methods (e.g. Pedro 2005). Studies focus on a variety of aspects of reflection, ranging from the broad – for example, the theories about practice that emerge (Jennings 1992), the sorts of changes students make in a reflective process (Hamlin 2004), the experience of reflection (Wong *et al.* 2001), issues of importance to students (Smith 1998) and developing models of reflection (Ixer 2000; Mamede and Schmidt 2004) – to the more specific, for example, changes in levels of thinking identified (Smith 1998; Whipp 2003; Thorpe 2004), student perceptions of specific tools (Langer 2002) and of course evaluations of specific reflective programmes (Pololi *et al.* 2001). Because the tools for and approaches to reflection, as well as the data analysed, varied markedly in each case, it is impossible to build up a composite picture of the nature and effectiveness of reflective teaching and learning strategies. This underscores one of the major current issues facing professional educators – how to ensure the continued quality development of critically reflective methods in an area of such diversity and complexity.

The concepts of reflection, reflective practice and critical reflection

Development of the ideas

The idea of critical reflection has ancient origins. Socrates, for example, stressed the centrality of critical self-examination, or living the 'examined life', for ethical, compassionate, humane engagement with the world and its moral dilemmas (Nussbaum 1997). The recent resurgence in interest may then be seen as a *return* to reflection after centuries of searching for stable truths and foundational knowledge. Most contemporary literature refers to the work of Donald Schön (e.g. Argyris and Schön 1974; Schön 1983, 1987), as being formative in their development of the idea of reflective practice, particularly for its application in professional practice learning. Some authors also acknowledge the work of Dewey (1916, 1933) as being pivotal to the development of our current notions of reflection (Mezirow and associates 1990; Redmond 2004). Of course, as the ideas have developed, and different people have engaged in successive reworkings of the concepts using and adding newer theoretical frameworks, it is possible to identify several different approaches. These may firstly be categorized based on the theorists used. Redmond (2004), for instance, traces the major influences on her work to Dewey, Habermas, Freire, Brookfield, Kelly, Polanyi and Boud. She argues that there is an interconnection between their work (all are concerned with metalearning and perspective transformation) and that it can be demonstrated that there is a clear chonological progression linking them (Redmond 2004: 26).

Using a more explicitly philosophical framework, Bleakley (1999: 328) posits that there are four main epistemologies involved, which can be used to develop the idea of reflective practice into a 'holistic reflexivity'. These are the technical rational (criticized by Schön), humanistic emancipatory (Schön), postmodern deconstructive (Usher) and radical phenomenological (post Heidegger).

In yet a third way of characterizing the different theoretical influences, Ixer (2000: 21) poses three different paradigms: 'reflection in action' (pragmatists Mead, Dewey and Schön); 'reflection as social process' (Kant and Kemmis); and 'reflection as dialogue' (Habermas and Freire). Ixer (2000) and others (Issitt 1999) have more recently attempted to draw up a framework for 'anti-oppressive' and feminist (Issitt 2000) reflective practice.

The above formulations appear to downplay to some extent the role of critical theory and perspectives in the development of the idea of critical reflection (although of course the works of Habermas and Freire are frequently cited as providing theoretical antecedents to current understandings). A more focused formulation of critical theory contributions to reflection is clearly evident and well articulated in the extensive work of Brookfield (1995, 2000) and Mezirow (2000; see also Mezirow and associates 1990) writing from the critical education tradition. In his writing, Brookfield (1995: 207–27) clearly distinguishes between the traditions inherent in the reflective practice literature, critical pedagogy, and adult education more broadly. There have also been more recent attempts to develop discourse analysis (Ellermann 1998; Taylor and White 2000; White and Stancombe 2003) and postmodern thinking in reflective practice (Parker 1997; Lesnick 2005) and of course to combine postmodern and critical theories as a basis for critical reflection (e.g. Fook 1999a; Grace 1997). The work of Fook (2002) develops these in relation to critical reflection within social work practice and also draws parallels between critical reflection and deconstruction/reconstruction. In fact, from a critical perspective (although this term of course has multiple usages) the use of critical theory, and its development for use in critical reflection, is probably one of the major defining features of critical reflection, and therefore one of the major factors which may differentiate it from reflective practice. In this sense, critical reflection involves social and political analyses which enable transformative changes, whereas reflection may remain at the level of relatively undisruptive changes in techniques or superficial thinking.

It is posited by some writers (e.g. Taylor and White 2000) that central to the notion of the critical reflection is an understanding of the capacity of language to construct the world and way we experience it. This is often known in social theory and philosophy as the 'linguistic turn' (e.g. Rorty 1992). The capacity for language to construct what it purports to describe has been theorized and researched empirically on a number of levels. Work in this area is often known generally as discourse analysis. The term 'discourse analysis' is often used as though it related to just one conceptual framework. However, it can mean a number of things. It may refer to ways of thinking about particular phenomena, such as terminal illness, childhood, bereavement, gender, race, the family, or mental health, and how these reflect particular historical, political and/or moral positions. So, at a societal level, or macro-discursive level, we can see how language produces dominant ideas, or 'forms of thought', or 'regimes of truth' (e.g. Foucault 1980) which are taken for granted but are in fact historically contingent. For example, in contemporary Western societies there are certain dominant notions about how mothers should properly behave towards their children. These are linked to specific forms of knowledge associated with attachment theory, for example. Critical reflection at this level is about understanding the technologies of power, language and practice that produce and legitimate forms of moral and political regulation. To reflect critically at this level, practitioners need to understand the historically contingent nature of their ideas. The familiar theories and practices need somehow to be 'made strange', so that they can be properly interrogated and so that people can build their own ethics out of this analytic process. That is, they can develop the capacity to resist and transgress.

However, discourse may also refer to language used in interactions between people, or written words (e.g. casefiles). At this interactional level we may look at how facts get assembled to do professional work, or how questions get asked. We may attend to how some phrases seem to be more powerful than others (Taylor and White 2000). We need to look at the work the talk does. This is often called the 'performative' nature of language. These kinds of distinctions have led a number of commentators to subclassify discourse analysis. For example, Walker (1988) uses upper and lower case to differentiate between 'discourse' as talk in action and 'Discourse' as a body of knowledge. Contributors to the present book have used both of these meanings. For the purposes of critical reflection, it is important to understand that these forms of discourse interact with each other. Discourses (forms of thought and knowledge, which may be, for example, theories or political ideas) are reproduced within discourse (talk) at 'the point of its articulation' (Walker 1988: 55). Therefore, when analysing any conversation it should be possible to look for Discourse(s) and also to examine how words are assembled and used for a particular audience and for a particular effect (Miller 1994).

More recently there is a beginning recognition of the spiritual and existential aspects of reflective practice (e.g. Ghaye 2004), and therefore there are related attempts to introduce approaches such as Buddhist and Native American lore in developing it further (Johns 2005; Varela 1999). As Betts (2004) points out, reflective practice can be aligned with theological, therapeutic or political benefits. In this sense, theorists of reflective practice may conceivably draw upon any theories which develop these aspects of the reflective experience. As Issitt (2000:121) notes, 'the flexibility of reflective practice leaves it open to appropriation by different stakeholders' and presumably different theoreticians.

Defining reflection, reflective practice and critical reflection

Given that a plethora of different theories may be drawn upon to develop the ideas of reflective practice and critical reflection, it is possible, to some extent, to trace different usages to the different theories or paradigms which underpin their usage. All attempts to define any phenomenon will of course vary depending on the aspects emphasized, such as the nature of the process, its purposes and motivating features. As Ghaye and Lillyman (2000c: xv) so aptly state: 'reflective practice stands for a collection of intentions, processes and outcomes'. And of course particular processes and outcomes may not necessarily be consistent with particular intentions.

A review of some of the most oft-quoted definitions of reflection or reflective practice will indicate some of these variations. Some commonly quoted definitions are as follows:

> the active, persistent and careful consideration of any belief or supposed form of knowledge in the light of the grounds that support it and the further conclusion to which it tends.
>
> (Dewey 1933: 9)

> a generic term for those intellectual and affective activities in which individuals engage to explore their experiences in order to lead to new understandings and appreciation.
>
> (Boud et al. 1984: 19)

> the process of internally examining and exploring an issue of concern, triggered by an experience, which creates and clarifies meaning in terms of self, and which results in a changed conceptual perspective.
>
> (Boyd and Fales 1983: 100)

As can be seen, these definitions vary depending on what aspects of learning are emphasized (cognitive, emotional, meaning, social, cultural or political), the motivating factors and the degree to which the process is systematically organized, the extent to which they specify the actual processes involved, and the inclusion of change. Stein (2000: 1) puts most of these aspects together nicely:

> Critical reflection is the process by which adults identify the assumptions govern-
> ing their actions, locate the historical and cultural origins of the assumptions,
> question the meaning of the assumptions, and develop alternative ways of
> acting.

It is possible to draw up from the foregoing definitions a full view of reflective practice or critical reflection which involves:

(i) a process (cognitive, emotional, experiential) of examining assumptions (of many different types and levels) embedded in actions or
experience;
(ii) a linking of these assumptions with many different origins (personal,
emotional, social, cultural, historical, political);
(iii) a review and re-evaluation of these according to relevant (depending
on context, purpose, etc.) criteria;
(iv) a reworking of concepts and practice based on this re-evaluation.

Different usages will vary in the number and type of assumptions focused on, the types of processes involved, the criteria for review of assumptions, and of course the purposes for which the process is used.

The contexts of the uses of reflection may include learning about and improving practice, learning to develop practice-based theory, learning to connect theory and practice, and improving and changing practice. One of the more confusing and complex aspects of reflection is therefore the fact that it can be used to serve many different interests, often simultaneously, some of which may seem contradictory. It may be used, for instance, both for greater or lesser conformity, as a way to increase accountability to existing norms, but also as a way to question the 'taken for granted' which may be implicit in those norms.

In its fullest sense, then, reflective practice or critical reflection appears to apply to the use of reflective abilities in the scrutiny and development of practice. This therefore implies the use of a framework for a reflective process involving different levels and stages, with one stage at least focused on the application of reflective learning to practice itself. This in a sense adds a context, complexity, purpose and depth to the simple exercise of reflective abilities. The implication is that it may be counterproductive to undertake any reflective process (in organized learning settings) without being clear about the specific purpose and process of reflection in relation to the particular context.

It has also been pointed out that the process as defined above implies that it is an individualistic, predominantly personal or self-oriented learning exercise (Reynolds and Vince 2004). There are therefore attempts to develop reflection as a collective experience, especially in organizational contexts (e.g. Gould and Baldwin 2004a; Reynolds and Vince 2004; Ghaye 2005).

To some extent, then, it is the way the abilities and process are theorized which provides some guidance as to the specific nature and goals of the process. Critical reflection, in this sense, may be seen as the use of reflective abilities to achieve some freeing from hegemonic assumptions (e.g. Brookfield 2000, 2001a), particularly those relating to power and its complex expression as exemplified by the work of Foucault (Brookfield 2001b). Adding a postmodern perspective allows for the hegemony to be recognized even in assumptions about the nature of knowledge and its generation itself. Recognizing this type of reflection often involves differentiating levels of reflection, distinguished by the levels of assumptions unearthed. The varying levels of reflection will be discussed further on.

Is it necessary to differentiate reflection and critical reflection? Perspectives on this question vary in the literature, since of course it is widely acknowledged that there is little consensus on the meaning and usage of these terms (Ixer 1999; Ghaye and Lillyman 2000a: xv). Some may simply see the two as intertwined (e.g. Redmond 2004), as building upon and complementing each other. Others emphasize the need to differentiate the two in order to capitalize on the emancipatory potential of critical reflection (Reynolds 1998; Catterall *et al.* 2002. Brookfield (1995: 8) argues that reflection is important in the daily business of living, but that critical reflection (with the express purpose of understanding how assumptions about power construct – and often restrict – practice) is vital if we are to make crucially relevant changes in the ways we work.

These issues will become clearer when we discuss the different levels of reflection outlined in the literature.

Levels of reflection

It is sometimes hard to distinguish between different types of reflection and levels of reflection. At the simplest level is perhaps Argyris and Schön's (1974) conception of single- and double-loop learning, where 'single loop' refers to learning regarding already accepted values, and 'double loop' refers to learning which questions accepted values. This relates to Habermas' three domains of knowledge (Redmond 2004: 13–14; B.J. Taylor 2000): the technical (instrumental), practical (communicative) and emancipatory. Habermas' categories may be seen as a typology of domains of reflection and are widely used as a theoretical base in differentiating types of reflection, all of which need to be reflected upon in some formulations (B.J. Taylor 2000)

However, formulations of levels of reflection usually assume a staged process involved in attaining successive levels of depth, transformation or criticality. Redmond (2004: 9) argues that most approaches to reflection assume at least two levels – a lower type of experimentation level and a higher order level of conceptualization – which are then fleshed out differently by different authors. In fact most schemas recognize at least three levels of reflection, beginning with a more descriptive level, advancing to what might be termed a more reflective level, and culminating in a critical or transformational level.

What differs of course is the way the detail of these stages is conceptualized. For instance, early schemas appear relatively simplistic in contemporary times (Mezirow 1991). The three levels of content, process and premise reflection are differentiated in terms of the focus of reflection (content of problem, strategies employed in the problem and underlying premises of the problem and a questioning of their relevance). Yeung *et al.* (1999) develop these slightly through their study of students' journals, from which they devised three different types of reflectors: non-reflectors (involving habitual action, thoughtful action, introspection), reflectors (involving content, process reflection), and critical reflectors (involving premise reflection).

A later formulation of Kember's (Leung and Kember 2003) characterizes four levels of reflection: habitual action, understanding, reflection and critical reflection. These refer to the ability to advance from a state of automatic performance with little consciousness, through understanding without relating to other situations, onto a systematic consideration of the grounds for knowledge and its implications, to a final level of awareness of what is behind thoughts and perceptions.

Hatton and Smith's (1995) stages of reflective writing are a little different in the way the critical level is conceptualized, in that they link this more directly to critical education perspectives as discussed earlier. Their four levels are summarized as follows: unreflective descriptive (ability to report and interpret in personal terms; reflective descriptive (demonstrating some effort to analyse from own or other point of view); dialogic (ability to step back, analyse from multiple perspectives); and critical (ability to incorporate ethical considerations based on social, political, and cultural questioning of status quo).

King and Kitchener's (1994) levels of reflective judgement are often used, and seem to be conceptualized primarily in terms of understandings of knowledge. Their seven levels begin with conceptions of knowledge as absolute (pre-reflective levels) and advance through levels where knowledge begins to be seen as uncertain or ambiguous (quasi-reflective), to a reflective stage where knowledge is seen as constructed by systematic inquiry and evaluation of evidence. Their schema is more explicitly rational than others.

The broad theme running through all these conceptualizations is the idea that it is possible to differentiate lower and higher order levels of reflection (usually advancing from purely habitual or descriptive abilities, through stages of being able to analyse situations from other and multiple perspectives, to finally developing an ability to gain ascendancy over knowledge use and to some extent an ability to create and manipulate its social use) through questioning the tenets upon which it stands.

These sorts of conceptualizations provide useful frameworks for differentiating the uses of reflection in different settings and also for the identification and possible measurement of the effectiveness of different reflective methodologies. What is problematic of course is that whatever framework is used (and presumably whatever features are taken as indicative of respective levels of ability) will be at least partly related to the sort of theoretical framework which guides the understanding of reflection. This will necessarily, at least in part, construct the phenomenon it sets out to investigate and describe. And since these frameworks are not necessarily shared, it is difficult to conduct research which builds upon the findings of previous studies.

Models and tools of reflection

How is reflection carried out – what models guide the process and what tools may be used within these models? Again, variety is the order of the day, although to some extent these variations appear to be less related to theoretical frameworks than other aspects of reflection. Ghaye and Lillyman (1997: 20) note five different types of models: structured, hierarchical, iterative, synthetic and holistic. To some degree these vary according to their levels of prescriptiveness, flexibility and the typologies of reflection upon which they are based. Stuctured models may use staged sets of questions to guide reflection (e.g. Johns 2002). Hierarchical models may focus on guiding students though succeeding levels of reflective abilities. Iterative and holistic models may be more cyclical, and focus more on the process of learning.

A plethora of tools and techniques for reflection has been written about in the literature (Osmond and Darlington 2005), and may be used in written or verbal form, either interactively or in self-reflection. These include critical incident technique (Fook *et al.* 2000), journalling (Bolton 2001), on-line discussions (Whipp 2003), case studies, reflective or critical conversations (Brookfield 1995; Ghaye and Lillyman 2000c), narratives or stories (Lehmann 2003c), poems (Bolton 2001), fiction (Rolfe 2002), metaphors (Hunt 2001), the body and movement as resource (Risner 2002), and the 'jotter wallet' (Longenecker 2002). In addition, the analysis of ethnographic data, naturally occurring case records and reports, or transcripts of meetings may also be useful for the interrogation of taken-for-granted assumptions (Riemann 2005a; Taylor and White 2000; White and Stancombe 2003).

The specific styles of group facilitators, and particular methods and questions for eliciting reflection used in conjunction with these tools, will presumably depend to some extent on theoretical frameworks used, but of course a plethora of other factors can come into play as well (since we recognize, as reflective teachers, that there may be a gap between theory and practice and the capacity for unarticulated assumptions to influence practice in unintentional ways).

There therefore appears to be a danger in concentrating too closely on the techniques for reflection, which may easily be co-opted for use by conflicting interests. Much of the literature therefore notes that simple techniques of reflection may not be effective if the culture or principles of reflection are misunderstood (e.g. Mezirow 2000), or indeed that the professional culture, with its capacity to shape and sustain activity and ideas, is itself taken for granted (Bilson and White 2004).

Conditions/requirements for reflection

Whilst the appropriate culture (group, personal or organizational) in which the effectiveness of critical reflection is maximized is often referred to, only some literature spells out in detail what this might entail. Mezirow (2000: 10–16) terms this type of climate 'reflective discourse', which includes access to accurate information, freedom from coercion, an ability to weigh evidence and assess arguments objectively as well as openness to other perspectives and new ideas. Elsewhere this has been termed 'critical acceptance' (Fook *et al.* 2000: 231), referring to a type of respectful climate in which it is safe to challenge old ideas and try new ones. Such a climate emphasizes processes of dialogue and communication, rather than closed judgements of learners' practices.

These elements are to some extent echoed in other formulations of the requirements for reflection (Brockbank *et al.* 2002; Brockbank and McGill 1998), which include features such as dialogue, holism and modelling (Brockbank and McGill 1998: 64). Most of the foregoing emphasize the value base of reflection and perhaps focus on the way the process is conducted. Other formulations are presented as 'principles' and include some of the more explicit assumptions regarding knowledge and the links between theory and practice. For example, Ghaye and Lillyman (2000a) discuss 12 principles of reflective practice, which include: 'reflective practice does not separate practice and theory'; 'reflective practice emphasizes the links between values and actions'; 'reflective practice generates locally owned knowledge' (p. 120). Sometimes an understanding of the experience of reflection also brings alive the type of culture necessary to its effectiveness. Bolton (2001: 200–1) notes features of the experience such as 'certain uncertainty', 'thoughtfully unthinking' and a 'process of letting go' which it may help participants understand to maximize benefits from the process.

Many of these features can be taken as referring to the sorts of values or beliefs which individual reflective learners need to accept in order to maximize the effectiveness of their reflection. However, there is also recognition that this resurrection of Socratic dialogue needs to be supported or created in a broader environment (team or organization or even more broadly) in order to foster reflection in individuals, and to maximize collective learning (Gould and Baldwin 2004a; Reynolds and Vince 2004).

Associated terms and ideas

As mentioned earlier, it is difficult to discuss the ideas of reflective practice and critical reflection in an isolated manner, since they are associated with many related concepts such as critical thinking, critical awareness, critical consciousness, critical inquiry, critical self-awareness, emancipatory reflection, and reflexivity. In some instances these concepts themselves may involve contested meanings. For example, the idea of critical thinking may be defined as similar in outcome to one of the goals of critical reflection as defined in critical theory terms: an awareness of how dominant thinking is created (Brookfield 1991: 2). On the other hand, it may be defined more in terms of the reasoning skills involved, encapsulating creative, reflective and judgement abilities in complex and uncertain situations (Ennis 1991; Plath et al. 1999; Resnick 1987).

In other instances the terms themselves involve their own set of complexities and theoretical developments (e.g. critical consciousness, which may be associated with the consciousness-raising tradition). In still other cases, what is common in many of the usages is simply conflated. For example, Payne (2005: 33) sees the concepts of reflexivity and critical thinking as developments of the idea of reflective practice.

It is not profitable or helpful to attempt to delineate and differentiate the separate meanings of this host of related terminology, but it is useful to note that presumably there is room for both clear and sloppy meanings of the terms to abound when such flexibility exists. Flexibility, whilst being inclusive of many traditions and theoretical perspectives, also makes it difficult to develop our understanding of such ideas, and rigorous research of them, when so many of our formulations are built upon different traditions and frameworks.

Complicating the situation even further is the fact that many conceptions of reflective practice and critical reflection are associated not just with different single terms, but in fact with different research or learning formulations or approaches themselves. In terms of learning traditions these would include: action learning (McGill and Beatty 1992); transformational learning (Mezirow and associates 1990; Mezirow 1991, 2000); consciousness-raising and critical pedagogy (Freire 1970; Hart 1990); experiential learning (Kolb 1984); the learning organization (Argyris and Schön 1978, 1996); and workplace-based learning (Boud and Garrick 1999). In the field of research associated traditions include: action research (Reason and Bradbury 2001; Bradbury and Reason 2003); co-operative or collaborative inquiry (Heron 1985; Heron and

Reason 2001); autobiographical/biographical, autoethnographical and self-study methods (White 2001; Chamberlyne *et al.* 2004); narrative methods (Hall 1997; Lieblich *et al.* 1998); and discourse analysis and deconstructive methods (Ellermann 1998; Taylor and White 2000). The idea of reflexivity seems to span both, as an approach which can both be used to research and learn from practice (Taylor and White 2000). And indeed, in a critical approach to knowledge making, the goal of becoming critical combines both educational and research functions. The classic work of Carr and Kemmis (1986) is written in this tradition.

Of the above ideas, those of transformational learning, action learning and research, narrative research, discourse analysis and reflexivity are probably the most interrelated with critical reflection. Transformational learning, as developed by Mezirow and others (see Mezirow 2000), places emphasis on how we make meaning (and decisions to act) from experience. Critical reflection is an essential part (but only a part) of this process. Likewise, in the action learning and research traditions, the focus is on learning from actual activities, and critical reflection is also an integral and articulated phase (but only a phase) of this process. Narrative research (and therapy) to some degree overlap with the idea of critical reflection in that by using the central tool of personal 'stories', some reflection on (and deconstruction of) personal experience is therefore entailed in any change process. Linking the ideas of language and discourse with our understanding of critical reflection, the process of critical reflection may be likened to a process of identifying and analysing how our language and discourse may indicate the influence of dominant discourses in our thinking and practices. With regard to reflexivity, it is possible to argue that a reflexive ability is central to critical reflection, in that an awareness of the influence of self and subjectivity is vital to an appreciation of how we construct and participate in constructing our world and our knowledge about that world (Fook 2004a).

Criticisms

What are some of the key criticisms of critical reflection and reflective practice which emerge from the literature? We have noted the confusing, sometimes undiscerning and uninformed, usage of the terms and their conflation. This has led some critics to assert that for the purposes of assessing reflective abilities at the very least there is no such thing as a theory of reflection (Ixer 1999). Certainly the atheoretical, particularly apolitical nature of Schön's original conception of reflective practice was observed long ago (Smyth 1988). Another key problem we have also already noted is the lack of research to provide empirical evidence of the value and outcomes of a reflective process. Many of the critiques centre on the actual practice of reflection. For example,

Brockbank and McGill (1998: 84–5) note that the process of reflection may simply function to reinforce or collude with current beliefs or practices, so that the quality of the experience and the facilitation of the process itself are crucial. Perriton (2004) highlights this last point by noting the difficulties in actually using critical reflection as a method. She also points up the tension, which is an issue in many educational frameworks, of how people may become critical without becoming indoctrinated. Brookfield (1994, 1995) notes the 'dark side' of critical reflection, pointing out the cultural and personal risks involved, and the fact that not all people may feel empowered by the process.

Conclusion

Reflective practice and critical reflection emerge from this review as popular, yet complex and contested ideas. They are used and written about in a plethora of professions, from a variety of disciplinary backgrounds, and for a variety of different purposes. They may be 'stand-alone' methods or approaches, or they may be envisaged as part of a broader approach of action learning/ research or transformative learning. In addition, they are often terms used interchangeably with others whose meaning may be equally contested.

Beginning in Ancient times with the Greek philosophers, and continuing in the thought of Kant and the hermeneutical philosophies and later in the work of Dewey and Schön, theoretical developments of the ideas have encompassed philosophy, psychology, therapy, social theory, and education, using a variety of formulations which most recently have expanded to include postmodern and deconstructive thinking as well as notions of spirituality and emotion (Nussbaum 2001). What actually happens in a critical reflective process is largely related to the particular theoretical formulations in vogue with its exponents. The degree to which transformative change, based on political analyses of social domination, or the interrogation of culturally and historically situated 'truths', takes place, depends in part on the extent to which exponents draw on critical or related theory as an underpinning. In addition, different models and tools may be used, and the effectiveness of the experience may also be influenced by the style and skill of the facilitator, as well as the group climate and broader context of the reflective process.

Our review highlights the relatively under-researched nature of reflection, given its extensive use. On the whole there has been very little research conducted on groups outside the researcher's own milieu. Furthermore, there is little empirical research seeking to identify the changes brought about by reflection, or outcomes of the process, compared with that found in other studies. Sometimes the published studies do not outline in detail the actual research methodologies used, or the details of the reflective process and approach under study. This makes it very difficult to progress our understandings across disciplinary boundaries, and indeed even to learn from each other in improving the effectiveness of our own use of critical reflection. This seems highly counterproductive in a growing field. How, then, do we account for such glaring gaps?

It may be that the very popularity of critical reflection is also its undoing: it becomes difficult to develop systematically the quality and effectiveness of reflection in a climate where its meaning and value are assumed and therefore relatively unarticulated and unjustified. Perhaps also the very educational culture which supports the value of practice experience in a reflective practice tradition, also works against its best interests by not also subjecting it to rigorous debate, systematic investigation using a variety of methods, and informed awareness of its complexities, differences and shared understandings. Perhaps we assume that reflective practice is simply a matter of practice, learnt best by doing it? And does this therefore preclude other, more academically inclined approaches to knowledge-making?

What is the way forward for an approach and set of teaching practices which have already gained ascendancy, perhaps before their 'academic' justification? How do we 'trouble' this less critical version of critical reflection? By asking this question we do not mean to suggest that critical reflection is not something of value and relevance in current workplaces and learning institutions, and indeed within broader social contexts. Clearly, the need for reflective abilities is evidenced by current workplace and social changes, and the degree to which they have caught the imagination of so many different groups. But how do we further the cause of critical reflection so that it is not used for purposes we did not intend, co-opted by contradictory interests, simply used in harmful or at best ineffective ways, or even written off as too sloppy or indeterminate?

Part of the answer to this may lie in our need to examine reflectively our own assumptions about critical reflection and the cultural practices and climates which may support its undiscerning use. Perhaps there is a need not only to value the practical nature of the approach, but also to develop more inclusive ways of understanding, representing and researching the great variety of benefits we know, from our own experience, that it provides. There may need to be more and other ways of representing our experiences of critical reflection; ways which can also speak to the more sceptical amongst us, and illustrate how such a process might be used to good effect in a variety of very different settings. The flexibility of reflective practice may in fact demand that there be much more inclusivity in the way it is researched.

2 Unsettling reflections: the reflexive practitioner as 'trickster' in interprofessional work[1]

Sue White

[T]rickster is a boundary-crosser. Every group has its edge, its sense of in and out, and trickster is always there, at the gates of the city and the gates of life, making sure there is commerce. He also attends the internal boundaries by which groups articulate their social life. We constantly distinguish – right and wrong, sacred and profane, clean and dirty, male and female, young and old, living and dead – and in every case trickster will cross the line and confuse the distinction. Trickster is the creative idiot, therefore the wise fool, the gray-haired baby, the cross-dresser, the speaker of sacred profanities. . . . the origins, liveliness and durability of cultures require that there be space for figures whose function is to uncover and disrupt the very things that cultures are based on.

(Hyde 1998: 7–9)

The 'trickster', as the anthropologists call the ubiquitous, mischievous, character in ancient indigenous folk-tales and myths from many cultures, is a marginal figure. Trickster is travelling, passing through, amongst and between, 'keep[ing] the world lively and giv[ing] it the flexibility to endure' (Hyde 1998: 9). Trickster is a boundary crosser, but also a boundary creator, exposing new distinctions, making the usual strange. Trickster is Hermes in Greece, Coyote in North America, Krishna in India, the Monkey King in China, the Raven in Nordic myths. Often breaching morals and mores, trickster invites the possibility of new values. Because of the association with breaches, the term 'trickster' carries pejorative connotations, as in 'confidence trickster'. Indeed, in the myths, trickster is often deliberately deceptive, and in invoking the metaphor of 'reflexive practitioner as trickster' here, I am not suggesting that professionals learn to lie and dupe, rather I am trying to bring to light another aspect of the trickster – trickster's ability to 'shift', to turn many ways.

Practice in health and welfare takes place in the context of powerful organizational and professional cultures. Yet, the concept of culture is often taken for granted and its capacity to shape what can be thought, said, or done is ignored. Culture is often referred to in policy documents as a medium relatively easily changed. Yet, research into teams in social care (e.g. Pithouse 1987; Hall 1997; White 1998), medicine (e.g. Bloor 1976) and nursing (e.g. Latimer 2000) shows how cultures are locally accomplished and reproduced and can sustain the tacit practices of occupations, organizations and teams, and indeed may be used to resist the sort of approaches to policy and practice change usually associated with rational approaches to governance.

For example, Paul Thagard's (2000) case study of the development and acceptance of the theory that peptic ulcers are primarily caused by a bacterium, *Helicobacter pylori,* illustrates how a complex range of activities, processes and events affects the production and acceptance of new ideas. The hypothesis, generated during the mid-1980s, that gastric ulcers were the result of bacterial infection was initially considered preposterous. The established belief at the time was that peptic ulcers were caused by excess acidity, which eventually eroded the stomach wall and caused lesions. Due to this established belief, which was treated by both clinicians and scientists as the only right and proper way to think, the new hypothesis was slow to gain acceptance. It was not until the mid-1990s that the idea gained widespread acceptance. Thus, until the discovery by Warren (a pathologist) and Marshall (a gastroenterologist) of the role of *H. pylori* had been argued and negotiated in an interactional context, it remained contested and fragile. Its entry into practice was initially blocked by the constraints imposed on thinking by the popularized 'excess acidity' explanation which operated as a culturally available resource, through which clinicians 'just knew' how to treat peptic ulcers.

What is true for medicine is arguably more so for domains of professional activity, which are more 'social' in nature. If we take the example of child care social work in the UK, there are numerous examples of particular orthodoxies taking hold. Examples include the rights and wrongs of transracial adoption, planning for permanency for children in care, and the use of 'anatomically correct' dolls to interview suspected victims of child sexual abuse.

Fashionable and powerful ideas, often supported by theory, or varieties of moral reasoning can interrupt the capacity of practitioners to engage critically with their endeavour. When making their case for this or that course of action practitioners may be unaware that they are invoking an 'idea', and that this idea exists amongst many alternatives which may have become obscured by the current settlement. I want to argue here that, in these circumstances, the trickster metaphor may be helpful in encouraging new thinking about everyday practices. Trickster's ability to shake up language and received ideas may be crucially important to critical reflexive practice. That is to say, professional accounts are contingent upon available vocabularies. Professionals may be free and purposeful agents, but not in conditions of their own making. Sometimes vocabularies need stirring up a little.

Lively talk and lively culture

Hyde says of the trickster:

> [W]hat tricksters quite regularly do is create lively talk where there has been silence, or where speech has been prohibited. Trickster speaks freshly where language has been blocked, gone dead, or lost its charm. . . . for usually language goes dead because cultural practice has hedged it in, and some shameless double-dealer is needed to get outside the rules and set tongues wagging again.
>
> (Hyde, 1998: 76)

Or again:

> When we have forgotten that we participate in the shaping of this world and become enslaved to shapings left to us by the dead, then a cunning artus-worker[2] may appear, sometimes erasing the old boundaries so fully that only no-way remains and creation must start as if from scratch, and sometimes just loosening up the old divisions, greasing the joints so they may shift in respect to one another, or opening them so commerce will spring up where 'the rules' forbid it.
>
> (Hyde 1998: 279–80)

To get the full sense of the complexity of this cultural agitator you will have to consult Hyde's excellent book (see also Radin 1956), but for our purposes here let me give an illustration of how trickster tales can work to destabilize boundaries. In an Indian folk-tale, Yasoda leaves her young foster son, Krishna, alone in the house. She has told him not to steal the butter whilst she is away. No sooner has she left the house than Krishna heads for the larder, unseals the jars and greedily slurps their pale yellow contents. On her return, Yasoda admonishes Krishna. To begin with, he gives a series of cunning retorts, such as 'there were ants in the butter jars, I was trying to save the butter', or he tries blaming his mother, 'these bracelets you put on my wrists were chaffing, I had to sooth the sores'. All to no avail, but his response 'I didn't steal the butter. How could I steal it? Doesn't everything in the house belong to us?' causes Yasoda to laugh, charmed by the child's ability to trouble her notions of property and theft. In so doing, Krishna reveals the artifice, the cultural specificity and the constructed nature of the distinctions, and suggests alternatives. The important message about the trickster myths, then, is that they are a celebration and a reminder of the need to open up dialogue and reflexive spaces within one's own culture, to be anthropological about one's own presuppositions. It is easy to spot the flaws in the practices of others, but the capacity of cultures to act as sustaining media for established forms of thought means that for us all, as members of cultures, many of our own taken-for-granted distinctions never receive scrutiny.

Troubling boundaries in professional work

In this chapter, I want to argue that we need to create contexts and spaces where these kinds of boundary-crossing and boundary-troubling activities can safely occur in professional domains. I use the phrase 'troubling' as both a verb and an adjective, to refer to the act of causing trouble to established distinctions in the current settlement, and also to argue that some boundaries are indeed 'troubling' in the sense that the boundaries themselves cause trouble. I will illustrate this with data taken from an ethnographic study of interprofessional talk in a child health setting.

I have spent a good deal of my personal and professional life at the edge of various cultures. Like the trickster, I have often had a sense of being both in and out and have told my tales about it. I am from working-class origins and, like many others who benefited from the financial support for study offered in the UK in the 1970s, I was the first person in my extended family to go to university (my elder son has just become the second). When I was in practice, I managed a statutory child and family social work service in a hospital setting, crossing organizational and disciplinary boundaries, sometimes invoking one set of mores, sometimes another. To be effective, I had to learn to represent the world using different vocabularies in diverse settings and to do this self-consciously and respectfully – though doubtless this was not always so. My doctoral research was an ethnographic study of child care social work. I became an ethnographer of my own practice (*cf.* White 2001; Riemann 2005a; Chapter 13, this volume). As an academic, I am ethnographer, sociologist and social worker, sometimes researching or writing sociologies of social work and other professions, sometimes using social science in an applied way to tell practitioners how to 'do' practice. I am now Director of the Centre for Health and Social Care Research at the University of Huddersfield and, despite the rapprochement between these domains in contemporary policy initiatives, I am again a liminal figure, moving within and between different cultures and sets of understandings. These are ambivalent positions and can be itchy and uncomfortable, but the experience of being a 'marginal native' has also been extremely helpful in creating critical distance from dominant and unquestioned beliefs in my own professional practice, as I have described elsewhere (White 2001).

It has sometimes created the possibility of dialogue (at least in my head) where there was orthodoxy and it has fashioned a sensitivity to, and suspicion of, attempts to seek closure and a final settlement on the complex matters we confront as health and welfare professionals, educators and researchers. This argument finds resonance with many themes in social science and in philosophical traditions, such as hermeneutical philosophy, philosophical pragmatism, social constructionism and the 'linguistic turn' in social theory, referred to in Chapter 1 of this volume. This is not the place for a whistle-stop tour of those domains; suffice to say that there are a number of voices calling for a return to dialogue and debate as means of settling problems of judgement, or of unsettling dominant assumptions, in an epoch, or in relation to practices, where science cannot deliver unproblematic answers. For example, Bernstein (1983) argues that this theme of dialogue and communality is a unifying anthem consolidating diverse positions. It is a

> defence of the Socratic virtues, ' the willingness to talk, to listen to other people, to weigh the consequences of our actions upon other people' . . . It means turning away from the obsession 'to get things right' and turning our attention to coping with the contingencies of human life.
>
> (Bernstein 1983: 203)

For Bernstein, it is a *moral* imperative to defend 'the openness of human conversation against all those temptations and real threats that seek closure' (1983: 204–5). Such a vision acknowledges the inevitability of conflicting perspectives, and it also highlights the dangers of monopoly positions on truth, which limit debate and threaten mutuality. It is a defence of 'lively language' and in this sense it joins nicely with the trickster myths and their capacity to trouble comfortable distinctions.

We can see traces of the trickster in the work of a number of social scientists and philosophers. For example, the ethnomethodologist, Harold Garfinkel is a trickster in his famous breaching experiments (e.g. Garfinkel 1967). Ethnomethodology is the study of 'folk' (ethno) 'methods' (ways of doing things) – in other words, of those complex forms of shared knowledge upon which we all draw in 'doing being ordinary' (Sacks 1984). Garfinkel pioneered the use of what he called 'breaching experiments' with his students. These were designed to break the taken-for-granted rules of everyday social order, as a way of making these explicit. One example might be shopping from someone else's trolley in the supermarket. The taken-for-granted routine is that once you have placed an item in your trolley, it belongs to you. The students who performed this 'breach' matter-of-factly took items from the trolleys of other shoppers. When questioned, they responded that the item in the trolley had been more convenient to reach than the one on the shelf. When assumptions are breached, people look for a 'reasonable' explanation – something that reaffirms the underlying assumptions, such as 'Oh, I'm sorry, I thought that was my trolley'. However, to act as if there is nothing wrong with taking items from someone else's trolley breaches the hidden rules and for a moment makes explicit the processes that are at work in rendering situations 'normal'. For Garfinkel (1967), breaches were aids for a sluggish imagination.

Hyde's reading of the cultural value of the trickster myths is that they grease the hinges and joints of whatever logic is in fashion, but do not offer anything prescriptive in its place. This is not a reforming mission, but a sense that knowledges and moral orderings are temporary and that other possibilities can be made visible. Hyde quotes Foucault as saying (but not in print) 'My job is making windows where there were once walls'.[3] Foucault (1994: 132) points to the need for agents to build an ethics based on an understanding of the socially and historically constituted nature of their knowledges:

> People have to build their own ethics, taking as a point of departure the historical analysis, sociological analysis, and so on that one can provide for them. I don't think that people who try to decipher the truth should have to provide ethical principles or practical advice at the same moment, in the same book and the same analysis. All this prescriptive network has to be elaborated and transformed by people themselves.

Foucault is suspicious of reforming zeal, seeing it as a means by which regimes of truth and power knowledge configurations become inverted and one substituted for another, a point echoed by Ian Hacking (1999: 7) in relation to the (mis)uses of social constructionism:

> One may realize that something, which seems inevitable in the present state of things, was not inevitable, and yet is not thereby a bad thing. But most people who use the social construction idea enthusiastically want to criticize, change or destroy some X that they dislike in the established order of things.

In this sense, the trickster's role is closely related to Rorty's 'ironist', who has a deep suspicion of 'final vocabularies'. Rorty argues that human beings carry about a culturally sustained vocabulary, which they employ to justify their actions and beliefs, and indeed their lives. Rorty calls these words a person's 'final vocabulary', as beyond them language breaks down – there are no more possibilities. Or, as Wittgenstein (1961:115) puts it, 'the limits of my language mean the limits of my world'. Professionals, like other human agents, have their final vocabularies. It is worth quoting Rorty (1989: 73–4) at some length here as he explains well the liberating effects of the ironist.

I shall define an ironist as someone who fulfils three conditions: (1) She has radical and continuing doubts about the final vocabulary she currently uses, because she has been impressed by other vocabularies taken as final by people or books she has encountered; (2) she realizes that argument phrased in her present vocabulary can neither underwrite nor dissolve these doubts; (3) insofar as she philosophizes about her situation, she does not think her vocabulary is closer to reality than the others, that it is in touch with a power not herself . . . I call these people 'ironists' because their renunciation of the attempt to formulate criteria of choice between final vocabularies, puts them in a position which Sartre called 'meta-stable'; never quite able to take themselves seriously because always aware that the terms in which they describe themselves are subject to change, always aware of the contingency and fragility of their final vocabularies, and thus of themselves.

Trickster myths are closely associated with polytheism, polyculturalism, openness to 'the other' and multiple possibilities. Trickster works away at the joints, the articulations between beliefs that are neither wholly separate nor fully unified. In this sense, there are analogies to be drawn with multi-agency and interprofessional work, in that what we want from such working practices is neither the assimilation of one professional group into another, nor endless identity politics with each defending a set of received ideas against exposure to the other. Reflexive practitioners need to be able to tell stories about *themselves* and others (and stories about those stories) that defend the openness of human conversation and create possibilities that things could be otherwise – not because they necessarily *ought* to be, but so that they *might* be. This requires a defamiliarization of the everyday, expectable professional routines of thought and action. Too often this does not occur. Exposure to difference in multi-professional contexts can all too often lead to humorous ironization of the practices of the other, in the form of various 'atrocity stories' (see Dingwall 1977; Taylor and White 2000; White and Stancombe 2003; White and Featherstone 2005), or claims to moral superiority of one's own ideas, at the expense of a reflexive engagement with the views of others or one's own presuppositions or prejudices. Let me give an example from the past.

Occupational liturgies: the 'new morality' in 1990s social work

> The shift – in the very broadest of terms – is from an individualism in which self determination and non-judgementalism featured as reference points for an ethical neutralism . . . to a more recent certitude and orthodoxy about the direction to be taken by social workers in constructing their own, and their clients', moral universe. . . . The qualities follow on inevitably from the requirement: the anti-racist or the anti-sexist is self consciously and deliberately censorious; to them the mundane is made serious, and the reassuring and comfortable 'sharedness' of the assumptive world is assaulted. Others become subject to judgement, and the exception-taker is set above those who are found wanting; an element of uprightness is embraced by the accuser, and the behaviour and sentiments of the tainted are held up as morally deficient.
>
> (Webb, 1990: 146–49)

David Webb caused something of a storm with this analysis of the impact of an anti-racist and anti-sexist 'new morality' on social work in the UK during in the 1980s and early 1990s, himself becoming branded as one who was 'found wanting' (Dominelli 1990). During this time, which coincided with my doctoral fieldwork, the use of expressions of various kinds became proscribed and the shared knowledge that a particular term was racist or sexist became a powerful component in associational claims, through which social workers affirmed their occupational identity and hence underscored the differences between themselves and other occupations. For example, a poster, displayed in the main reception of one office, carried the following cautionary words to visitors:

> People are reminded that racist/sexist behaviour, which includes language, jokes and the display of literature, artefacts and/or the writing of racist/sexist graffiti is contrary to the objectives of this department and will not be tolerated.

The 'exposure' of certain expressions as oppressive could, of course, have been an emancipatory triumph. In many ways, it was social work's deconstructive turn, but problems arose in defining what constituted racist/sexist behaviour, language, jokes, literature, or artefacts. For example, during my fieldwork (in 1993–4), the relationship between the police 'child protection team' and (some) social workers was disrupted by a claim, made by the social workers, that the expression 'nitty-gritty' was racist, and the police should refrain from using it. The relationship was usually fairly harmonious as, because of a shared commitment to child protection, the police officers were held in reasonably high regard by social workers. However, on this occasion, some social workers had argued that the etymology of 'nitty-gritty' had been traced to the slave trade, where it was ostensibly used by white owners to refer to the lice-infested pubic hair of female slaves. Hence, the argument went, the expression 'getting down to the nitty-gritty' meant the rape of a slave by a white owner.[4]

I was unable to discover the source of this interpretation, but it soon became impossible to hear the utterance without wincing and awaiting the expressions of moral opprobrium. Any 'unknowing' social workers were soon inducted into the majority, either by friends who would gently tell them of the offence they were likely to cause should they continue to use the term, or because they were party to stories told by their colleagues about the transgressions made by another. The police were unconvinced and erected a poster in their offices proclaiming 'nitty-gritty is not a racist expression'. Of course, this reaffirmed social workers' opinions of the police as shameless racists.

Although the battle was played out amongst only one or two major protagonists, the ramifications were sufficient to render the term 'nitty-gritty' unspeakable within social services and, no doubt, to give it new significance as a badge of resistance within the police. Other problematic expressions were black coffee, blackboard, and the use of 'girl' or 'lady' to describe women. On one occasion, during a multi-agency meeting, a social work team leader was urged by a colleague to 'select another metaphor', after using the expression 'it's not a black and white case'. What is important about this story, is that, whilst the problematization of languages of oppression may have elements of trickster's ability to create lively talk, what happened on this occasion was a stifling of dialogue and a discursive reinforcement of occupational boundaries. At no point were the categories of race and gender problematized. 'If it only mirrors the thing it opposes, it discovers no secret passage into new worlds' (Hyde 1998: 271).

Some of this problematization has happened subsequently due to the impact of varieties of postmodernism (e.g. Fawcett *et al.* 2000), which have encouraged, not without controversy, a playfulness (and perhaps some mischief-making), about categories. Perhaps the most striking example of this is queer theory, which is based on the idea that identities are not fixed and deterministic. It proposes that we deliberately challenge all notions of fixed identity in varied and unpredictable, indeed 'tricksterish' ways (e.g. Butler 1990).

Health and welfare work is riddled with ambiguity and it needs trickster figures to prevent these ambiguities from being pushed into the background, as Hyde (1998: 11) notes:

> We may well hope our actions carry no moral ambiguity, but pretending that is the case when it isn't doesn't lead to greater clarity about right and wrong; it more likely leads to unconscious cruelty masked by inflated righteousness.

In the example above, I would argue that Webb shows elements of trickster's ability to spot a new orthodoxy and trouble its unintended consequences, which, in this case, Webb saw as the petrifaction of professional discourse and debate. However, the rather haughty manner in which he 'troubles' the new morality makes it unsurprising that he perturbed some of his contemporaries in social work academe.

This is of course, the crucial problem. How does one create the possibility of 'lively talk' and reinvigorate sterile slogans and liturgies without causing offence or humiliation and thereby reinforcing behind stronger fortifications the very vocabularies that one is trying to tickle and make squirm into novel form? The propensity for the ironic redescription of stable vocabularies to provoke humiliation has been discussed at length by Rorty. For him, humiliation is the companion of irony, and the public use of irony therefore carries with it a liberal ethic – a sense that humanness is defined by sensitivity to humiliation. So the ironist must avoid humiliating others through an awareness that her own vocabularies may also be subject to potentially humiliating redescription. For Rorty, this means being exposed to as many final vocabularies as possible in order that we constantly recognize the contingent nature of our own. In the 'nitty-gritty' example above, we can see clearly the role that public humiliation played in both 'the new morality' of which Webb writes and in Webb's redescription.

If we compare this with Krishna's playful redescription of the concepts of property and theft discussed at the beginning of this chapter, we can find clues as to how organizational tricksters may tease new vocabularies into life. Humour and playfulness are powerful tools in trickster's repertoire. Think of Shakespeare's wise fools. The fool often helps destabilize notions of class and propriety. The noble characters take seriously themselves and their melodramas, romances and tragedies whilst the fool is having a good time *making* a fool of them (and of himself). The role of the sage fool is to challenge hubris, to say what could not otherwise be said. This requires humility: 'the wise man knows himself to be a fool' (*As You Like It*, Act 5, scene 1).

> Holy fools and jesters through the ages have always known that the first step toward liberation and enlightenment is to escape from lives that are overgoverned by the ideals of efficiency, predictability, control, and rationality. The essential ingredients of being human are always upside down, mirror-imaged,

and reversals of common sense. Do not trust anyone, for example, who says 'Trust me'. Crazy wisdom helps us question leaders who lazily invoke metaphors of patriotism, law, and duty to fight a war or lock up alleged troublemakers.

(Keeney 2004)

I have already noted the use of humour and storytelling in interprofessional and multi-agency work and said how they often take the form of ironic banter about 'the other'. In fact, while as social actors we are extraordinarily good at spotting the idiosyncratic routines and typifications of unfamiliar cultures, it is much harder to spot our own, as they are already camouflaged against the familiar thickets of our professional imagination and final vocabulary. Seeing ourselves as others see us requires us to grow eyes on stalks that can look back at us with scepticism. At this point, I should like to present some data which exemplify the capacity of social actors to be sensitive to, and adopt alternative vocabularies within, different cultural contexts. This skill potentially provides opportunities, in the comparative way Rorty has described, for people to become more humble and playful with their own final vocabularies, not so they can abandon them necessarily, but so they can debate them and create lively talk. However, as we shall see, boundary crossing may be a necessary condition for creating lively talk, but it is not sufficient.

A morning in the liminal world of the boundary crosser

During the fieldwork for my last ethnographic study (see White 2002; White and Stancombe 2003), I spent some time with a nurse whose explicit function was to bridge the boundary between paediatrics and the child and adolescent mental health service (CAMHS). I was wearing a lapel microphone (with informed consent) as the nurse went about his daily round, visiting first the paediatric ward on which various children and young people with mental health problems were placed in designated child psychiatry beds. The recent closure of a separate child psychiatry inpatient unit was, at the time, controversial. After our tour of the paediatric ward, we visited the CAMHS day unit. Like the trickster, the liaison nurse must be an identity shifter, performing his different identities as we walked betwixt and between these cultural domains.

Extract 1. *Conversation with paediatric nurses on the paediatric ward: the ally*
LN: Sally's doing her mental health training. She's one of my stars.
Paed.: I'm just doing Kieran's lithium levels?
LN: Are you doing the lithium levels?
Paed.: Yes.
LN: That's very good of you. [To SW] Kieran was a client who was on the ward with manic depression and he's now down at [child

psychiatry day unit], so even though he's not an inpatient you've still got links with him by taking his blood then. How did you find him? He was quite down last week wasn't he?

Paed.: He's quite up.

LN: Is he?

Paed.: Yeah, yeah.

LN: Yeah, a bit bubbly?

Paed.: Yeah he is a bit.

LN: You like him though on here, don't you? You've got a bit of a soft spot for him?

(*Laughter*)

LN: Do you think things have changed? I was just telling Sue about the role and strides that people have made. Do you think things are [better]

Paed.: [Def]initely. I think were all a bit scared when we first started dealing with mental health patients cos we had no experience of it at all really, did we?

LN: No and you're going to be trained up and you're gonna have my job.

Paed.: Yeah, I'll know everything won't I (*laughs*).

LN: I can hand the mantle over cos there's Jan and Mary doing a mental health course and I'm gonna hand the mantle over to you two at one point aren't I and move onto bigger 'n' greater things.

In this exchange, the liaison nurse, whom I shall call Andrew, is displaying a reverence towards a paediatric nurse who has shown a particular interest in mental health. The invocation of the patient 'Kieran' is respectful and the opinion of the paediatric nurse is sought, reinforcing the idea that she is the holder of particular expertise, such that she is 'gonna have [his] job'. The selection of the informal phrase 'a bit bubbly' as opposed to 'quite up', or 'high' potentially signals a greater familiarity with the condition 'manic depression', but one that includes his new ally and accepts her clinical view of Kieran's condition that morning. The paediatric nurse is recruited as an ally in the aspiration for cultural change on the ward: 'Do you think things have changed? I was just telling Sue about the role and strides that people have made. Do you think things are better?'

As we move away from the nurses' station and progress down the ward out of earshot, the following exchange takes place between Andrew and myself:

Extract 2. *On the way to the day unit: the ironist*

LN: My profile here [ward for younger children] is not as high as it should be to tell you the truth and I don't know why that is. It just tends to be a crisis thing, so I'm very aware I'm not over here as much as I should be.

SW: They refer to you though, don't they, the paediatricians?

LN: Yeah, they do refer to me – far too much! (*Laughs*) I was down here the other day and I've been here nearly nine months and the staff nurse said 'who are you anyway' (*laughs*), so I was very aware that my profile was a problem (laughs).

LN: I very struck as a CPN by the formality of it – the way everyone has uniforms and badges and everyone's referred to at times as staff nurse this or that and that's something I find very strange. Especially when doctors come on the ward and everybody's sort of 'oh here are the doctors'. I mean one of the problems is that I can be in the middle of a conversation with a nurse and they'll just leave me. But they don't only do that with me, they'll do it with Harry Singer [child psychiatrist] or Dick Tarrant [child psychiatrist] as well and they're consultants, but they'll just say 'oh excuse me the proper doctor's here' . . . I was quite taken aback. I'm still puzzled at the way they jump up when someone comes in, cos obviously psychiatry's a lot more informal. You get 'Oh he's a busy man. He saves lives'.

LN: We had a lot of arguments about an anorexic girl we had – toe to toe and nose to nose arguments about how she should be moved at 17.

SW: What about how she should be moved?

LN: Well with paediatric nurses there's this thing about wanting to be liked and ingratiating themselves to clients – where they thought they were helping she was doing her own blood pressure, weighing herself, she was doing her own meals and stuff, but you can't – she was saying 'I've put three pounds on'. She was doing that, you know and to get them to confront her and say 'no you're lying' was incredibly difficult. I used to take them along to the meetings with me as much as possible and talk to them afterwards and they'd say 'you were really nasty to her and really nasty to the parents' and I didn't think I was, you know . . . But it's the element of confrontation you know, but they don't get a lot a need for that you know cos everybody's in for physical illnesses, everybody wants to be there and wants to get out and ours don't want to be in and don't want to be out and manipulate the situation. That's the other thing the paediatric nurses are doing this mental health training I was told I couldn't be their mentor because I'm RMN and think differently. So I met this tutor at a thing in Newcastle and had a bit of a go at her and she started to back-pedal.

The shift in vocabulary and repertoire here is striking. The nurse variously ironizes the formal hierarchy and alleged professional dominance of the doctors. Paediatric nursing staff are described as 'wanting to be liked' and 'ingratiating' themselves with clients. There is a noteworthy increase in the ironic use of reported speech to amplify cultural and professional differences, for example, 'oh excuse me the proper doctor's here', 'Oh he's a busy man. He saves lives', 'you were really nasty to her and really nasty to the parents'. Here, the tough professional savvy of the specialist psychiatric nurse is displayed. I have noted elsewhere how this kind of humorous banter is also a vehicle for identity work in child care social work (e.g. White 1998).

While collegial consensus is performed and displayed in the preceding dialogue between Andrew and the paediatric nurse, cultural and conceptual differences are amplified here: 'We had a lot of arguments about an anorexic girl we had – toe to toe and nose to nose arguments'. The 'untrustworthy anorexic' and the naivety of the paediatric staff are contrasted with Andrew's seasoned, sceptical, straight-talking, challenging know-how. The categories 'physical illnesses' and 'ours' (meaning patients with mental health problems) are contrasted and the boundaries between them reinforced.

We continue on our walk to the CAMHS day unit.

Extract 3. *Child psychiatry day unit: the insider*

LN: [referring to child psychiatrist who is on the telephone] This is interesting, you'd never get a doctor actually doing his own phone calls upstairs (*laughs*)

CP: He's a bit agitated, isn't he, Kieran. I've just spoken to him.

Nurse: He's flatly high, if you can be flatly high (*laughs*) – he's a bit flat but he is quite high (laughs).

LN: I know he's had his blood done upstairs. Jan took his blood upstairs.

Nurse: He's annoyed with me.

LN: What, why?

Nurse: I wouldn't let him go upstairs and he's hanging round the office and I'm like there's confidential stuff here.

LN: He's looking for that Bob Marley tape (*laughter*). See that's another difference with upstairs like they let them hang around the nurse station and stuff and with generic poorly kids that's ok, but with our kids they're like rooting through the notes. Upstairs they just get ingratiated really. The anorexics do it, don't they, sit round.

Nurse: Like if we have got someone difficult, the ability to wander in this building is very great

LN: and ability to find them is very low (*laughter*). Do they know upstairs he's not to go up?

Nurse: Yeah he's not doing it as much. It's circular down here as well. Like he goes off and he's gone, but you can head him off (*laughter*).

LN: It's designed for anorexics here, cos they just do laps of the bloody place (*laughter*).

Here, the tenor of the talk and the jokey repertoire continue and are reinforced by the co-narration by the other nurse of humorous anecdotes about the exploits of 'the anorexics', which are contrasted again with the less problematic behaviours of 'generic poorly kids'. There are further references to 'ingratiation' of young people by the nurses on the paediatric ward. Clinical information is delivered in an informal, but subtly nuanced style 'flatly high, if you can be flatly high' which invokes a shared specialist familiarity with the volatile mood shifts of the manic depressive. Shared jokes based on past knowledge are used: 'He's looking for that Bob Marley tape (*laughter*)'. The skilful management of 'difficult' behaviour is a strong identity claim, supported by gallows humour. The shared understanding that young people with anorexia often want to exercise is displayed, again using humour about the circular geographical structure of the building:

> Nurse: Yeah he's not doing it as much. It's circular down here as well. Like he goes off and he's gone, but you can head him off (*laughter*).
>
> LN: It's designed for anorexics here, cos they just do laps of the bloody place (*laughter*).

This is artful boundary crossing with a highly performative aspect, but, whilst he displays trickster's ability to tease, Andrew is not a trickster since the familiar world of the psychiatric day unit, with its less rigid formalities and banter, is immune from ironic redescription. Instead, for example, the categories 'physical' and 'mental' illness are reinforced. Contrastive rhetoric is used to ironize the paediatric *modus operandi*, which serves to reinforce the shared assumptive world of the child psychiatry unit.

An important feature of contrastive rhetoric . . . is the sometimes humorous but always dramatic definition of normality by reference to its opposite, deviance; and thus the demarcation (albeit a hazy one) of the outer limits of existing practice.

(Hargreaves 1981: 312)

Andrew has evolved a *modus vivendi* that enables him to rub along and function across the paediatric boundary, without troubling that boundary in any sense.

Bruno Latour (1987: 22–3) distinguishes between 'positive and negative modalities'. In the former, claims are made which do not invite the interrogation of their conditions of production, whereas in the latter, inquiry leads us towards the conditions of production of a claim and thereby invites us to comment on its usefulness and veracity. If I may use an example invented by my colleague Chris Hall (Hall and White 2005), the statement 'foster placements work best where families do not have children of similar age' takes for granted the nature of foster care, whereas the statement 'there is little difference between a foster placement and a small residential unit' allows the nature of foster care and its similarities and differences in relation to residential care (whatever that may be!) to be questioned. My contention is that, in situations where cultures are unquestioned, there is a greater propensity for the issuing of statements with positive modalities, which invoke categories in ways that stabilize and allow swift disposals. We can see this in operation in Andrew's use of the categories 'physical illnesses' and 'anorexics'. Andrew does not notice the ways in which the informal banter in the CAMHS service supports the shared assumptive world. We are well equipped as social actors to spot the idiosyncrasies of the other – it is part of how we create a sense of belonging within our tribes. Trickster's skill is to tickle the imaginations of his kinsfolk.

I should at this point give an exemplar of an exchange that I think did have 'tricksterish' properties. Again, during fieldwork in a child psychiatry setting, I attended a planning meeting held in order to consider whether Rebecca (aged 14) should move from a foster placement where she had been living for 9 months. Rebecca was happy there and did not want to move; nor did the foster carers want her to leave. However, they had been approved to look after young people 'short term', and the family placement worker needed Rebecca to move in order to release a valuable placement. This was couched in terms of the young person's welfare, best interests and wishes and feelings. The family placement worker invoked attachment theory in the following manner:

> [Rebecca]'s made a good attachment here. That's good. A lot of kids don't have that. It will help her when she moves. She needs a forever family now.

The popularized version of the theory posits that the ability to form one good attachment will facilitate others in the future (Fahlberg 1994). Attachment theory is extraordinarily dominant in UK child and family social work and it is often invoked in this kind of unproblematic way and is frequently unchallenged. On this occasion, however, a social worker, who was based in a multi-disciplinary CAMHS team said very humorously:

> Yes, that is good news. Attachments are important, in fact I have a really good attachment to my husband, I wonder what he'll say when I go home and tell him he's set me up so well, I'm going to try another man!

In this way the causal connection between a good attachment and 'resilience' to cope with a move was broken so that the terms of the debate changed and the bureaucratic, resource and other pressures were engaged with more explicitly. I congratulated the social worker later and she remarked that her work alongside psychiatrists and psychologists had made her aware of how social workers, including herself, relied on attachment theory as a monolithic explanatory framework. Once it was problematized in that way, she was no longer able to invoke the theory without being self-conscious about so doing. Being exposed to other final vocabularies made her use the theory more critically.

Nurturing tricksters

Nurturing is used here as a verb and an adjective – how can we nurture trick-sters' talents so they can, in turn, nurture the liveliness of ideas amongst their own. It would certainly be against the grain of the trickster in me to prescribe a set of trickster competences, or establish an Academy of Trickster Excellence to train people to eat hubris!

I hope the exemplars I have offered will give you a flavour of what the benign trickster needs to do. Identifying your own 'final vocabularies' is a job you will need to attend to yourself within your own cultural domains. There are some clues in the work of the classicist, Martha Nussbaum, who defends a broad vision of education (Taylor and White 2005). In her various writings (e.g. Nussbaum, 1997, 2001, 2004), Nussbaum makes a powerful case for the opening up of dialogue through the encouragement of Socratic self-questioning. She advocates the value of literature and art in fostering the 'narrative imagination' which she considers to be essential to this criti-cal engagement, but she goes further in suggesting the need for continual questioning of assumptions. For example, she argues:

> Books are not 'alive'. . . . they certainly cannot think. Often, however, so great is their prestige that they actually lull pupils into forgetfulness of the activity of mind that is education's real goal, teaching them to be passively reliant on the written word. Such pupils, having internalized a lot of culturally authoritative material, may come to believe that they are very wise. And this arrogance undercuts still further the motivations for real searching. Such people are even less likely than ignorant people to search themselves, looking for arguments for and against their culture's ways of doing things. So, books, when used in education, must be used in such a way as to discourage this sort of reverence and passivity.
>
> (Nussbaum, 1997: 34)

Humour, art, irony, theory and formal knowledge are all essential, but it is how they are taught, read, deployed and made sense of that makes a *critical* difference in making you critical! It is important that life is allowed to rub at the edges of our theories, as my trickster friend and colleague Brid Featherstone (2005: 10) notes:

> I have argued that versions of feminism, which insisted that all men were power-ful and all women powerless victims, quite simply did not tally with my own experiences of strong women and invisible men. I also found it hard to reconcile what often felt like a rhetoric of sisterhood with my own experiences of relation-ships between women. Furthermore, and this was crucial, my relationship with my mother, particularly with the death of my father at an early age, was not easily reconcilable with what appeared to be sanitised accounts of victimised mothers who always loved their children unless prevented by patriarchal constraints.

Brid has from time to time pulled some threads from the smooth, com-fortable fabric of certain varieties of feminism, and has thus fashioned a new pattern in the cloth, but she has left the edges deliberately unfinished – there is always a danger of a new orthodoxy (e.g. Featherstone and Trinder 1997). She has been troubled by impossibly final settlements, but throughout she has remained a (trickster) feminist. It is incumbent upon those of us who are edu-cators to become tricksters, not so that we can stand outside and reject the settlements that others have left for us, but because 'the only theory worth having is that which [we] have to fight off, not that which [we] speak with profound fluency' (S. Hall 1992: 280). To nurture the trickster we need to learn to watch the world, its liturgies, contradictions and occasional absurdities, whilst knowing our own fallible place within it, as Dewey (1910: 177) notes:

> Genuine ignorance is profitable because it is likely to be accompanied by humil-ity, curiosity, and open mindedness; whereas ability to repeat catch-phrases, cant terms, familiar propositions, gives the conceit of learning and coats the mind with varnish waterproof to new ideas.

Spending time, either physically, or virtually through film, theatre, litera-ture, history or anthropology, in other cultural domains is important, but finding ways of slowing down the action in our familiar haunts and watching our own world from within it is also vital (Taylor and White 2000). Attending to how we use humour, for example, can give us clues about the sorts of iden-tities we are trying to fashion for ourselves. So, tape your team meetings and look for where the laughs are. Who are you laughing at? Why? What are you not allowed to say? Why? Try saying it. When were you last shocked by something a colleague or other professional said? Why were you shocked? Look at the everyday – tickle the bits of your imagination that have gone stale. Wake your monkey mind!

Acknowledgements

Data extracts were taken from a study funded by the Economic and Social Research Council, grant number R000222892.

Notes

1   I am grateful to Dave Wastell for introducing me to Hyde's book, which has been described as a study of 'the grand and squalid matter of all things human'. Dave and colleagues discuss the role of humour in organizational change (McMaster *et al.* 2005) and also introduce the trickster theme in a paper of the same name presented at the International Federation for Information Processing (IFIP) Conference, Atlanta, Georgia 2005.

2   In using the word *artus* here, Hyde is himself acting as trickster to destabilize meanings. He is drawing upon the Latin roots *ars* (skill, craft, crafty action, liberal arts, performance, art) and *artus* (a joint in the body), which in contemporary English coalesce in words such as artisan (a joiner and maker), articulation (an act of speech) and artifice (a made object). So here he is referring again to a worker who makes and remakes the articulated world.

3   This was overheard by Hubert Dreyfus, who mentioned it in a talk that was heard by Lewis Hyde, who wrote it down – another mischievous appropriation!

4   More recently (2002) controversy arose when a Home Office Minister, John Denham, used the term when addressing the Police Federation Conference. He was told by a delegate that officers were banned from using the term under race relations law, as it referred to debris at the bottom of slave ships at the end of a voyage. This reading is disputed by lexicographers (see http://news.bbc.co.uk/1/hi/uk/1988776.stm).

3 The 'critical' in critical reflection

Jan Fook and Gurid Aga Askeland

The importance of reflecting on practice appears to have become firmly entrenched in the professions. It is one response to the need for professional practice to become more responsive and effective (Gould 2004: 1; Redmond 2004: 1) and therefore to generate knowledge directly from the specific contexts of professional practice (Ghaye and Lillyman 2000a: xii). The idea of constructing professional knowledge by reflection on practice is attributed to Argyris and Schön (1976). Schön, however, developed the idea further into a model of reflective practice that has been well accepted and found useful in a range of professions such as education (Lauvås and Handal 2000; Brookfield 1995), nursing (B.J. Taylor 2000; Wisløff 1998), and social work (Napier and Fook 2000).

We find, however, that the concepts of reflection or reflective practice are often used interchangeably with the idea of critical reflection, implying that they have the same meaning (Lauvås and Handal 2000; B.J. Taylor 2000; Fook 1999a; Brookfield 1995). There have been efforts to clarify the distinction between the two ideas (Askeland, forthcoming; Brookfield 1995: 8; Reynolds 1998; Brookfield 2000), but we believe the distinction is important enough to visit again, particularly as the two terms become more frequently used. We therefore aim in this chapter to differentiate between our understandings of 'reflection' and 'critical reflection'. In particular, we discuss the dimensions of the 'critical' aspect of critical reflection, and clarify this by outlining how it might be experienced by some people when reflecting on their professional practice.

In the first section of this chapter we start by defining and differentiating reflection and critical reflection, and follow this by elaborating the theory involved in the 'critical' aspect of critical reflection. We finish the chapter by describing the results of some research which indicate how this 'critical' aspect might be experienced by participants in the critical reflection training groups one of us has run.

'Reflection' and 'critical reflection'

When we speak about being critical in combination with reflection it means, for us, to reflect through the lens of critical theory (Hillier 2002; Brookfield 1995; Carr and Kemmis 1986). Critical reflection is thus a process of reflection which incorporates analyses of individuals' thinking with regard to the influence of socially dominant thinking. It potentially builds on Schön's basic model of reflection through the incorporation of a more substantial analysis of the links between individually held beliefs, socially imposed ones and the ways power is exercised accordingly. In critical reflection, the material that is being reflected upon is filtered through an analysis based on critical theory. We will elaborate on this further in due course.

Reflection

It can be argued that 'reflecting' is something we do all the time without noticing it. For instance, in a professional context we often reflect consciously to create meaning or new understanding when something surprises us or is unfamiliar or problematic. However, we might not necessarily explicitly label the process (Schön 1991). The process of reflection involves examining our experiences anew and assessing what is reflected back. This may also involve constructing a new meaning, or one which makes sense in new or different circumstances. What is important, of course, is that if we are to harness this learning, we must become more aware of the process and the new meanings we are making. This is in essence the basic idea behind 'reflective practice'.

Behind Schön's development of the model for the reflective practitioner was his recognition of a gap between the 'espoused theory' and the 'theory in use' by many professionals (Schön 1991). His aim was to create a model by which professionals could develop their own practice theory by reflecting on their experience. By creating knowledge through reflection he was posing an alternative to the ruling epistemology, which tended to privilege knowledge created through a more 'objective' research process. In simple terms, Schön's model involved the comparison of 'espoused theory' (the ideas which we consciously believe we are working from) and 'theory in use' (the ideas which are embedded in, or implied by, what we actually do). By unearthing the assumptions implied by our actual practice, we are able to compare the theory we actually enact with the theory we may wish to believe we are enacting. This effectively exposes the gap between our theory and practice and thereby provides a template for how we may need to change either our practice or our theory. In this sense, Schön's model becomes a model for both the improvement of practice (and theory) but also for the creation of theory directly from practice experience.

This process of examining the hidden assumptions that are embedded in practice may also be used in a critical reflection process. One of the criticisms of Schön's model, however, is that it is inadequate in terms of providing direction regarding what assumptions should be unearthed and what should be changed (Adams 2002). This direction is provided by the use of critical theory. However, we first need to examine the idea of critical theory before we can flesh out in more detail how a critical reflection process might look.

Critical theory

The 'critical' component of reflection, for us, is provided by critical theory as the basis or direction for the reflection. Whilst there may be some debate about the complexity of critical theories, they may simply be seen as social theories that challenge the positivistic understanding of the world and the society (Brookfield 2001a; Agger 1998; Carr and Kemmis 1986). Critical theory results from processes which reveal contradictions in the rationality and the argumentations for social actions (Carr and Kemmis 1986:144). The central idea is that the new insight and knowledge gained through reflection would result in societal changes.

The latest generation of critical social theories combine critical theory with postmodernism and feminist theory (How 2003). Agger (1998) highlights some common characteristics, such as an opposition to positivism and acknowledging knowledge as constructed and value-based. All objectivity is not rejected, but science is considered situated and historical, a philosophical and politically contextual activity (most recently there have been further developments of these ideas, for example in critical realism; see Houston 2001). The socio-critical theorists convey a belief in progress and social change. By consciousness raising and the generation of new insights and analyses it will be possible in the future to destroy dominant structures and institutions which result in hegemonic opinions governing the society. An important message is that the social changes begin in people's everyday lives, in their families and at their workplaces. Even if structural conditions are important in people's lives, people have personal and collective power to change the society when they obtain insight through new knowledge (Agger 1998).

In relation to critical theory there are three issues we would like to highlight in this chapter as particularly important for critical reflection: knowledge, power and reflexivity.

Knowledge

Habermas (1981) distinguishes between three kinds of knowledge: the technical, developed through empirical analyses; the practical, developed through language and hermeneutic interpretation; and the emancipatoric, developed by reflection based on critical theory. He claimed that the various kinds of knowledge did not exclude each other, but depended on each other, and would serve different interests (Carr and Kemmis 1986). Causal knowledge might even be necessary to reveal how societal structures might influence and obstruct human development and actions. By combining causal and hermeneutic knowledge with critical social theory he wanted to show how people could see through, understand and explain social conditions and how they are created, and thereafter change them (Carr and Kemmis 1986).

The way we understand the relationship between knowledge and power from a critical perspective is spelt out succinctly by Fay (1977). He argues that individuals' understanding of themselves is embedded in the social structure and that therefore if choices about social circumstances are revealed, then opportunities for personal control are provided.

Foucault's work provides a more complex understanding of the operations of knowledge and power. He is concerned with the *relationship* between knowledge and power (Foucault 1983: 210). For Foucault, discourses are important as structures of knowledge created at a historical moment in a socio-political context. Because discourses are contextual, they are not static and may contradict formerly accepted ones. Foucault claims that a discourse leads to the possibility that some opinions gain authority over others. Because Foucault is concerned with the relationship between knowledge and power, he is preoccupied with how knowledge structures are created and how some discourses gain authority over others.

---

discourse can be both an instrument and an effect of power, but also a hindrance, a stumbling-block, a point of resistance and a starting point for an opposing strategy. Discourse transmits and produces power; it reinforces it, but also undermines and exposes it, renders it fragile and makes it possible to thwart it.

(Foucault 1990: 101 in Chambon *et al.* 1999).

In critical reflection the idea of discourse is useful in providing an analysis of how people's knowledge (assumptions) may be linked to power.

In relation to knowledge creation it is necessary to distinguish between Habermas' and Foucault's concept of discourse. A discourse in Habermas' terms is a democratic process where decisions are not ruled by power, but by the rationality in the argumentation. In a discourse it is therefore important to unearth the underlying norms that guide the communication. A discourse should be without hegemonic domination, everybody should exercise equal rights to speak, and the aim is to arrive at consensus on how to act (Carr and Kemmis 1986). In a discourse it is therefore important to unearth the underlying norms that guide the communication. In critical reflection groups, therefore, communication should have these qualities of discourse. However, a

shortcoming in Habermas' theory is his emphasis on the rational argumentation and the resulting neglect of irrational, emotional, social and cultural
aspects of human communication (Aamodt 1997).

Power

Foucault has contributed immensely to our understanding of power and the
dynamics of its operation (Brookfield, 2001b). According to him, power is not
structural or an institution in itself. Power is not something people have or
can acquire, but something they exercise. '[I]t is the name one attributes to a
complex strategical situation in a particular society' (Foucault 1990: 93). It is
everywhere, and only exists in relationships, on micro as well as macro levels.
How power is exercised is often disguised, and we therefore have to hunt for it
using a process of critical reflection to help reveal it. In social work and health
professions, laws, rules and procedures that regulate their work might be considered to disempower people. In Foucault's terms the exercise of power takes
place in relationships between the people. The social and health workers who
operate laws and regulations do not necessarily have to do so blindly but use
their professional judgement. However, to use their power purposefully they
must become conscious of it as a first step. This is one of the functions of
critical reflection, to enable awareness of the one's own use of power. A further
function of critical reflection is to enable changed actions based on these new
insights about the operation of power.

Foucault considers power to have productive aspects in that it produces
knowledge and action. Yet professionals often deny their own power or are
uncomfortable with the idea of having it (Napier and Fook 2000). Power is
often seen as something negative instead of productive, which might also be
seen in the light of Foucault's (1990: 94–5) claim that 'Where there is power,
there is resistance'. If that is so, it is important to account for the resistance.
Examining how and why power works (or does not), the sources and maintenance of resistance, can lead us to replicate practices which have the potential
to challenge and change dominant power. Thus critical reflection performs a
valuable role in analysing professional's own use of (and resistance to) power.

Professionals hold positions that allow them to define other people, such
as users' situations and how to handle them (Askeland, forthcoming; Howe
1994a). Professionals operate at the interface between treatment and control
and therefore must exercise a great deal of professional judgement (White and
Stancombe 2003). They therefore have to be extremely concerned about how
they perform their professional roles, what they do or do not get involved in,
and how they mutually contribute to create the situations in which they play a
part. Therefore critical reflection can assist in exposing their choices and the
assumptions behind them.

In a roundtable discussion with Foucault, Paul Thiband said: 'Wherever
there is social work, the social worker is always tied to a source of authority'

(Foucault 1999: 91). In this sense, any professional, no matter what their position in the hierarchy or their source of power, will exercise some type of authority as well as being under the authority of superiors. Therefore critical reflection is vital to unearth an understanding of these sources of authority and how it operates in everyday practice and decision-making. A deconstruction of understandings of authority can lead to a reconstruction of it.

Reflexivity

The idea of reflexivity is important in our approach to critical reflection, since it adds a dimension to the understanding of agency, or personal ability to act upon or influence a situation. Reflexivity can simply be defined as an ability to recognize our own influence – and the influence of our social and cultural contexts on research, the type of knowledge we create, and the way we create it (Fook 1999b). In this sense, then, it is about factoring ourselves as players into the situations we practice in. This specifically involves: recognizing the influence of ourselves as the lenses (physical, emotional, social and cultural) through which we see and interpret ourselves and our contexts; recognizing that our contexts themselves may influence what knowledge is available and how we interpret it; acknowledging the role of our own selves and perspectives in selecting the knowledge which we believe is important; and, finally, understanding the *reactivity* element, that is, how the world we see may in fact be a direct function of the methods we use to see it and therefore a function of the environmental reaction to our actions and presence.

Using the idea of reflexivity, then, critical reflection can be seen as a way of researching personal practice or experience in order to develop our understandings of ourselves as knowers or makers of knowledge. This in turn helps us make specific connections between ourselves as individuals and our broader social, cultural and structural environment, by understanding how our ideas, beliefs and assumptions might be at least partially determined by our social contexts. This therefore increases our awareness of how we participate in constructing existing power relations in our social contexts, by showing how the ideas we hold may do this.

The idea of reflexivity is filled out further when we refer to Beck's (1992) idea of 'reflexive modernity' and Giddens' (1992) concept of 'life politics'. 'Reflexive modernity' is Beck's way of characterizing the current social period. We will discuss the concept of 'life politics', which is important in reflexive modernity, further on. The main features of reflexive modernity include a breakdown of the predictable life stages, social rituals and norms because of uncertain social conditions. In addition, there has been a rise in access to information, both through increased educational opportunities and through technological advances. The resulting shifts in social boundaries, categories and borders, and the increased opportunity to remake them, have placed an emphasis on the importance of individual identity-making and life choices.

Contexts therefore become more important, and because traditional boundaries are broken, people derive their sense of community from a wide range of networks. There are therefore different sources of power, which are less hierarchical and more mixed.

However, in this climate of increased choice and fluidity, there is also increased risk in charting a life course through uncertain and new conditions. Social institutions themselves are not able to monitor and control these risks in personal lives, so there is an increased need for individuals to find their own sources of meaning and solidarity. And overall it is the construction of the self within these fluid social contexts, which becomes the crucial task of living. Thus in reflexive modernity the self is a reflexive project (Giddens 1991), a biographical project in which 'critical reflection and incoming information are constantly used by people to constitute and (re)negotiate their identities' (Ferguson 2001: 45).

This task of living, to create a sense of self which is meaningful, has been termed by Giddens (1992) 'life politics' (Ferguson 2001: 48). The idea of life politics is essentially an attempt to conceptualize the experience of individuals in negotiating their existence within a breakdown of traditional structures. This is not to deny that there are still structures which to a large extent determine life chances – however, the form, expression and force of these structures may be changing. In this context, the concept of life politics becomes important. It places emphasis on the idea that people also have to make *choices* about how they engage with, and relate to, the sorts of *chances* they encounter. This distinction between *chances* and *choices* that Ferguson (2001: 47) makes is useful in our understanding of our central question of 'how to promote a theory of human agency whilst at the same time taking account of the impact of social structure' (Houston 2001: 849). For in this climate of changing structures, it may also be possible to make choices which involve challenging, resisting, and remaking the ways in which some of these structures play out in the lives of individual people. The idea of life politics, then, may be useful in providing a framework for understanding how critical reflection may assist in remaking the ways individuals engage with social structures in their lives.

The critical theory in critical reflection

How do the above theories translate into the theory we use in guiding our critical reflection learning groups? First we should emphasize, as stated earlier, that the processes of reflection and critical reflection will be similar, in that both seek to unearth underlying assumptions, or the hidden theory embedded in specific professional practices. However, the particular theory guiding the reflection will influence the kinds of assumptions which are focused on, and the specific changes in practice which are flagged as a result. Thus the particular guiding principles will directly influence the stated purposes of the reflective process. In a critical reflection approach, therefore, the specific purpose of the reflective process is to expose or unsettle dominant assumptions with the expressed purpose of challenging and changing dominant power relations.

This involves the following more specific principles:

- Linking personal experience with social and political contexts and influences – including an understanding of the social construction of individual perception and experience, or how individuals are socially made, which also involves an ideological analysis, or how domination works at individual and everyday levels, and a connection between knowledge and power.
- An analysis of the dynamics of power and its operation/exercise at different levels and in different ways, particularly the level of personal power, including an awareness of personal power and influence (sense of agency).
- Praxis or an ongoing linking of theory and practice, especially the micro practice possibilities (i.e. practice which is immediately possible in the current context of a person's work).
- A focus on the transformative or social change possibilities (i.e. change in one's social context), particularly focusing on how changes in the immediate context may build into changes at broader levels.
- Valuing both empirically generated knowledge and alternative (non-positivist) and inclusive ways of knowing, which includes valuing contradictory perspectives as well as knowledge created through experience (personal, social and professional).
- An analysis of how people negotiate life chances within a context of choices – how people use critical reflection to make and remake their identities.

The changes brought about by critical reflection

Using the above critical framework, is it possible to trace transformative changes brought about through a process of critical reflection? Most of our experience in working with critical reflection has been in using the process in small groups to assist with professional learning, in social work education at undergraduate and postgraduate level, and in interprofessional continuing education. In this section we report on some research conducted by one of us with interprofessional groups (involving mostly allied health and human service workers). The study attempted to trace the details of some of the changes in thinking which group participants reported at the end of the learning programme.

The learning programme involved participants in small groups reflecting on a specific practice experience with the assistance of other participants as peers and colleagues.

A framework of critical reflective questions was used based on the critical theories outlined above (Fook 2004b). A collegiate and trusting climate was established in order to facilitate openness to learning. Sessions ranged from 1 day to 2½ days in length (the latter normally spread over a period of a month).

Written evaluation forms were completed at the end of the sessions, and included semi-structured questions such as 'what did you learn?', 'how will you use the learning?', did you learn something directly applicable to your practice?', as well as room to provide extra comments. The responses to these questions were analysed (using both a thematic and content analysis framework) with regard to the themes of identity construction, types of choices constructed, views about the connection between participants' selves and their social worlds, changes in a personal sense of mastery or control, and other aspects of self-actualization. There were 154 completed forms from participants in 20 different groups (all conducted in Australia in the years 2002–4). Participants included professionals from a range of roles and backgrounds (nurses, counsellors, teachers, social workers, occupational therapists, human resource managers, child protection workers, policy officers).

The broad question the study attempted to investigate was: How do people challenge, resist and remake themselves in relation to structures? Many of the responses to this question did not easily fall into clear categories, often sharing overlapping aspects. Therefore, they were initially categorized in relation to some of the specific themes included in the framework of life politics: self-constructions; mastery, control and self-actualization; choices in relation to chances; and the connections between personal and social domains. These are discussed in more detail below.

Peoples' constructions of themselves: themes regarding self and identity

In broad terms people moved towards a broader, more encompassing, more holistic, more complex sense of professional self (one which can include their own emotions and personal experience and beliefs), and a more affirmed, reflexive and empowered sense of themselves. Specifically, this involved:

- Developing a self-directed sense of self – moving from other-directed to self-directed identity construction: the ability to move from a sense of self which is relatively defined and determined by social environment (especially those devalued in a devaluing environment) to recognizing the source of this self-definition; separating these sources of definition from their own choices; then making a conscious choice to define and value themselves more in their own terms (e.g. 'I learnt to maintain a sense of self within a departmental framework'; 'being able to identify the value of the work that is done even when it is not seen as productive by the organisation'; 'learnt how we allow ourselves to take on others' expectations'; 'the importance of knowing yourself well enough to know how to reaffirm the sources of confidence generating').

- Developing an integrated sense of self – moving from experiencing tensions between different aspects of themselves to being able to construct a reintegrated sense of themselves as workers and people, which incorporates formerly oppositional characteristics or domains, such as personal and professional (e.g. 'I felt less of a fraud'); see also the section below on choices.
- Developing an empowered sense of self – moving from seeing themselves as relatively powerless or as marginal individuals, to seeing themselves as reflexive social agents, with an ability to act and influence a situation, and whose sense of self affects both approaches and outcomes.
- Developing a sense of self-affirmation – moving from doubts about personal or professional suitability or value to feeling freer to be themselves, more confidence in own abilities and authority, and more acceptance and value of their own personal characteristics (e.g. 'I felt affirmed in a new way as a social work practitioner'; 'I felt proud to be a social worker again').

Mastery, control and self-actualization: themes regarding empowerment

Broadly, people moved towards reframing their ideas about power (to include different types – non-hierarchical, personal and emotional) in ways that allowed them to feel more powerful and therefore to act in more powerful ways. Specifically, this involved:

- Developing a more complex view of power and themselves as potentially powerful – moving from hierarchical and positional views of power to recognizing many different types and expressions of power.
- Developing a sense of personal power and authority – moving from feeling constricted by organizational situations to an awareness of personal authority, the potential to take control, and feeling a greater courage to be themselves.
- Developing a sense of personal and emotional legitimation and power – moving from a denial or non-acceptance of personal and emotional experience to a recognition, acceptance and integration of emotions/personal experience and harnessing this for use in professional practice.

A sense of new choices created (within a framework of chances)

In broad terms, people were able to move from a sense of restricted (sometimes paralysing) choices to find new ways of seeing which in turn created new opportunities for action. This was experienced as 'liberating' or 'freeing'. This typically takes the form of moving from 'binary' or 'oppositional' constructions or 'forced choices' – for instance, seeing situations as involving unresolvable dilemmas – to allowing for more complex, multiple, or different constructions (e.g. 'I see practice dilemmas as an opportunity for positive change'; 'I developed the ability to look at other options and not be afraid'). Often work with service users might be conceptualized within clear parameters. For example, within a hospital setting, one social worker believed that there were set ways of dealing with the husband of a female patient (i.e. that the patient's interests come first). This led her to assume that their interests were necessarily different and mutually exclusive. This made her apprehensive about seeing the husband. However, through reflection she realized that these were her own assumptions, and partly caused her to feel defensive towards the man and his own needs and requests. She was able to see that if she remained more open to the husband's perspective she may be able to find multiple ways of addressing both the woman's and the man's needs.

Specifically, this involved:

- Reconstructing an integrated framework of choices – moving from a sense of 'personal versus professional' tensions to professional work which integrates the personal; moving from a 'consensus' framework for practice to a framework of consensus which can incorporate conflict.
- Reconstructing a more flexible and complex frame of choices – moving from a sense of clear boundaries to a more flexible orientation (e.g. 'no right or wrong way').
- Reconstructing a more attainable frame of choices – moving from 'perfectionist' constructions to frameworks which enable action (e.g. limits of responsibility – not taking responsibility for everyone's happiness or for 'getting it right all the time').
- Reconstructing possibilities for multiple choices or ways of seeing (e.g. 'a strong reminder that there are many ways to view situations').

Connection between the personal and social

This involved what might broadly be termed a more 'contextual' way of working. It involved people's ability to move from seeing themselves as isolated or powerless individuals, differentiated from others in unworkable ways, to locating themselves as responsible actors within a context of other players. They were able to differentiate themselves in acceptable ways which allowed further practice possibilities. (e.g. 'I learnt to effectively challenge my own assumptions so that I can get the most out of interactions with others').

Specifically this involved:

- An openness to other views and perspectives – reconstructing an accepting sense of self in relation to others: moving from a sense of differences in others as paralysing action to the ability to recognize and accept difference in others so as to allow the person to separate their own needs/desires and then work in a more accepting way, e.g. 'managers are people too'. This allows for improved practice: letting clients tell their own story (e.g. 'not allow the views of one to cloud my view of all the others') and an acceptance and realization of other people's perceptions of the situation and a 'oneness' with other social workers in our feelings, concerns and ideals ('I learnt to let go of other people's values that conflict with mine and accept the differences between mine and theirs, rather than being disturbed like I used to.').
- Developing a reflexive sense of self – the ability to see their own influence on clients and outcomes and change: greater recognition and acceptance of personal influence; recognition that aspects of the self might need to be incorporated into practice in order to produce better outcomes; an ability to see how a sense of self and difference affects their approach (e.g. 'I have learnt how much I impact on my clients and therefore am very much a part of the outcomes')
- Developing a sense of context which influenced criteria for practice (e.g. 'I learnt the notion of helping in the context of achieving fairness and equity. not just trying to help the individual all the time'; 'reframing the helping relationship in an organisational context').

In broad terms the findings from this analysis demonstrate that individual workers can use critical reflection to reconstitute themselves as potentially powerful, able to exercise agency in influencing situations. This involves a revaluing of self through: shifting the source of self-value from social environment to themselves; valuing characteristics which were formerly thought to be non-professional; and reintegrating these characteristics into their professional identities. Choices are also reconstructed, moving usually from framing choices in 'forced choice' terms to provide multiple choices, and sometimes from a more fatalistic frame ('dilemma') to a more empowered frame ('opportunity'). These ways of reframing understandings of practice provide more opportunities for new practices. In this process participants also experience a 'liberation' or empowerment, as if freed from ways of constructing a situation, which restrict options and ways of doing and being.

How do participants experience the process of critical reflection? What is 'critical' about it? This above analysis provides a little more detail to our understanding of how individual people might challenge, resist and remake the ways social structures play out in their lives. Part of the process involves creating an awareness of how hidden assumptions behind our practice may be directly influenced by social contexts or social learning, be it cultural, professional, structural or workplace. Second comes a recognition of how this thinking may be undesirable or restrictive, thus limiting the range of options for practice, and sometimes for self-recognition. For example, sometimes such thinking leads us to deny or devalue important personal characteristics in professional settings, leading people to feel that there is no room to incorporate their personal integrity into their work lives. Third comes a reframing of professional practice (and professional self-identity) to include these possibilities.

These findings allow us to theorize the critical aspect of critical reflection process as following four stages:

1   Creating an awareness of how hidden assumptions behind our practice may be directly influenced by social contexts or social learning, be it cultural, professional, structural, political or workplace.
2   A recognition of how this thinking may be undesirable or restrictive, thus limiting the range of options for practice, and sometimes for self-recognition (e.g. sometimes such thinking leads to a denial or devaluation of important personal characteristics in professional settings, leading people to feel that there is no room to incorporate their personal integrity into their work lives).
3   A more empowered identity, as professional practice (and professional self-identity) is reframed to include these possibilities, and as there is a growing awareness of how we as individuals are able to ourselves create and reframe our thinking freed from social expectations.
4   An awareness of new skills/strategies which become possible with this new way of thinking.

Conclusion

We have argued that the critical aspect of critical reflection is underpinned by a clear theory, based on broad critical theory and informed by aspects of Foucauldian theorizing regarding power. Fundamentally, this provides an analysis of how people make (and remake) themselves in relation to social context and structure, and how they gain a sense of personal power or agency in this process. In this sense, for us, the aim of critical reflection, or what makes the reflection critical, is the allowing of more control and choice in individual lives through the exposure of dominant social assumptions (which had partly maintained their power through their hidden operation). We have illustrated how this happened in detail for some participants in critical reflection training workshops conducted by one of us.

We do not wish to argue that fundamental and transformative changes may not happen for people who critically reflect but theorize it in other ways. For example, critical reflection may be theorized as being primarily about the making of meaning (e.g. Mezirow 1991). We do not see other meanings of critical reflection as being mutually exclusive with our own. In fact it may be that the power of critical reflection for any individual cannot be maximized unless its meaning is theorized in a way which is relevant for that person. However, we would argue that part of the power of critical reflection in opening up new perspectives and choices about practice may only be realized if the connections between individual thinking and identity, and dominant social beliefs are articulated and realized. If we do not theorize the meaning of the 'critical' aspect of critical reflection in the way we have done, then the power of critical reflection may only be partially realized.

PART II
Professional Learning

4 Reflections on building a reflective practice community in China

Pauline Sung-Chan and Angelina Yuen-Tsang

The establishment of the Socialist regime in mainland China has not freed China from social problems related to poverty, social inequality, and corruption. In the Maoist era, families, local communities, *danwei*,[1] and state agents attempted to tackle such problems (Yuen-Tsang 1997). However, since the introduction of the market economy, the functions of the above groups have gradually eroded. In response to the social and welfare needs created by the economic reform, the Ministry of Civil Affairs of China and several semi-governmental bodies, such as the All-China Federation of Women[2] and the All-China Youth Federation, as well as some non-governmental organizations, have emerged to provide social services. There is an increasing demand for professionally trained social work personnel and a corresponding need for professional training programmes in social work.

In view of the urgent need to 'train the trainers', the Department of Applied Social Sciences of the Hong Kong Polytechnic University developed a Master of Social Work (China) program (MSW) in 2000, which aimed to train social work educators who could assume leadership in promoting social work education in the future. Dissatisfied with technical-rational educational paradigm based on positivist philosophy, our programme endeavours to cultivate 'scholarship in practice' among its students and to develop reflective social workers who are able to think, articulate, be self-critical, evaluate their use of theories and knowledge constantly in different socio-cultural contexts, and evolve their own personal perspectives and approaches to professional practice.

Our teaching staff are committed to evaluating and developing innovative projects intended to train competent and reflective practitioners. Staff members regard practicum as the mechanism most conducive to strengthening students' competence in integrating theories with practice through critical reflection. In 2000, we used practicum training to implement our first action experiment to educate reflective practitioners in Beijing. We considered it imperative to build a community including our MSW students, the local social service workers, and the local residents that would be competent in reflective practice. Since 2000, the 11 teaching staff have built up seven practicum sites in different parts of China. To date, we have trained a total of 73 social work educators with satisfactory learning outcomes.

In this chapter, we first discuss the meaning of reflection underlying our teaching model. Second, we present our experiences of implementing the conceptual understanding of reflection in Beijing from 2000 to 2002. We conclude with a critical discussion of the risk and potential of educating reflective practitioners in Chinese society, and its implication for social work practice and education.

Different facets of reflection

What does it mean to educate a reflective practitioner? This hinges on our understanding on the notion of reflection. Different philosophical paradigms offer different understandings of the term. In this chapter, we present the theoretical and philosophical traditions that have shaped our understanding of reflection. These include the views of John Dewey and Donald Schön, as well as the theories of social constructionism and cybernetics.

Relating reflection to thinking, Dewey understood reflective thinking as experimental inquiry. Dewey (1933) defined experimental inquiry as 'the controlled or directed transformation of an *indeterminate* situation into one that is so *determinate* in its constituent distinctions and relations as to convert the elements of the original situation into a unified whole'. As Argyris and Schön (1996: 31) put it: 'Inquiry begins with an indeterminate, problematic situation, a situation whose inherent conflict, obscurity, or confusion blocks action. The role of the inquirer is to seek to make that situation determinate, thereby restoring the flow of activity'. Inquiry involves both mental reasoning and action. The Deweyan inquirer is not a spectator, but an actor who stands within a situation, actively seeking to understand it so as to change it.

Since the 1970s, Donald Schön, with his long-term partners Chris Argyris, Martin Rein and Jeanne Bamberger, have expanded Dewey's conception of reflection (Argyris and Schön 1974, 1978, 1996; Bamberger and Schön 1991; Schön 1983, 1987; Schön and Rein 1994). Schön regards Dewey's definition of reflection as related to two significant concepts, namely problem-setting and experimental inquiry (Sung-Chan 2000b). Further, Schön has noted the potential contribution of hermeneutics, constructionism and cybernetics to a robust understanding of reflection. Specifically, Schön expounds the notion of reflection in terms of framing, frame reflection, reciprocal frame reflection, frame conflict, reframing, and frame experimentation (Sung-Chan 2000a).

According to Schön, a reflective practitioner regards any situation in terms of her 'underlying structures of belief, perception, and appreciation', or her unique *frame*, which influences how she constructs a sense of coherence within vague, indeterminate practice situations (Schön 1983; Schön and Rein 1994: 23). Eventually, the practitioner thus constructs a *social reality* from a particular frame, engaging in two complementary processes that fulfil a *problem-setting* function, naming and framing. In so doing, she first highlights certain features from the often overwhelmingly complex practice situation. Then she engages in judging the problematic elements of the situation as well as the direction for future transformation. She then makes a *'normative leap* from data to recommendations, from fact to values, from "is" to "ought" '(Schön and Rein 1994: 26). Thus, not only theoretical knowledge but also, most importantly, normative values shape the construction of a practice reality.

Frame reflection is a crucial step in the reframing that helps resolve conflicts and controversies practitioners meet in practice (Schön and Rein 1994: 38). The frames that influence practice are tacit in nature; they 'exert a powerful influence on what we see and how we interpret what we see, they belong to the taken-for-granted world . . . we are usually unaware of their role in organizing our actions, thoughts and perception' (Schön and Rein 1994: 34). All interpretations or frames are necessarily conditioned by the particular society, historical period, and social status in which they originate. Metacultural discourses also influence the ways individuals frame situations. For example, policy-makers are influenced by *metacultural frames*, which are themselves shaped by cultural understandings of social need, the market, and social control, when they conceive and construct housing policy for the homeless (Schön and Rein 1994: 41).

Conflicts arising from different ways of interpreting problematic situations often trigger frame reflection (Schön and Rein 1994: 57, 170). Noting different and conflicting interpretations of any one situation affords the practitioner the opportunity to examine critically the different frames. The practitioner may also engage in frame reflection when she discovers that her initial frame differs from the frame in which her work in any particular situations is developing (Argyris and Schön 1996: 40). It is the 'discovery of the mismatch between outcome and expectation that triggers awareness of a problematic situation and sets in motion the inquiry aimed at addressing the discrepancy' (Argyris and Schön 1996: 31). This awareness leads to new thinking and acting.

Frame reflection involves two processes, *frame construction* and *frame appreciation*. Since one's frame is intrinsically tacit, an individual cannot critically reflect on it without first making it explicit. This involves identifying how one 'selects things for attention and organises them, guided by an appreciation of the situation that gives it coherence and sets a direction for action' (Schön 1987: 4). The frame organizing one's action is the *frame-in-use*. It consists, for example, of a practitioner's set of theories, values, metaphors, images and assumptions that guide her reasoning and ultimately her action.

A complementary and essentially evaluative process, frame appreciation, follows frame construction. It requires the practitioner to regard her frame and the frames of the significant others as 'texts' for critical reading, seeing each in terms of 'its adequacy to the emerging intentions, values and interests of other stakeholders and herself' (Schön and Rein 1994: 173). Taking a critic role, the practitioner thus evaluates the different consequences – along with their aesthetic, pragmatic, ethical, and political dimensions – that would result from seeing the situation according to each frame.

Frame reflection is necessarily a social process. When the practitioner and her counterparts are trapped in frame conflict (e.g. when each person views the situation differently and cannot see the situation in terms of the other people's frames), their ability to reach agreement is compromised. To reach resolution, each individual must understand the ways by which others frame the situation. This need results in reciprocal frame reflection (Schön and Rein 1994: 45).

One of the logical outcomes of frame reflection is *reframing*. The critical reflection process enables all involved, including the practitioner, to identify the parameters of their initial frames, as well as those of others' frames. Through inquiring into the intentions and meanings of those involved in the conflict, the practitioner reframes the problematic situation, thus modelling future reframing. As Ricoeur (1976: 88) highlighted, interpreting a text 'goes beyond the mere function of pointing out and showing what already exists. Here showing is at the same time creating a new mode of being'. Frame reflection is thus an ontological process that gives rise to a different ways of 'making' the world (Goodman 1978).

Reflection remains incomplete without action. *Experimentation* is a useful test of the viability of the frame ultimately advocated by the practitioner. By subjecting the frame to rigorous experimentation, the practitioner can discover any flaws: experimentation then serves at least two functions: first, it explores the situation with a view to gaining new knowledge; second, it encourages change (Argyris *et al.* 1985: 63–7).

The understanding of reflection underlying our training model for reflective social work practitioners draws on some insights of social construction theorists and scholars of second-order cybernetics as well as those of Schön. According to social constructionism, reflexivity is a 'turning back of one's experience upon oneself' (Mead 1968). Further, the self under scrutiny is socially constructed. Second-order cybernetics is concerned with inquiry into circularity and recursive processes (von Foerster, 1974). Cybernetics originally focused on studying circular relationships in observable systems. Second-order cybernetics deals with *observing systems* instead of observed systems. The practitioner, in her observing role, becomes part of any system of description and intervention via reflection. The focus of reflection thus shifts from the participants as the basic unit for intervention to both the practitioner and the participants, thus stressing how the practitioner can gain understanding of her effect on others.

This process demands the practitioner become willing to make explicit the contradictions and paradoxes implicitly embedded in her own observational process. Revealing these hidden contradictions through conversation, the practitioner becomes conscious of herself as an other, as the subject of reflection. By engaging in this process, she not only models critical self-reflection for others, but enriches the experience for all involved (Steier 1991: 7). Reflexivity is an organizing and reconstructing process of self-reflection and communication, a 'dialogue' between oneself and one's community rooted in language (Gergen 1985). Constituting a kind of community, the practitioner and participants can reflect on their ways of understanding themselves and listening to others' stories, ultimately learning that they are not privileged interpreters of the situation or of others' texts (Steier 1989).

Social constructionists emphasize that these multiple perspectives and conversations constitute multiple realities. Reflection invites the individual to see both the constraints and potentials across these multiple interpretations. This promotes an expansion of understanding which is social in nature.

Our narrative of building a reflective practice community in Beijing

How we narrate our experience of instituting and evaluating a programme to train critically reflective practitioners reflects our theoretical and philosophical orientation and biases. Our main narrative plot does not fit typical storytelling genres, such as the success and failure narrative, the happily-ever-after or the tragic narrative, or the epic hero narrative (Gergen 1991: 162). Our story emerges from a collection of voices belonging to a number of characters/ actors. Together, these voices co-constructed a drama of reflective practice against a highly complex backdrop of massive unemployment arising from the economic reform in China. The drama does not have one main protagonist. We present the voices of different characters in order to create a mirroring effect, allowing different facets of reflective practice to emerge in the presence of others.

The overall aim of this project was to build up a community of reflective practitioners so that they could develop, after critically reflecting on the reality which they helped create in the past, different ways of constructing realities in the future. The 'characters' of our story include eight local, untrained social service workers (commonly referred to in China as 'cadres'), four social work student practitioners (henceforth refered to as the 'practitioners'), 13 unemployed women; and two social work teachers. We have selected a number of episodes to illustrate how the practice of reflectivity among these actors encouraged them to reflect on the way their choices constructed reality.

By sharing this story, we hope our readers will themselves reflect critically on the struggles of these actors and on their search for appropriate approaches to coping with the unemployment issue facing women in China. Hopefully, these actors' reflections will motivate readers to explore what they can do differently with respect to this marginalized group of women.

Episode 1: Frame reflection and reframing of local cadres and student practitioners

What was the background against which the practitioners engaged in critical reflection? Their process of reflection began when they accepted an invitation from the All-China Federation of Women to participate in a consultancy project. Since 1949, the state had played the lead role in providing employment and comprehensive welfare for workers and their families. But the launch of the open-door economic policy in the late 1970s resulted in a fundamental restructuring of the traditional socialist economy, greatly affecting the livelihood of workers. With the introduction of the market economy, most of the state-owned enterprises became uncompetitive. This caused massive unemployment, especially in the urban areas. The unofficial unemployment figure was as high as 50 million in 2003.

For the most part, the government has relied on the market to solve this emerging problem. However, some local governments have proven more receptive to collaborating with academics to solve the developing unemployment problem. In 2000, the All-China Federation of Women formed a tripartite relationship with the Chinese Women's College and the Hong Kong Polytechnic University, launching a project to develop a practice model to improve the services offered to unemployed women in a local neighbourhood in Beijing.

Confronted with this local expression of the general unemployment problem, neither the social work teachers from the two universities nor the student practitioners had a predetermined intervention model before their entry into the community. Nonetheless, they were explicit in their direction of practice. They subscribed to a participatory action research paradigm based on two core commitments: promoting reflection and its resultant action by the collaborators; and respecting local knowledge. They were cautious of practising from an expert-oriented frame. They emphasized strengthening the capacity of the local cadres to meet the increasingly complex demands of the unemployed women through developing a culturally sensitive practice model. The cadres received no formal social work training.

In order to reflect on the frame underlying the cadres' practices, the practitioners took oral histories (Mills 1959; Slim and Thomson 1995; Ku and Yau

1997). This method gave the cadres a public space to describe their perceptions of the social issues and problems encountered by the women; to tell of the approaches they employed to deal with these problems; to explain the rationales underlying their choices; and to detail their appraisals of the strength and weakness of the approaches. The stories captured their approaches to working with women in general and with the unemployed women in particular. The practitioners were successful in organizing eight cadres and collecting a total of 15 stories. They thus began forming these cadres into a reflective practice community.

The practitioners became extremely excited while listening to the cadres narrate their frustration and excitement in working with the unemployed women. After collecting stories, they were supposed to guide the cadres in reflecting on the stories by reconstructing the cadres' underlying frame that influenced their practice with the unemployed women. Instead, however, the practitioners took over, interpreting the situation without the cadres' reflection. The practitioners spoke primarily from the position of experts, strongly criticizing the cadres' approach to practice. Interestingly, the practitioners focused their attention narrowly on the negative aspects of the cadres' indigenous practice frame. Without thoroughly reconstructing the features of the cadres' practice, they judged the practice as backward and unprofessional. On the basis of this evaluation, they advocated replacing the cadres' practice with a Western social work model.

While listening to the practitioners' reflection on the cadres' frames, I[3] became curious about what might have contributed to their hasty suppression the cadres' voices. I then recognized an interesting paradox: reflecting for others was indeed unreflective. I invited the practitioners to reflect on their way of working with the cadres, and on its unintended consequences. Through reflection, the practitioners discovered a gap between their frame-in-use and the practice frame they espoused. They had practised an expert-oriented and culturally insensitive approach instead of a participatory approach that stressed a respect for local knowledge. This discovery was a shocking realization, but it motivated them to explore others ways of looking at the cadres' practice and its usefulness in serving the unemployed women.

The critical reflection triggered a reframing of the practitioners' expert-oriented frame. With the desire to espouse a participatory frame, they designed a plan to have the cadres reflect on their indigenous practice frame. The frame reconstruction afforded an opportunity to identify the major components of the cadres' practice frame, including its strengths and weakness. Three major features emerged. First, the cadres had themselves adopted an expert orientation. The cadres acted as problem assessors and problem-solvers, without involving the service users as collaborators. They were authoritative and directive. Second, the cadres' intervention emphasized primarily tangible service, with little stress on psychological and social considerations. Their analyses of problems were supported by 'common sense', with almost no reference to any professional theories. Third, the cadres relied on family and work organizations to help their service users make changes. The cadres were extremely resourceful in mobilizing social support networks that could provide tangible assistance to their service users. Through critical reading of the cadres' practice, the practitioners realized that local practices had positive aspects that they could maximize further.

Episode 2: Frame reflection and reframing of local cadres and student practitioners

The cadres' frame reconstruction was to be followed by a reframing of the cadres' practice. Nonetheless, the reflection effect was rather short-lived. A surprising phenomenon emerged. The practitioners were supposed to collaborate with the cadres to develop a practice framework that, based on the understanding and insights generated from the frame reconstruction stage, would be congruent with the needs of the unemployed women within the Chinese socio-cultural context. Instead, the practitioners reframed the situation for the cadres. The practitioners proposed adopting a social support network approach through which the unemployed women would help each other cope with the psychological stresses arising from the process of being laid off (*xiagang*) and regain psychological strength. Listening to the practitioners, the cadres became eager to take immediate action to implement the new model. I reacted differently, however. I considered it important for the practitioners to evaluate the appropriateness of advocating a psychologically oriented frame.

My invitation to have them reflect on their suggestion took them all by surprise. However, once they evaluated the appropriateness of the psychologically oriented approach, the practitioners recognized that they had explained the women's failure to seek employment within the context of a model emphasizing deficiency and pathology. They had regarded the unemployed women as deficient in adapting to the rapidly changing social environment. The practitioners had assumed that learning new ways to manage the psychological stresses was the key to women regaining the psychological strength needed to face the harsh reality that they might not return to the market.

As the practitioners realized, their advocated frame, however, did not take into consideration the macro-economic, social and cultural forces contributing to the individuals' predicament. In addition, the belief underlying this frame was very similar to assumptions underlying the indigenous government's policy that some individuals are losers and should sacrifice their personal welfare for that of the country. This 'self-sacrifice' frame was shaped by two prevailing discourses, namely the 'grand narrative of progress' and the 'obedience to authority' discourses. The latter has historical roots in the traditional Chinese philosophy of Confucianism. In order for China to make progress in the midst of globalization, some citizens have to make sacrifices in order to show allegiance towards the open door policy and related policies set by the state.

Through frame reconstruction, the practitioners made explicit the professional, social, and cultural discourses shaping their practice. They explored the potential unintended consequences resulting from their advocated frame. Their implicit frame contradicted one that would emphasize capacity building through supporting the women's network and in which women could make use of action research to solve their own problems. Reflection sharpened the practitioners' awareness of this discrepancy in their practice. On the one hand, they claimed to practise an approach that stressed promoting the capacity of the women and changing women's victim position. On the other hand, they acted in the opposite way by encouraging the women to subjugate themselves to the domination of the professional, social and cultural discourses that reinforced the marginalization of middle-aged and uneducated women and encouraged their obedience towards the Socialist government.

Recognizing that they had once again acted on an expert-oriented frame, the practitioners decided to join the cadres in constructing an alternative framework for improving the cadres' practice with the unemployed women. They all were committed to synthesizing local practice with Western theories in an effort to develop a culturally sensitive, theoretically justified practice frame. The cadres and the practitioners debated their options rigorously, which helped them identify the most appropriate framework to adopt. Through a process of reflective practice, the group interrogated the underlying assumptions of the options before them, as well as the relevance and contradictions of the proposed frameworks within indigenous Chinese culture.

The group identified communal networking, a key component of the cadres' existing indigenous practice, as the major skeleton of an alternative practice frame because it was congruent with Chinese values and relational patterns, and therefore would not be regarded as culturally foreign and insensitive (Yuen-Tsang and Sung-Chan 2002). In order to fortify this positive element of the cadres' indigenous practice, the practitioners realized they had to make more effective use of the social work and related theories they learned in the MSW programme. They intensely re-examined the theories they had learned, focusing on integrating theory and practice more creatively. Subsequently, they introduced the cadres to two additional theoretical insights they might incorporate into their communal network approach. The first focused on setting women's capacity building through networking as the ultimate goal. Emphasizing a 'strength perspective', this tactic concentrates on the positive potentials of the women rather than on their problems and weakness (Saleesby 1997).

The other theoretical insight suggests adopting an action research approach as the main methodology for strengthening the capacity of women in dealing with the problems arising from the process of unemployment and re-employment. Contrary to the expert-oriented approach adopted by the local cadre, the action research approach emphasizes women's participation and self-directedness. They would be expected to be involved actively in the process of problem identification, analysis and planning, as well as in the implementation and evaluation of solutions. The reframed practice model was named 'communal networking through the action research approach.'

Episode 3: Frame reflection and reframing of unemployed women

The practitioners' and cadres' reframing experience afforded the cadres a new direction in constructing their practice reality. Instead of practising from an expert-oriented frame, they were keen to strengthen the women's capacity to cope with the unemployment problem by introducing them to reflective practice. They were dedicated to including this marginalized group in the community of reflective practitioners. They recruited a total of 13 unemployed women as their collaborators to conduct 33 oral history interviews, interviews that provided a group of socially isolated women with a public space in which to describe their work experiences from a life-course perspective and to reflect on the role of historical, political, cultural, social and economic forces deter-mining their work experiences. These stories provided the unemployed women with 'texts' they could 'read critically' in order to identify and evaluate their underlying frames.

Their process of listening to the voices of these 33 women changed the cadres and collaborators' perception of the unemployed women as well as of themselves. In the beginning, they perceived the women as having failed to meet the market's demands. This was similar to the public image, portrayed by the media, of unemployed women as incompetent, unmotivated to learn new skills, unrealistic about job demands, and as nostalgic for the 'good old days' when they were still fully employed. In fact the narratives betrayed a strong sense of powerlessness and social exclusion:

I do not want to go out of the four walls of my home because I feel ashamed that I have no job and no danwei[2] to depend on. I do not want my neighbours and relatives to ask me about my present situation since I do not know what to say. I used to feel proud that I belong to a danwei which takes care of me and everything. But now I belong nowhere.

(Wang)

Through listening to the voices of other unemployed women carefully, however, our collaborators gained an intimate knowledge of the women's unspoken narratives, and the unemployed women who helped gather these stories gained new insight into their own situations. They identified many positive features of other unemployed women's stories, such as risk-taking, active agency, self-reliance, ambition, and controlling one's destiny. In addition, they came to realize that their stories shared these features, and that all stories were situated in similar historical, social, cultural, and economic contexts. They were able to see the interconnectedness between individual stories and collective stories. Thus, they could see that they were not inferior to others as individuals, but were collective 'victims' of the change in government policy from planned economy to market economy. The following narrative captures vividly their sense of connectedness:

> The life of women in our generation is tough. My experience was similar to many others in the same age group. We have gone through the Cultural Revolution and were deprived of the opportunity for education . . . and now we have become unemployed. I think the open door policy is good for those who are ambitious, but not for those who prefer stable and secured jobs. Before, the government determined our destiny. We did not have to look for jobs and we were assigned to our workplace. . . . But now everything has changed. We have to take care of ourselves but without any support. All of us feel abandoned.
>
> (Ma)

However, the women spoke differently when they moved from the context of listening to each other's stories to the context of analysing the 'texts' with a view to explaining the problems facing the unemployed women. Interestingly, the majority of the unemployed women adopted the same bureaucratic perspective as did the government when explaining what caused their unemployment. Basically, they framed their situation within a pathological-deficient perspective, assuming that those who became unemployed were unemployed because they did not possess the necessary skills required by the market. The solution was simple: institute comprehensive skill-training programmes, including those teaching job-hunting skills, for the unemployed to enable them to make up for their deficiencies. This solution was based on the 'grand narrative of progress' which stressed that women should strive to increase their competitiveness in the open market through all kinds of self-improvement strategies (Gergen 1991: 30). This perspective is illustrated succinctly by the following narrative:

> Can you organize some classes for us, such as learning basic skills for working at the beauty salon, traditional craft making skills, etc.? I think by learning more of these skills I will become more competitive when I have to fight for a low-paid job with the younger girls . . . We cannot fight the system. We have to survive by accepting the reality and lowering our expectations.
>
> (Huang)

Some women suggested another solution, one based on a paternalistic discourse that emphasized that the ultimate solution was for women to 'return home'. The following is a good example:

> Maybe we can consider returning home and resuming the full-time housewife role. It is very difficult to fight with the younger women as they ask for less money and are more skilful. We will eventually lose out to them. I cannot even get a temporary job at McDonald's. Maybe we have to face the reality of returning home. This is what I am doing. I comply with my husband's wish that I stay home . . . Our skills are obsolete. Our golden age is gone. We are useless.
>
> (Ko)

Instead of encouraging the women to accept their present reality as a finality and to comply with public expectations, the practitioners suggested that they turn their life stories into 'texts' that they might read critically and reflexively. The practitioners guided the women to reflect on the reasons why they suddenly took on the voices of 'the other' and invited them to develop reflective skills and reframe the situation. The practitioners also engaged the women in a series of intensive deliberations on the social and cultural assumptions underlying the pathological-deficient model.

The unemployed women ultimately became dissatisfied with their pathological frame. However, they lacked ideas about how to reframe their situation. The practitioners invited them to do a thorough reconstruction of the underlying frames of all the women, based on the belief that the rich experiences of these women would expand the repertoire of ways to reframe the unemployment challenges facing them. Through rigorous analysis, the practitioners and the unemployed women identified a total of three narrative types in the stories of women's coping with unemployment (Sung-Chan *et al.* 2003). The first type was the *obedient followers*, who were characterized by their dependency on the state and their husbands to solve their problems and who exhibited the tendency to suppress their own voice for the sake of preservation of harmony. The *ambivalent path-finders* were torn by the tension between their longing for independence and their need to get approval from their families and significant others. They were at the crossroads of difficult choices about complex tensions and dilemmas. The third type were the *courageous risk-takers*, a small group of women who dared to make a difference in the midst of unemployment crisis by fighting against the domination of the authorities. Reading stories of the three different typologies together, and reflecting on these stories triggered different emotional reactions among these women and generated self- and social reflexivity.

The critical reconstruction of these three typologies allowed these women to realize the ways in which dominant discourses dictated their ways of framing and understanding their predicaments. In addition, the reflection offered them a promising direction for reframing their situation. They recognized there was at least a minority of women, the 'courageous risk-takers', who framed their situation innovatively. They were inspired by the risk-takers' effort to make a difference in their seemingly intractable unemployment problem. Comparing their own plight to those depicted in the three typologies, they were able to reflect on and analyse the strengths, weaknesses, and social and cultural underpinnings of their own responses. The following illustrates one woman's reflection on a risk-taker's story:

> The story of Madam Yang touched my heart. She was laid off by her factory after twenty years of dedicated service. She quit her new job and returned to the factory to help to complete an urgent task because of her sense of loyalty. But she was sacked two weeks after the task was completed. She felt betrayed, but she did not give up and started her small business (a corner store). Her fighting spirit inspired me . . . I know that we cannot expect the environment to change to suit us, but we have to try hard to change the environment. If I continue to consider my unemployment as 'bad luck' . . . all I do is to reinforce my inferiority and regret over my poor life . . . From now on I must take active steps like Yang to change my own destiny and not regret the past.
>
> (Song)

In order to make a more comprehensive reframing, the practitioners suggested the unemployed women expand their repertoire by learning from the experiences of unemployed women in other parts of China and the world who were coping with unemployment and poverty. At the end of their diligent search, they were most interested in women's co-operative experiences in rural China, India and Japan, and they took an active role in collecting and reading information about the co-operative movement. The capacity-building perspective and strength perspective (Eade 1997; Li *et al.* 2001; Moyer *et al.* 1999; Plummer 2000) also offered new insights into their situation. As a result, they no longer perceived themselves as victims of the social structures. They were active agents who had the capacity to construct a different meaning about work and family and who did not need to follow the paternalistic and grand progression discourses. With this new way of understanding their situations, they decided to form a women's co-operative and to develop income-generating endeavours.

Conclusion: Reflections on our experiences of building communities of reflective practice in China

What does it mean to practice reflection as a teacher? We, as those who observe, must reflect upon our experiences and ourselves, with a particular emphasis on making explicit the contradictions and paradoxes embedded in our process of grooming communities of reflective practice. From our rich, five-year experience, we highlight two areas for reflection: the meaning of introducing a Western conception of reflection into the Chinese context; and the role of metacultural discourses in influencing the frames of social work practitioners and local residents. These areas of reflection can be regarded as cultural considerations which are pertinent to our endeavour of educating reflective practitioners in a Chinese society.

The meaning of introducing a Western conception of reflection into the Chinese context

We had not engaged in any critical reflection about the meaning of advocating a Western approach to reflection with our Chinese students until some of our students did not respond positively to the training in 2003. Interestingly, none of the student practitioners, cadres or unemployed women challenged openly the reflection approach we advocated for the two-year period in Beijing. Perhaps their eagerness to learn Western approaches to social work practice blinded them from seeing the potential incompatibility of these approaches with Chinese cultural characteristics.

However, when we attempted to introduce our preferred approach to refection in 2003, we hit a brick wall. At least five students hesitated to engage in frame reflection and identifying the beliefs, perceptions and values under-lying their practice frame. They were reluctant to look closely at the kinds of professional and socio-cultural discourses shaping their framing, preferring simply to refer uncritically to the grand theories they espoused. Instead of engaging in frame reflection, they essentially engaged in historical revision-ism, or 'reading back onto the beginning of a process what has emerged only at its end' (Schön 1992: 4). Whenever we tried to guide them to do the frame reconstruction and appraisal, they returned to telling their practice story, reciting the theoretical concepts they espoused and that underpinned their practice model. We were greatly affected by their resistance to make explicit the assumptions, values and images underlying their practice. We became curious about why they told their story in this particular way.

We did not invite our students to inquire into their way of responding to the Western approach to reflection. Rather, *we* engaged in critical reflection, which enabled us to see that we put such excessive value on the practice of reflection that we failed to see the possible risk doing so might incur. Having been educated in the West, we took for granted that 'reflection' was core to social work practice. We suddenly realized that the reflection we consistently advocated was basically from the West and that our students might bring a different Chinese meaning to the concept of reflection. We suddenly felt vulnerable because we knew so little about the Chinese conception of reflection. We asked ourselves: What would our teaching practice be like if we accepted the fact that there is more than one way of understanding and doing reflection?

This reflective question suddenly opened up new possibilities for creating reflective practice realities. We took immediate action, asking the students to share their culturally specific understanding of reflection. Some attributed a negative connotation to the idea of reflection that had historical roots in the Cultural Revolution. During the ten-year period of the Cultural Revolution, individuals were forced to go through self-criticism in order to show their allegiance to Communism. Reflection implied a strong criticism of one's weakness. Their experiences of self-criticism during the Cultural Revolution had left with them a repertoire of negative images that evoked terrifying emotions.

Through dialogue, our students and we deepened our understanding of the social, cultural, and historical contexts under which these different conceptions of reflection evolved. Though our reciprocal reflection uncovered differences between two conceptions, our frame reflection did not result in a synthesis. Rather, we learned that we should not advocate an approach to reflective practice without inviting counterparts to reflect first on their own definitions of reflection. More generally, we learned that teachers involved in disseminating Western theories must be culturally sensitive. Another implication is that the teachers should not overlook any feedback given by the students, especially negative responses. Without the input from our students, we would not have reflected on the risks accompanying the approach to reflection in which we had invested so heavily.

The role of metacultural discourses in influencing the frames of social work practitioners and local residents

Despite their different backgrounds, the cadres, the unemployed women and our student practitioners interpreted the unemployment problem very similarly. They referred to the similar social and cultural discourses when framing the problem as well as when constructing solutions. We saw that the metacultural discourses exerted a powerful influence on how individuals constructed their frames. The success of reproducing these discourses does not rest only on the Chinese government's sophisticated publicity mechanisms. The members of our project also reproduced these ideas when going about their daily practice. As teaching professionals, we are interested in the role reflective practice can play in facilitating these actors to resist the tyranny of these metacultural discourses.

The ways in which metacultural discourses shape perception and interpretation often remain unrecognized. One implication for social work education is that the teachers must be knowledgeable in providing students with basic frame-reflection and reframing knowledge and skills, so that they can make explicit the kinds of discourses actually determining their frames. Through identifying the links between the metacultural discourses and individual framing, the students can openly critique the risks these discourses pose, which may result in a reframing. Indeed, the reflection of our student practitioners in the Beijing experiment allowed them to realize that their frames reproduced the values, beliefs and assumptions underlying the 'grand narrative of progress' and 'obedience to authority' discourses. By engaging in the complementary process of reframing, the student practitioners were able to find ways to remedy the flaws of their original framing. Their active search for a model that would address the inadequacy of the social support intervention helped them find ways to truly enhance women's psychological strength and hence to improve their own social work practice. Consequently, they gained concrete experience in integrating theory and practice.

Notes

1   This refers to work units in Socialist China established in 1949 and modelled after Socialist egalitarian principles. The *danwei* are mini-communities which provide comprehensive welfare for the workers from cradle to grave.
2   This is a semi-governmental organization with a nation-wide network to meet the social service needs of women and their families.
3   'I' refers to the first author of this paper, Pauline Sung, who was one of the two social work teachers responsible for developing the reflective community in Beijing.

5 Practising reflexivity: narrative, reflection and the moral order

Carolyn Taylor

I start from the presupposition that working in health and welfare is a messy and complex business for much of the time. Jobs in health and welfare tend to fit all too easily into the category of 'tough jobs that someone has to do'. This is partly attributable to the very nature of the work and the sorts of problems that practitioners are asked to deal with – in child care social work, for example, serious alcohol and substance use are having a major impact on parenting capacity and many more cases of child neglect are now being identified. These difficulties are perhaps exacerbated by the changing context where managerial imperatives are increasingly holding sway and where pressures on the health and social care workforce to perform efficiently and effectively seem to be increasing. Although I am writing from a UK perspective, I am sure that this will resonate with readers elsewhere, given the many similar developments in welfare in response to globalization (Fook 2002). This creates something of a difficulty for practitioners. On the one hand, they need to get on with the job and get through the work as speedily as possible. On the other hand, in order to function well they need to have time and space for thinking about and reflecting on what they are doing, how they are doing the work and how they are using knowledge in their practice. As Sue White and I have argued elsewhere (Taylor and White 2005), when working under pressure, practitioners need to avoid closing down discussion prematurely and operating with too much certainty in their decision-making. Instead they need to develop their ability to remain in uncertainty and to adopt an open and questioning approach to their work, thinking through the processes by which they make categorizations about cases and patients/service users and how they make knowledge about themselves (Taylor and White 2001).

For this reason I have taken the view that a degree of *reflexivity* is necessary in professional practice in order to avoid it becoming routine and taken for granted.

How is reflexivity relevant to this 'staying in uncertainty'? To answer that I first need to explain my use of the term. I will then go on to explore a way of being reflexive, using the example of reflective practice. In this way I want to suggest that, whilst reflective practice is undoubtedly important, it can sometimes take the form of 'benign introspection' (Woolgar 1988: 22) and therefore not go as far as it might do to help with managing uncertainty and understanding the process of knowledge-making.

What is reflexivity and why is it relevant to health and welfare practice?

'Reflexivity' is in fact a rather slippery term, used in different ways from differing perspectives, but I use it in the way it has been used by ethnographers and interpretative social researchers to acknowledge the active involvement of the researcher in the processes of research. Such a view stands in opposition to the positivist notion of the researcher as distanced, disinterested and unemotional observer of the object(s) of study, capable of avoiding bias, error and distortion by adhering to standardized, objective methods of data collection – the stance most associated with the natural sciences. I should quickly add that the association between positivism and science is a complex one. The practice of science is not necessarily positivist, and many scientists acknowledge the uncertainty of their enterprise and the provisional nature of their findings (Fleck 1979; Kuhn 1962). Nonetheless the positivist view has gained canonical status and has come to be regarded within many quarters of health and social care as the gold standard for scientific endeavour, with its emphasis on generalizability, causal explanation, prediction and control. In contrast, the interpretivist tradition of hermeneutic inquiry emphasizes sense-making and deeper understanding of social processes and human interactions.

Earlier interpretative researchers thus rejected the quest for objectivity and instead signalled the significance of experience and the need to study and describe the social world 'as it really is' in naturally occurring situations (for discussion of the 'new language of qualitative method', see Gubrium and Holstein 1997). They suggested that people construct their world through interpretations and actions based on those interpretations (Hamersley and Atkinson 1995). This insight, however, led researchers to question their own position in relation to their research. Was their task simply to relay the facts about whatever aspect of the social world was under scrutiny, without influencing them in any way – in effect, to report objectively the subjective meanings of their respondents? Or did they need to recognize the logic of their position on the way social actors construct their world and apply this reflexively to research and its products? An affirmative answer to the latter question would mean accepting that 'research procedure constructs reality as much as it produces descriptions of it' (Gubrium and Holstein 1997: 9). The sociologist/ethnographer Paul Atkinson (1990: 7) suggests:

> [T]he notion of reflexivity recognizes that texts do not simply and transparently report an independent social order of reality. Rather, the texts themselves are implicated in the work of social construction. This principle applies not only to the spoken and written texts that are produced and interpreted by social actors, but to the texts of social analysts as well.

This has proved to be an important insight for anthropology, sociology and ethnography. It has led to a shift of focus from the *content* of talk and texts to a study of *how* texts produce knowledge of the social world. Key examples include writing 'culture' (Geertz 1973; Clifford and Marcus 1986) and writing and reading ethnography (van Maanen 1988; Atkinson 1990). Importantly, as well, sociologists of science and technology began to apply similar approaches to study the ways in which scientists make knowledge in their laboratory work and their writing (Knorr-Cetina 1981; Gilbert and Mulkay 1984; Latour and Woolgar 1986). These studies of science are significant because they suggest that scientific work actually parallels the sort of sense-making activities engaged in by social actors in their everyday lives.

How is this relevant to health and social care? My response is that we can apply similar principles to professional practice. This is not to say that qualitative research and health and welfare practice are identical; nonetheless, I do want to argue that they have things in common. Both are engaged in forms of social inquiry that have to make sense of ambiguous and indeterminate situations where the 'truth' is hard to come by. Practitioners, like researchers, may be seen as 'mining for the truth' (Kvale 1996) when they make assessments and diagnoses, but this view is not without its problems. Practitioners, just like researchers, are implicated in the work in which they are engaged. They do not simply observe in a neutral fashion and gather objective facts about people and their 'problems', they construct versions of cases and, in this sense, make knowledge about patients and service users (for a more detailed discussion of this point, see Taylor and White 2000, 2001). For this reason I want to argue that reflexivity is also required by practitioners just as much as it is by social scientists: to paraphrase Gubrium and Holstein, cited above, 'health and welfare practice constructs reality as much as it produces descriptions of it'. If we accept that this is the case then we need to engage in analysis which interrogates the process by which interpretation has been produced; in other words, 'reflexivity requires any effort to describe or represent to consider how that process of description was achieved, what claims to "presence" were made, what authority was used to claim knowledge' (Fox 1999: 220).

This may seem a tall order, taking us into new and unfamiliar territory. However, I want to suggest that we have many helpful guides since we can deploy methods for scrutinizing practice developed within the social sciences and, I should add at this point, the humanities in recognition of its important contribution to the understanding of speech and texts. What, then, might a reflexive approach look like in practice? Inevitably, in the space of a book chapter, I can only sketch a partial answer to this question. Fortunately, many others in this volume have also addressed this issue, and other analyses are available elsewhere (e.g. Hall 1997; Taylor and White 2000).

Taking a reflexive approach to reflective practice

I became interested in applying a reflexive approach to reflective practice whilst Sue White and I were writing our book on reflexivity (Taylor and White 2000). A central plank of our argument was to point up the inadequacies of the conventional evidence-based practice approach and its potentially very narrow and hierarchical treatment of 'evidence'. This seemed to herald a return to positivist methods and the marginalization of qualitative methods. It thus reinforced a realist approach to knowledge, disregarding the difficulties with this position not only in relation to its presuppositions about knowledge but also about the way practice is actually accomplished. Practice in fact involves much more than the simple application of formal knowledge to problem situations. In contrast, we wanted to suggest that constructionist methods of social inquiry, drawing on methods and techniques drawn from microsociology and discourse analysis, could be used in a fruitful way to understand how practice is conducted in a variety of ways: in client–worker interactions, in backstage collegial talk and in documents produced within an institutional environment. In doing so we were focusing on the performative aspects of talk and text and emphasizing that descriptions do things in the world. Practitioners make knowledge about clients and their moral worthiness, whilst service users attempt to display their moral worth. Because of this it is valuable to study the interactional and rhetorical strategies deployed in talk and text.

We used the complex court case involving Louise Woodward (the British nanny accused of murdering the child in her care) that took place in the United States in 1997 to pull together our argument that the judge was faced with a plethora of competing versions of the medical evidence and of the characters of the various protagonists (the parents' credibility was also on trial). Deciding who and what to believe was immensely difficult and challenging given that neither the judge nor the avid followers of the trial could ever really know, at some remove, 'what really happened' to Matthew Eappen, the baby who died. What we could understand was how the various protagonists constructed their arguments to appear credible authors/narrators

of authoritative accounts. We could then see how they made particular knowledge about the case and what resources they used in order to do so. In doing so
we were arguing that what we need to know about practice goes much further
than simply what makes for an effective outcome and how it can best be
achieved.

However, as we were coming to the later stages of the writing we came to
realize that it was not simply evidence-based practice that we ought to question. There were also things about reflective practice, often seen as the antith-
esis of evidence-based practice, which called for a similar process of reflexivity,
of understanding the processes by which knowledge gets made about an individual's practice in the process of producing a reflective account. Having
begun this process of inquiry in *Practising Reflexivity* (Taylor and White 2000), I
have continued it by looking at other, different ways to analyse reflective
accounts (see Taylor 2003; Taylor 2006). In what follows I will set out some of
my ideas using an example of reflection. First I will briefly outline what I
intend by the term 'reflective practice'. From this you will note the parallels
between debates about knowledge in practice and in the social sciences.

Reflective practice: a new epistemology of practice

Within health and welfare there is of course a long-standing debate about the
nature of the relationship between the way that knowledge or 'theory' is generated and practice. In one view, which might be regarded as the conventional
one, knowledge is treated as a 'substance that can be sent, received, circulated,
transferred, accumulated, converted and stored' (Gherardi and Nicolini 2003:
204). The knowledge required by practitioners in order to perform their job
effectively is generated exterior and anterior to practice according to the
canons of positivist, scientific procedures. This knowledge is then transmitted
via various educational media (books, lectures, handouts and so forth) and
intermediaries (teachers, academics, trainers) to practitioners who acquire and
store this knowledge in memory for subsequent retrieval and use. In effect
knowledge is contained in the authoritative text that is to be 'followed,
attended to, known, mastered, copied' (Schneider and Wang 2002: 75) and
intermediaries exist to make this process possible. This assigns prime importance to the role of generator of knowledge and assumes a certain passivity on
the part of the reader/receiver of knowledge. The latter's task is the more
straightforward and technical one of understanding and applying in specific
instances what is already formulated as generalized knowledge.

The conventional view of the knowledge–practice relationship of course
accords with the view of the professions as purveyors of specialized and eso-
teric knowledge whose worth to society lies precisely in their command of
knowledge outside the ken of ordinary or lay people. At one level this stance

has proved enormously attractive to many health and welfare professions, as the current espousal of the evidence-based practice movement indicates. However this *technical-rational* conception of professional knowledge is not without its critics. A 'new epistemology of practice', based on the concept of reflective practice, challenges the view of practice as the achievement of fixed, unambiguous ends using rule-governed thinking (Schön 1994: 243; see also Benner *et al.* 1999). Instead it insists upon the ambiguity and indeterminacy of practice situations: things are rarely what they seem; change can be difficult to achieve; problems are not easily amenable to change; and success is elusive. As Schön (1983) puts it, practitioners are dealing with the 'swampy lowlands of practice', which are mired in confusion and uncertainty. Contrary to popular belief, the 'high, hard ground' of knowledge generation may be more clear-cut and manageable in comparison.

In thus revaluing the world of professional practice it is argued that the off-the-peg solutions of ready-made knowledge are not the most appropriate. For much of the time when they are working with and for patients and service users, practitioners simply get on with the job, using methods and techniques that they intuitively know will work in a manner designated as *knowing-in-action* (Schön 1983). It is only when problems and puzzles disrupt the flow of this work that a process of *reflection-in-action* occurs (Schön 1983).[1] At such times practitioners have to think through how to conduct an action or piece of work and work out a solution to the problem in question. Whilst an essential part of practice, such reflection is not always sufficient, and a third form of reflection – *reflection-on-action* – occurs when practitioners take time after some activity to reflect on what has happened and how they conducted themselves in a given situation. In essence the reflective practice approach confronts the view that rigorous thought (i.e. of the abstract, deep, theoretical kind) is only possible if one is completely removed from action, that one must take 'a standpoint outside the game' (Arendt, cited in Schön 1995: 36). Schön (1995) is concerned not to dismiss the artistry and intuition of professional practice as simple 'know-how', nor to privilege technical-rational forms of thinking.

The new epistemology of practice has proved extremely appealing to both educators and practitioners. Why might this be so? There are several reasons. First, a reflective practice approach values action and on-the-job activity – what practitioners do in their everyday work is of prime importance (in this respect it may of course encourage, albeit unwittingly, a form of anti-intellectualism). Second, it treats practitioners as experts in their own right rather than rule-bound technocrats whose work is devalued by designating it as merely practical and technical. Third, a reflective approach acknowledges the complexities and ambiguities of practice and the taxing and demanding nature of working with patients and service users. Fourth, politically (in the non-party political sense) it promises a more democratic practice based not on the distanced, emotionally uninvolved expert associated with certain readings of the medical model of practice, but rather the emotionally engaged, committed, warm, empathic practitioner attuned to the needs and feelings of patients. It is thus consonant with an ethic of care (Benner and Wrubel 1989) since intuition and artistry are used in the service of patients rather than in a self-serving or bureaucratic manner. In this respect it can be seen not only as the equal of the technical-rationality of the 'medical model' but even as its superior, an important issue for those (semi-)professions allied to medicine. Added to this, from an educational perspective it highlights the importance for students of reflecting on their learning experiences in order to know themselves and their practice better. Lastly, it offers a standpoint that suggests that knowledge is not something that is simply learned, stored and retrieved by practitioners but actually made in practice:

> [A] reflective approach posits that contrary to traditional conceptions, 'theory' is implicit in the way people act, and may or may not be congruent with the more formalised theory that they believe themselves to be acting upon. In a reflective approach theory is induced from practice in more of a 'bottom-up' manner'. The best way to access this 'theory' is thus through processes of reflection on specific actions, and a linking of these with unacknowledged assumptions and features of the specific context. (Napier and Fook 2000: 7–8)

Reflective practice has become an accepted part of the curriculum for professional education and training. Indeed, reflection is now regarded as so important that a whole host of books are being produced to cater for the need of educators and students to understand the nature of reflection and how it might be done (e.g. Ghaye and Lillyman 2000a; Rolfe *et al.* 2001; Jasper 2003). As part of a programme of study students are expected to reflect on their practice verbally in (clinical) supervision, to keep learning diaries or logs, to produce reflective commentaries or to integrate reflection into practice assignments. Assessment of some or all of these endeavours forms part of the evaluation of a practitioner's fitness to practise. In this sense what the student says or writes is taken to correlate with or correspond to 'an objective, external, real world or to a realm of subjective, inner, authentic experiences' (Kvale 1996: 4). Now, it may be that for assessment purposes we must take these at face value as authentic representations of reality and judge them accordingly (but see Ixer 1999). However, I want to argue that the processes of reflexivity that I outlined above could and should also be applied to reflective practice. After all, this now forms such an important part of professional education and development. Moreover, reflective accounts are significant because they provide a space for practitioners to leave behind the third-person narratives of the case record and to develop a first-person narrative of their work.

Narratives of practice: Analysing reflective accounts

In my study of reflective accounts I began by looking at them as descriptions of practice. From a constructionist perspective this did not of course mean taking them at face value as literal depictions of practice. I was concerned with what the writer produced as a version of themselves as a practitioner, and possibly as a person, as well as a version of the service user or patient. However, as I extended my reading, I began to see them as descriptions written in a storied way and felt that this should be acknowledged in my analysis (readers will note at this point the storied nature of my description!). That reflective accounts should take a narrative form is perhaps not surprising given that many commentators would agree with the statement that 'telling stories is as basic to humans as eating . . . stories are what makes our life worth living. They are what make our condition *human*' (Kearney 2002: 3, italics in original; see also Polkinghorne 1987; Plummer 2001; for an alternative view, see Bell, 1990).

Narratives are regarded as a way of ordering the scattered and temporally dispersed events of our lives. Indeed, the historian Hayden White argues that narration provides a solution to 'the problem of how to translate *knowing* into *telling*' (White 1989: 1 cited in Riessman 1993: 3). Stories, it is suggested, create coherence and unity in the face of 'discord and dispersal', they are a 'stay against confusion' (Kearney 2002: 4). Why is this point about the ubiquity of narrative regarded as important? It links back to my earlier discussion about knowledge; recognition of the importance of narrative is intended as part of the rebuttal of positivism in favour of interpretative understandings of the social world. As Riessman (1993: 2) states:

> Nature and the world do not tell stories, individuals [or groups] do. Interpretation is inevitable because narratives are representations. There is no hard distinction in postpositivist research between fact and interpretation . . . Human agency and imagination determine what gets included and excluded in narrativization, how events are plotted and what they are supposed to mean.

To underline this point, attention has also been drawn to the ways in which narrative is used beyond the confines of everyday talk and fictional forms, for example within the social and physical sciences (Harré 1990; McCloskey 1990). It is further argued that identities are enmeshed in narrative: personal stories are not simply told to others or even oneself to create coherence, they also create identities (Rosenwald and Ochberg 1992). As Sacks (1986: 105) put it: 'We have, each of us, a life story, an inner narrative – whose continuity, whose sense, *is* our lives. It might be said that each of us constructs and lives "a narrative", and that this narrative *is* our identities.'

Sack's statement of course raises issues about representation and reality. Should we regard narratives *tout court* as 'overt manifestations of the mind in action ... windows to both the content of the mind and its ongoing operations' (Chafe 1990: 79 cited in Edwards 1997: 269)? Such a narrowly cognitive formulation is probably a minority position within the social sciences and humanities nowadays. Generally it is acknowledged that narratives are creations – not all narrative analysts adopt a constructionist position by any means, but they tend to adopt a nuanced position in relation to the issue of reality and referentiality (the representation of the world in speech and writing): 'what is clear is that the narrative of a life is not *the life*; and life narratives conform much less to the contours of the life as lived than they do to the conventions and practices of narrative writing' (Plummer 2000: 186).

Studying the conventions and practices of narrative is now widely recognized as giving us access to understandings and interpretations of the social world. Indeed, in the 'postpositivist' era there has been an explosion of interest in narrative and reference has been made to a 'narrative turn' (Plummer 2001). However, this is not to deny the heterogeneous nature of the field. There is certainly disagreement about definition. Some support an inclusive definition in which narrative is deemed to be present in a variety of genres such as myth, legend, drama, paintings and cinema, Barthes (1977), for example, is a strong exponent of this view. Others, notably those interested in the formal, structural properties of narrative, such as the linguist Labov, adopt a more restricted definition of narrative as 'a means of representing or recapitulating past experience by a sequence of ordered sentences that match the temporal sequence of events which, it is usually inferred, actually happened' (Cortazzi 1993: 43). This definition can then be deployed to explore narrative structure using a six-part framework: abstract (what was this about?); orientation (who? when? what? where?); complication (then what happened?); evaluation (so what?); result (what finally happened?); and finally, optionally, coda (the return to the present moment). I am constrained by reasons of space from further discussion, but readers might wish to consult Cortazzi (1993) and Riessman (1993) for further explication and some worked examples using this model (see also Edwards 1997).

What is significant about these differences of definition? The key point to make, in my view, is that the latter position exemplified by Labov takes us into the analysis of the structure of narrative as an autonomous entity which divorces the narrative from the context of its telling. The key distinction is between story (the actual events) and the narrative (the telling of the events). Because I am less interested in the structural properties of narrative than their performative aspects I have found an *interactional* approach of the kind advocated by Smith (1981) more compelling (for a different view see Chatman 1981; see also Edwards 1997). Smith (1981: 228–9) suggests that 'every telling is produced and experienced under certain social conditions and constraints and that it always involves two parties, an audience as well as narrator'. This seems particularly apposite in respect of reflective practice since reflective accounts are generally written in order to be read by and commented on by practice and/or academic assessors, indeed typically they are compulsory elements of a programme of study. In many instances they are produced using prescribed frameworks – Borton's framework, Gibb's reflective cycle and John's model for structured reflection are all examples (for discussion, see Rolfe *et al.* 2001; Jasper 2003). Interestingly, these frameworks invite the construction of narratives in the manner of Labov's evaluation framework cited above. For example, Borton's (1970) questions ('what? so what? now what?') connect precisely to orientation, complicating action and result. They thus invite reflection in a narrative form. Without them practitioners may struggle to move away from ingrained ways of telling the case where the focus is on the patient or client's story to a more introspective examination of the worker's own thoughts, feelings, reactions and responses.

In order to work, these reflections on practice must be accepted as authentic representations of 'what really happened'. But how does this happen? How do 'reflectors' make us believe in their story? It is to these issues of authenticity and credibility that I want to attend. Reflective accounts are not usually written simply to 'get things off one's chest'. Storytelling to colleagues, family and friends usually performs that function. Instead reflective accounts are written with particular purposes in mind. They seek to persuade the reader of the writer's fitness to practice and worthiness to be accepted within a professional community. Let me now amplify this by working through an example. This is a short written account, taken from a learning diary produced by a nurse, subsequently published within learning materials for a nursing and midwifery department, and more recently reproduced in a textbook aimed at health-care professionals. I have chosen this piece partly because it is fairly short and space is limited here and partly because it is in the public domain. Readers are therefore able to consult the published version and to compare it with other writing, including their own.

Example: A nurse writing about wound care

One entry describes a patient who has a slowly healing sinus which we had been treating for several weeks with slow but positive results. This particular day, the Registrar had seen the patient, was concerned with an increase in exudate [discharge] from the area and ordered TDS dressings, which the nurse had implemented. I felt annoyed at hearing this, questioning what is to be gained and why put the patient through the discomfort. Literature and my own experience confirm that daily dressings are sufficient. I approached the Registrar and explained the facts. His reasoning was the patient had mentioned the increased discharge so he felt he should be seen to change things! The patient was concerned that I was changing doctors' orders. However, after explaining my reasoning he was happy to continue. I also made him responsible for the care of his skin, frequent pad changes and cleaning of the surrounding skin to protect it from the exudate. Later when I wrote about this incident in my journal I was aware of several issues; no one (myself included) had given this patient an explanation of the principles of wound healing, nor had we allowed him the responsibility for some of his own care in this area. The nurse on the morning shift and the patient had both believed that the doctor knew best, and when I explained my reasons to the doctor he agreed and was willing to hand over responsibility. I had been irritated by the lack of control I had in the situation until I realised that I did have the ability to change things and feel I have now earned the doctor's respect.

(Richens 1995: 3 cited in Ghaye and Lillyman 2000a: 25–6)

It is possible to analyse this extract in a number of ways, for example using discourse-analytic techniques (Taylor and White 2000; Taylor 2003; Taylor, in press). Here I want to address the extract in a somewhat different way in order to extend the field of my analysis. I hold strongly to the view that reflective accounts are performative, that is they do business in the world and are intended to persuade the reader of the moral worth of the author. I want to focus on some of the ways that credibility is established in the construction of the account.

In case notes and records the presence of author is obscured by virtue of the 'disinterested voice and the assertoric style' (Harré 1990: 81) just as it is in scientific writing. In contrast, reflective accounts are characterized by first-person writing, although the degree of self-revelation is varied. In one example I came across, a worker in a microbiology laboratory, reflecting on the way MRSA was being dealt with, resisted the urge to get personal:

Borton's framework [see above] enabled me to explore the situation rationally by using the cue questions. It is not complicated, and can be used with any type of situation. A more complicated framework would have put me off; many of these ask about feelings and personal action, which, to be quite honest, isn't appropriate in this sort of situation.

(Jasper 2003: 100)

Similarly, there is considerable variation in the amount of information given about cases and work settings in reflective accounts. Many structured frameworks invite the person to begin their writing by setting the scene and some respond by giving a lot of detail about their area of work and/or the patient in question – several examples in Jasper (2003) conform to this pattern. In the above extract we have very little information about the patient and their slowly healing sinus, we are told nothing in relation to their age, gender, case history or their personality and ways of relating to staff. However, what we do get is a story and in this way it is entirely typical, although clearly non-narrative forms of reflective writing are possible (Johns 2004). In this account it is the nurse as the first-person narrator who has the authoritative voice. She controls the storyline and knows the ending. In this sense narratives have a teleological structure, they are ordered around and to build up to an ending (Mattingly 1998). The plot, the sequencing of the structure of events, is therefore highly important since the events narrated need to be congruent with the ending.

Analysis of narrative has blurred the boundaries between fictional and non-fictional forms of writing (Atkinson 1990). It is commonplace to acknowledge the similarities in the ways narratives are constructed using particular conventions. For example, in reflective accounts just as in fiction, the plot revolves, as our example does, around a period of equilibrium: a beginning (an agreed treatment and the slowly healing patient, a sequence of disturbance and disequilibrium); a middle (the patient expresses concern, the registrar alters the treatment, the nurse challenges this and negotiates an alternative, leading to a restoration of stasis); an ending (treatment back on track, the nurse –patient relationship realigned, the nurse–registrar relationship realigned). But, I would suggest, there is much more to this story than this synopsis of the plot would suggest. Although it lacks the artistic pretensions of an overtly literary piece of work, it nonetheless seeks quite skilfully and artfully to persuade the (implied) reader of the authority and credibility of the narrator. Here is a nurse who admits that she got annoyed and challenged a senior doctor and yet manages to convey to readers a 'solid wall of integrity' (Harré 1990: 84). How is this achieved? Character and communication with an audience are a vital issue here and I want to address this in some detail. This does of course mean that I must forgo discussion of other aspects I might have dealt with here.

Storytelling has been referred to as 'dialogic narration' (Mattingly 1998) because narrative meaning does not rest with the narrator alone, instead it is co-constructed in a social interaction (Smith 1981; Mattingly 1998). Reflective accounts try to persuade listeners/readers of the narrator's authoritative voice. In what follows I intend to draw on Rom Harré's discussion of narrative in scientific discourse which has some salience to my analysis of reflective accounts. Essentially Harré argues that scientific statements perform a specific function; they are intended to generate trust. Before a scientific statement, we can insert a 'ghostly performative operator' (Harré 1990: 81) such as 'Trust me (us) . . .' or 'You can take my word for it that . . .'. In other words, statements invite faith on the part of the reader, asking them to commit themselves not simply to the statement but to an act of trust or belief in the probity of the person making the statement. As Harré points out, trust cannot be a matter of empirical induction – peers can review the findings without having observed the scientific experiments upon which they are based. For this reason it is useful to think of the scientific community as a 'moral order', that is, 'a solidary whose internal structure is based upon a network of trust and faith' (Harré 1990: 82). Harré (1990: 84) goes on to argue that:

If trust and faith are the operative principles, so to speak, then the wherewithal for displays of character must be an important part of a scientist's repertoire. I mean character in the moral sense. An upright character must be readable in the accounts . . . If 'I know . . .' is to become 'trust me . . .' that character becomes an epistemological variable, for on the assessment of character hangs one's readiness to give that trust, to have that faith.

Clearly scientific discourse, used to present research findings, is expressed differently (much more formally, for instance) than the personal tones of reflective accounts, but there is a similar process at work in terms of the engagement of readers' trust. The work of writers of reflective accounts may be similarly invisible except via the *post-hoc* written or verbal account. Reflective accounts therefore perform an important function in terms of persuading readers of the competence and moral worth of the writer. If we consider the wound care extract above with this in mind, we can see how the nurse establishes that she is a 'competent subscriber to the moral order of which she wishes to be seen as a member' (Harré 1990: 99). She does this by using several devices. One is to begin by using the term 'we', implying that she is part of a community, although whether this is solely of nursing staff or inclusive of medical staff is somewhat ambiguous. Nonetheless, a sense of belonging is indicated rather than a practitioner who is acting as a lone, maverick operator. Second, we have the nurse as protagonist engaging in conflict, possibly rivalry with an antagonist, the registrar. This is the pivotal relationship in the story, and perhaps this is why the details of the patient are unimportant. To challenge a senior member of the medical team could of course be morally questionable since 'nothing shifty or perverse, self-serving or self-deceiving must leak through the solid wall of integrity' (Harré 1990: 84). Here, however, we have a challenge to the registrar based on the best interests of the patient and a better way of dealing with the problem, supported by 'literature and my own experience'. It therefore suggests strong moral worth.

Harré (1990: 91) suggests that in science 'the moral status of persons determines the epistemic status of the results'. The trustworthy 'good guys' in science are those who follow 'the Big Ell – logic' and who exert effort ('show guts'). The untrustworthy 'bad guys' are those who are so pushy and anxious that they engage in wishful thinking or are prepared to accept sloppy results, who reject collaboration, or who fail to display effort and willingness to take risks. On this basis there is a 'marked asymmetry' in the criteria by which one's own hypotheses and those of rivals are judged. Statements by 'good guys' are *de facto* to be accepted, ones by the 'bad guys' are discredited. In the reflective account there is a similar contrast between moral worth and moral laxity. In the nurse's account the registrar is depicted as a 'bad guy' because he adopts a rather lazy, 'gutless' response to the patient's concern, emphasized by the use of an exclamation mark. He proposes a change for the sake of it so as to be seen to be doing something. This also fits the category of 'failure to exert effort'. By contrast, the nurse acts as 'good guy' in adopting a more thoughtful and energetic campaign to effect a better solution. This involves not only sorting out the treatment but also gaining the agreement of the registrar and converting the patient to her point of view. Indeed, she shows a preparedness to go to considerable lengths to educate the patient and make him more active in his own treatment. As readers we are asked to see the story from the narrator's perspective and to believe her story: 'trust me, I know about wound care'. It goes rather further than this, however. This nurse is not only proficient in wound care but also very skilful in her dealings with both patients and medical staff, prepared to do the right thing rather than opt for a quiet life or an acquiescent position *vis-à-vis* the doctor. In this she is displaying a good 'clinical grasp' and aligning herself with expert nursing practice (Benner *et al.* 1999). She is asking us to believe that she is able to: 'make qualitative distinctions (recognizing what is salient in the specific situation); engage in *modus operandi* thinking ('keeping track of the specific situation, the way the situation unfolds, the meanings of the patient's responses that have occurred at the time they occurred, what has been tried, and what has worked or not worked with this patient') and clinical puzzle-solving; recognize changing clinical relevance; and develop clinical knowledge in specific patient populations (Benner *et al.* 1999: 28–39).

I want to make one further point about this notion of a moral order before I conclude, and that is to emphasise that I do not see it as something fixed and stable in which novitiates simply have to insert themselves. I disagree with those analyses that define professions in terms of traits and attributes and see the process of becoming a professional as the one-off internalization of those attributes and traits. Instead I want to suggest that the moral orders of health and welfare professions are much more indeterminate and provisional. A moral order is something that is in process, enacted and re-enacted in the written and spoken texts of professional groupings. It is subject to change and discontinuity. As part of claiming membership of the moral order of a profession, practitioners are always engaged in a process of fixing their identity, of proclaiming their moral worth and establishing the validity of their claims to professional status. Reflective practice is but one medium for doing this, albeit one of increasing importance.

Conclusion

I hope I have gone some way to persuade readers of the value of reflexivity and have indicated a way of analysing written texts that can help with this process. In approaching practice in this way, my work has some affinity with writers who use the term *practical reflexivity*, defined as a 'dialogical and relational activity' (Cunliffe and Easterby-Smith 2004), and with work on team-based experiential learning (Gherardi *et al.* 1998) and on 'communities of practice' (Lave and Wenger 1991). Along with many others I want to argue for the value of 'critical reflection' as a tool for making sense of and developing fresh insights into professional practice (Fook 2002, 2004a; Baldwin 2004).

One final question I perhaps need to answer: is this approach only possible within the academy? My answer is no. I think Eraut (1994) is right to signal a distinction between hot and cool action. When workers are in the thick of things they will need to get things done quickly and efficiently. There may be little or no time for reflection under such conditions. But such routinized ways of working cannot, or rather should not, be the only way of practising. Some reflection on action is essential if practice is not to become stale and unproductive. What I wanted to suggest here is that reflection on action needs to be taken further than simply the forms of 'benign introspection' that reflective practice can sometimes take, where the form of that reflection and the function it serves are deprived of attention. Just as sociologists and ethnographers regard it as crucial to adopt a reflexive awareness of their writing and to examine their textual practices and the 'processes and products of [their] self-description' (Atkinson and Coffey 1997: 45), so too do health and welfare practitioners need to analyse the ways in which they produce knowledge about themselves as practitioners in their talk and writing. By showing how a practitioner writes herself into the moral order of the community of nurses I have attempted to shed some light on these processes in the hope that readers will wish to take this further as part of a process of critical reflection. In doing so I want to emphasize the importance to practitioners of developing a different way of understanding practice and the processes by which team and occupational cultures are reproduced. Given the changing nature of health and social care and the considerable challenges currently facing practitioners, this is a vital task.

Note

1   Benner *et al.* (1999) prefer the term *thinking-in-action.*

6 Thinking with the body: artistic perception and critical reflection

Lynn Froggett

'Reflection' as metaphor refers to the production of an image that captures its object as faithfully as possible (even though the light of understanding is refracted or constructed through self and society). It tends to evoke a moment of stillness required to perceive the object as a whole, before the mind busies itself with analytic deconstruction. There is an inherent tension in critical reflection between the mental movement which precedes critique and the steady state of reflection. This chapter has been stimulated by my observation that the critical reflection literature struggles to hold the tension between critical analysis and reflection. This weakens its impact on the micro-interactions of practice and interprofessional relationships. I shall suggest that critical reflection is most useful if it is understood as a recurrent and necessary moment in a fluctuating cycle[1] which requires *uncritical* perceptual immersion in the object of contemplation followed by reflective distance and contextual critical awareness. It is this that allows the practitioner to maintain an empathic, embodied engagement with the experience of the other at the same time as challenging conditions of oppression. This balance is particularly difficult to achieve within current audit and outcome-led forms practice and management. I shall illustrate the point with a detailed example based on art work in a health and social care setting. The conjunction of art and care throws into relief the ways in which a holistic practice is positioned at the complex intersections between body, mind and the socio-political order. However the remarks that follow have implications beyond arts-based agencies for the development of a critical creativity in professional development.

I shall draw on a qualitative research project in a community development setting (Froggett *et al.* 2005)[2] which has evolved a distinctive approach to reflective cross-professional practice. In many ways this mirrors its work with volunteers and the people who use its services. The research was initially commissioned to characterize and evaluate the Bromley by Bow Centre's integrated model of community regeneration. During the course of the three-year project the relations between care, creativity and critical reflection gradually came to the fore. It became clear that the organizational culture produces a mindset which helps to overcome the divisions and boundary disputes that sometimes bedevil interprofessional relationships and complicate lay–professional interactions. It also facilitates working with emergent processes in a target-driven environment.

The Centre, which characterizes itself as an arts-based and storytelling organization, is a visually compelling setting amidst decaying inner-city estates. For over 20 years it has launched imaginative projects which have caught the attention of the media and national policy-makers. The Centre has been a critical force in relation to public services and at times relations with local state providers have been abrasive. It has regarded these agencies as enmired in bureaucracy – whether of the old public service or new managerialist variety – and as unwilling or unable to meet the challenges of working across professional boundaries. In the Centre's view, public services have been remote from local aspirations in which health, social care, leisure, economic and cultural needs are experienced as interrelated. Nevertheless, it maintains a range of local partnerships and is a healthy living centre and a children's centre. Further and higher education courses are franchised from local colleges and disabled adults are catered for through a major community care contract with social services.

The Centre's model of personal and professional development depends on a distinctive approach to learning which evolved organically as it negotiated ground-level tensions between diverse local needs and a politically centralizing, managerialist welfare regime. Work at the Centre is generally driven by a sense of a critical link between creativity and care. Although it is fair to say that there are times when the organization idealizes its own practice, it has also developed a capacity to use external pressures to stimulate critical self-reflection within the context of a 'conversational community'. This has enabled it to adapt to a changing policy agenda whilst remaining to a large degree consistent with its moral and political mission. Guiding principles are interpersonal responsiveness and recognition, a conviction that everyone has something to contribute, a quest for a genuinely holistic practice and a sense that community self-regeneration depends on facilitating individual and collective creativity (Froggett 2005). This last principle underpins all the others and has been foundational in the sense that the organization was an arts centre before it evolved into anything else. The link between creativity, embodiment and the reflective faculty is the main focus of this chapter.

The research team used a variety of observational and biographical methods and added visual methods as aesthetic aspects of organizational life came into focus. The full report and a number of related publications are available elsewhere.[3] At issue here are those dimensions of the organizational culture which facilitate a particular quality of perception and reflection throughout the organization as a whole. The emphasis is on helping professionals, users and volunteers to find a means of self-expression adequate to their contribution, and the arts are often, though not always, the medium of choice. It is important to stress that art is regarded as just a particular instance of creative living in which aesthetic experience which is always at play, though frequently unacknowledged, is the vehicle of an embodied engagement with the world. An individuated expressivity is encouraged, but this is fostered through the life of the group and it is understood that it cannot survive within relationships of hierarchy and domination. The Centre's way of operating leads to a practical critique of the kind of working relationships which are common in the local public service apparatus, and offers a challenge to the highly instrumental, performative, target-driven methods of service implementation favoured by current New Labour policy.

Creative activity and reflective learning

Consider the following extract from an interview in which an artist in the community care project speaks of her work with profoundly disabled adults:

A: An' it broke *my* barriers of people with different abilities, some of them quite severely disabled. I've never worked with somebod– I've worked with autistic children before, while I was doing my degree an' my postgraduate in teaching I worked with people with slight err with learning difficulties, but not physically disabled, it's completely different. I mean, how do – I was thinking how would they understand that I'm *doing* anything with them, like rolling the clay. They're just touching the clay. I just didn't understand if – how they understood – what they were thinking when they were touching the clay. I just thought: 'they're not *learning* anything, they're not *doing* anything',

I: Mhm.

A: err, but err I was completely wrong. Cause it taught me of . . . just how much a little . . . a little bit of touch with the wet clay – you – you saw the – how *happy* that person was, re– *really happy* just – you could see how they were *enjoying* – just by touching the clay that they were *part of that pot*. – An' that was when all my barriers of – or my – what I thought was just like . . . 'Oh my God, this is fantastic!' – And umm – it it was brilliant. An' then I looked forward to go to work every day, and being part of them, and being honoured really.

This extract comes from an interview from which we can extrapolate a relationship between creative activity and reflective learning which is well embedded at the Centre. I shall summarize its key features and follow this with a more detailed discussion of its relation to critical reflection which will be seen as a specific moment in a rhythmical learning process that also depends on empathic identification.

Personal change occurs through sudden or incremental shifts, involving some reorganization of one's personal (inner) relationship to the external world. The artist is involved in 'double-loop' learning (Argyris and Schön 1974) whereby her assumptions and appraisal of the situation change, leading to a change in relatedness to others and consequently to value change. At first, she perceives the people she is working with as profoundly 'other' and feels anxiety and discomfort – not understanding their experience leads to mounting frustration as she doubts whether they are learning anything. A latent conception of an acceptable 'learning outcome' refers to an educational discourse in which such outcomes must be clearly specified and demonstrated. In the first part of the artist's narrative she and her class seem to be estranged. Then her relationship with her students shifts to empathic identification so that she perceives a shared pleasure. The relationship and the nature of her responsibility for the class changes as she becomes part of a group. Power relations and emotional relatedness are realigned, leading to a different form of educational practice.

The learning process starts with 'creative illusion': the ability to imagine something which does not yet exist and to think or act 'as if' it were possible. We do not have a verbal account from the students of what they experience as they begin to work. The clay provides an alternative medium of bodily self-expression and it is highly likely that any premature attempt to verbalize what is going on would detract from the sensuous immediacy of their activity. In the artist's account the class achieves an intimate physical relationship to the clay which allows something to be conceived and take shape in a way which others can share. The student potters create for themselves a 'potential'[4] or 'play' space in which they are temporarily free of the constraints of having to produce in accordance with someone else's notion of how it should be. During this part of the creative process a suspension of the critical faculties is essential in order to preserve the capacity for illusion. However, the artist, distracted by performative expectations, is tempted to invade this space with demands that her class demonstrate learning. To the extent that she persists, the quality of feeling and attention that sustains the illusion of 'being part of' the clay is in jeopardy in that the product will be changed in accordance with her own conception rather than that of her students. The relations of power in the classroom in the initial phase of the process are potentially determined by her status as educated, able-bodied professional, situated within a dominant discourse of outcome-led education. There is little sense that she is drawing on her own experience of imaginative self-expression, even though it is normally essential to her own creative output.

Learning is only partly a cognitive rational process. Deep learning occurs when the whole self is brought to bear on the task, including emotions and perceptions which are linked to bodily states. The quality of the experience described in the pottery class depends on a phase in which cognitive processes of planning, design and evaluation are held in abeyance whilst a libidinal relation to the medium is established. During this phase it appears that the pleasure the students experience is one of coming together with the medium in an imagined merger which allows them to apprehend its properties and potentials. The qualities of the clay are initially felt rather than analysed and described. Later, when an object emerges with a separate existence to which others can relate, its distinctive properties will be recognized and compared to other objects.

The artist, who begins with critical appraisal of her students, undergoes an analogous process in reverse. She has to achieve an empathic identification with her group – a form of psychological merger – before she can 'read' their expressions and appreciate the tactile and emotional experiences of working with the clay. She does not surrender her position as teacher, but she negotiates a more ambivalent relationship of merger and separation – being part of the group and being separate from it. She can then identify with their experience, understand it and take a critically reflective stance towards the product and her own role.

Learning involves projecting a part of the self into the external word and experiencing that the world can be changed by it. In working with the clay the students bring an inner conception to bear on a medium outside of the self and thereby change it. A bit of the world is then experienced as malleable rather than resistant. What is produced 'passes through' the medium of the self and is invested with the vitality of their creative endeavour. The pots or moulded forms that result then have an independent existence – a life of their own. This process confers a sense of agency and reinforces learning. Similarly, the teacher allows the experiences of the group to 'pass through' herself and, in reflecting their experiences and getting 'closer' to the group, she recognizes their independent vitality and gains in ability to communicate with them.

Not knowing, and learning from others, evoke early dependencies and vulnerabilities and the need to relate to external authority before one acquires an internal authority of one's own. The students have never before worked with clay – it is an entirely new and strange experience where they need guidance. The impression of tactile merger involves in the first instance a kind of surrender to the clay in which they feel its properties rather than attempt to impose something of themselves upon it. In this childlike position of not knowing about it and not yet knowing what they can create, they are open to its possibilities and willing to occupy a position of dependency before an independent creativity emerges.

The artist has difficulty managing her role and her efficacy as a teacher. Her lack of experience of working with physically disabled people is a source of anxiety and she defends herself by 'othering' them. Eventually she gives up her attempt to impose externally defined learning criteria on the group in order to understand their capacities and motivations and work alongside them. She surrenders power but gains in influence and hence in authority. The implicit 'contract' between teacher and students changes to one of interdependence within a common project.

The learning process evokes anxiety which requires containment. Surrendering control within the learning group seems to be more difficult for the artist than for the students, although we can only surmise this through her account. It may be that the disabled adults in her class can deal better with the situation because they are experienced in negotiating the tensions between dependency and self-determination whilst relying on others for physical care. At any rate she perceives their enjoyment of the texture and plasticity of the clay. We know from the general organization of the community care project at the Centre that they are familiar with each other and are undertaking a freely chosen activity in a containing environment. The artist is initially considerably more anxious – concerned with her own performance and theirs. The group becomes a container for her only when she is able to free herself of performative expectations. The fact that she does this suggests that she herself is working in an environment which will allow her this creative space, and in which interdependence is supported.

One sees what one has learned when it is recognized by others. The relationships between artist and student evolve from one of non-recognition to one which is based on seeing the particular qualities and capacities of the other who is then no longer alien but is someone who can then in turn confer recognition. In 'seeing the other' and 'seeing themselves in the other' the group sustains an emotional environment in which each contribution is valued. The group relationships form a background matrix against which the individuals invest their work with a personal creativity and hence achieve individuation within a collective enterprise.

The example throws into relief the relationship between embodied experience, reflection and critical reflection. This relationship is seldom discussed in the critical reflection literature, which tends to concern itself with the higher cognitive functions (Mezirow 1990; Brookfield 1995). However, it is latently problematized the moment critical reason is counterposed to 'gut reaction'. For the purposes of this chapter I shall take embodiment to mean the linking of bodily excitements with consciousness, so that the body expresses inner states while inner states contain bodily representations. Since the embodied self is what others relate to, embodiment is a means of putting our inner selves into a social world.

I shall discuss three dimensions of the learning situation which bear on the relation between embodiment and reflection: firstly, the importance of a holding environment; secondly, the ability to work with emergent 'organic' processes; and thirdly, the alternation within the creative process between identification (often evoking a sense of sense of 'merger') and the reflective distance needed for critical appraisal and contextual awareness.

The reflective space

The Centre is a strikingly beautiful enclave, which at first sight seems something of a retreat from the run-down mean streets of Bromley by Bow (Figure 6.1). What does this do for the people who use it, apart from pleasing the eye and providing some respite from an ugly and sometimes dangerous environment? How might it help them think? The architect's guiding principle, 'the first task of any public building is to give pleasure' (Gordon McLaren, personal communication), recognizes the embodied sensuous existence of its users and implicitly affirms that the life of the mind – the symbolic and reflective faculty – is indissolubly linked through perception and fantasy to the senses. Spatial metaphors are often used to depict the optimal conditions for thinking in that people frequently refer to 'making space', 'crossing boundaries' and maintaining a 'critical distance'. Whereas many healthy living centres are without walls, mental space within the Centre is seen as intrinsically related to the quality of physical space.

The buildings which surround the central courtyard form a permeable 'membrane' of contrasting textures: timber, glass, brick and slate, full of entrances and exits which enclose a meeting place with water and climbing foliage. The paths paved with tiles fired in one of the workshops wind through to a park and playground reclaimed from dereliction. The setting seems to lend itself to pleasurable associations in any cultural idiom: paradise garden, stage-set, romantic retreat, cloister, Mediterranean courtyard – providing a place where people from a multi-ethnic neighbourhood can encounter one another and converse. The dominant sense seems to be of tranquillity, while the curving structures which flow into the spaces beyond preserve a sense of fluid movement. A strange benign stone creature guards the entrance with a child dreaming on its back (Figure 6.2). The sensation is one of being 'held'.

In describing 'holding' as the pre-condition of symbolic thought and hence of language and cultural life, Winnicott (1965, 1971) grounded the higher mental faculties in the sensuous embodied experience of being cared for by another. By holding her infant in her arms and in her mind the first caretaker, usually the nursing mother, helps her baby to deal with the chaotic, fragmented impulses and emotions of infancy – bits of bodily experience which it cannot organize through thought because it has yet to develop a thinking apparatus. Effectively, she provides a physical and emotional container that it cannot provide for itself. Becoming 'self-contained' and being able to hold together its own mental contents is the first step towards separating and developing a reflective consciousness. In later life the ability to access

Figure 6.1   The Bromley by Bow Centre courtyard

Figure 6.2 Stone feature in the Bromley by Bow Centre courtyard

internalized containers remains essential for reflection. However, for most people these are stabilized or reinforced to a greater or lesser extent by external containers which are often found in pleasing aesthetic form, whether in art work, landscape, music, building or garden. Bollas (1987) suggests that the transformative potential of aesthetic experience derives from the way in which it evokes early experiences of being soothed, caressed, cleaned and comforted in the context of our earliest experiences of containment through the mother's personal idiom of care. Schore (1994), who provides a compatible view by combining neuro-scientific and attachment perspectives highlights the complex bio-psycho-social nature of holding which establishes through bodily interactions the early neural pathways of affect regulation.

Bion (1967, 1970) accounted for the early development of thinking in metaphors of digestion, reflecting the overwhelming importance of feeding in early life. The infant projects (expels) into the nursing mother its inchoate sensations – and (in good enough circumstances) she is able to absorb them and process them with the dreamy attunement or 'reverie' that is often observed in the early phases of mothering. Despite the appearance of tranquillity, reverie is an active process whereby the infant's projections are 'metabolized' and, as it were, returned in a 'digestible' form. This primitive process of containment is a prototype of the symbolic function which involves finding both the conditions and the forms within which unprocessed mental contents can become thinkable.

This account of the early development of thinking is compelling because it resonates so closely with later experience of finding a space in which to think – in which the senses are at ease and the head clears. The reflective space is an aesthetic space which contains because (as the holding mother once did) it provides form which the mental contents at that point lack. The sense of internal integration provided by a setting, such as the room where one feels 'at home', is the sensuously mediated counterpart of the internal mental landscape in which thoughts can take form.

The Centre works with the untheorized intuition that the setting provides more than a 'feel-good' factor – though in London's East End this is desperately needed. It sees care of the environment and care of the self and others as intimately related. The optimal space for thinking and communicating is a space for bodies as well as minds, and stimulating the senses also stimulates mental faculties. For this reason a new project group is as likely to begin its work by visiting an art gallery as by holding a meeting. The sharing of images which resonate with bodily and emotional states precedes the intellectual work of the group which may then proceed according to the time-honoured format of the formal meeting.

The potential of an organization to sustain a reflective containment for creative work is generally discussed in terms of its ability to impart a particular quality of emotional life, whereby conflict and tensions that arise between individuals and factions can be processed within the very institutional structures that provide durability and reliability. Public service bureaucracies attempt to do this via reliable and consistent procedures, but in these settings the formal structures too often work against the caring or expressive role of the organization particularly when driven by a technical-rational logic and the impulse to shore up power structures. In the mismatch between form and function, containment is more likely to turn into restraint and the reflective space is 'compressed' as institutional hierarchy asserts itself.

Empathic identification and critical reflection

The pottery class provides a detailed illustration of a process of professional learning in which reflective distance is one moment in a learning process or cycle which also rests on identification or immersion in the object. In his early work on reflection, Schön (1987) conceptualized the components of this process in terms of knowing-in-action, reflection-in-action and reflection-on-action. He stressed the spontaneous and intuitive nature of knowing that leads to the 'artistry' of the competent practitioner followed by immediate, and then longer-term, reflective processes. He also drew attention to different types of knowing in his often cited metaphor contrasting the 'swampy lowlands' of practice with the 'hard high ground' of research and theory. Taylor and White (2000) find this dichotomy misplaced – in that fantasies of high ground are generally delusional in health and welfare. At any rate, the ambivalence of the swamp metaphor should occasion pause for thought. It highlights the indeterminacy of practice where there is no firm foothold, but a swamp is worse: it is where you sink under your own weight and where mounting panic accompanies the remorseless suction. The swamp is a sticky, fetid, infested place, a breeding ground for disease and corruption that traps you against your will and threatens to draw you under. You would be ill advised to linger there, much less abandon yourself to its slime. On the other hand, legend has it that the primeval slime is where we all originated, before we crawled on shore – it was fertile and generative as the maternal body.

I am not just indulging in extended metaphors for their own sake. A good metaphor is semantically dense, resonates in the body and condenses multiple layers of experience. The imagery here – including the ambivalence towards immersion – is pertinent to my argument: that professionals and academics alike often experience an anxiety about merger, fusion and self-abandonment, but that a practically useful critical reflection also rests on this capacity. While the literature acknowledges the importance of tacit and intuitive ways of knowing (Polanyi 1970; Benner 1984), it has difficulty saying very much about it. There remains an implicit hierarchy of virtue between the resources of body, emotion, imagination and intellect, but an examination of the creative process suggests they are very closely interrelated.

The artist is engaged in reflective learning when her theory-in-use (Argyris and Schön 1974) changes as a result of her experience of the class. It is double-loop learning in which she questions her early assumptions and her values shift. It is a precursor to critical thinking in that learning is transformative (Mezirow 1991) and situated in a community of practice (Wenger 1998). Furthermore, it clearly results in more symmetrical power relations between teacher and students (Fook 2002). In the context of the organization the artist is located at a point of tension between the two pedagogic discourses with which the Centre struggles. It has developed within a tradition of social pedagogy influenced by Freire (1970) which situates learning within an emancipatory value-base in the lived experience of communities. However, accreditation as an educational provider depends on a curriculum and assessment-led approach, which was emphasized in the artist's own pedagogic training. This particular group impels her to revert to a dialogical model of learning more consistent with the Centre's mission as a community develop-ment organization. She can make this switch because she is in an organiza-tional environment that makes space for emergent process while continuing to operate within a system which is target-driven and outcome-led. If she is not to simply swing between competing paradigms she needs to empathize with the group while extending reflective capacity and critical contextual awareness.

Let us look at the alternation of empathic identification and critical reflection a little closer. The artist watches her group undergo a perceptual immersion in the clay. She probably recognizes this sensuous experience because as a professional ceramicist she has often 'lost herself' in the clay, rather like a child 'lost in play'. In this state there is the sensation of being 'at one' with the medium while feeling curiosity about it. For Winnicott (1971) this possibility arises when the child occupies a 'potential space' in which there is an illusion of being both inside and outside of something – being part of it while knowing it to be separate. In this state of mind it seems as if the object of play 'comes alive' for the player because it is subjectively endowed with the possibility of what it might objectively become. Winnicott suggested that the ability to occupy such a mental space free from external impositions is the key to the development of a personal sense of creativity in the infant. In the adult, potential spaces allow us to use our imagination and to tolerate and enjoy the paradoxes of a complex cultural life. I would suggest that the ability to make use of this intermediate area of experience between inner and outer reality is also the hallmark of the reflective practitioner and helps to explain how it is that practitioners can 'think on their feet' or use intellect and emotions in action. Ixer (1999), writing without any reference to potential space, was discomforted by the ambiguity of reflection and concluded (provocatively) that there is no such thing.

Potential space is an area of illusion where the distinction between me and not-me is momentarily suspended before being reconfigured and reasserted. It is therefore a condition of a reflexive consciousness (Taylor and White 2000) where the question of what the practitioner brings to the situation can be sensed and become an object of awareness. In the classical model of supervision (Mattinson 1975; Hughes and Pengelly 1997) – which I take to mean one where there is space for reflection and reflexivity unhampered by the instrumental demands of the agency – the potential space is 'held' by the supervisor. In this role she allows indeterminacy and uncertainty and knowingly colludes – for a while – in the suspension of organizational imperatives as she 'ingests' and 'digests' the material brought to the process. At times the quality of attention may need to be a form of 'reverie' in order for her to remain sufficiently open to this material. Only when its novelty and particularity have been fully apprehended does a specifically critical phase of the reflection process begin. If it takes place without this open awareness the supervisor will not be able to use her perceptual 'radar'. Nor will she attune emotionally to her supervisee whose experiential account will be lost as the sense-making is foreclosed. Attempts at premature critical reflection are at best quite irrelevant to practice because there is a failure of perceptual awareness and emotional engagement. At worst they become immature critical reflection of a sort that results in ideological prescriptiveness.[5]

Reflecting on her own processes of creative blockage in her book *On Not Being Able to Paint*, Marion Milner (1950) highlighted this problem of being too quick to ask what something is or what it is for – thus failing to allow the object to emerge as if it has a life of its own. Whenever she rushed to produce a recognizable figure Milner was struck by the unpleasant meretricious quality of her own art which seemed forced or contrived and lacking in freshness and vitality. There are important parallels here between the nature of inquiry in the artistic process, and in practice and qualitative research grounded in data. Suspending preconceived categories of thought and attaining an 'evenly hovering attention' (Bion 1970) allows the inquirer to develop ways of knowing that are more adequate to the object. However, 'negative capability'[6] is not always easy to achieve as we are likely to be distracted by external agendas and personal inclinations, prejudices and desires. Milner remarked that occupying a potential space required a particular kind of discipline – not to force her work to take on the shape of a recognizable object too soon. Her best results were when she was able immerse herself in the painting and to suspend her goals for long enough to allow her own unconscious idiom to infuse the work. After a while she would stand back, establish a reflective distance and interrogate her latent and explicit intentions. Her subsequent analyses were subtle, perceptive and contextually aware.

Something very similar is suggested by the artist in the pottery class who needs to allow time and space to immerse herself in her group's experience as they immerse themselves in their task. Having done this, the way in which she appraises their learning process changes. Because she stands at an intersection between the arts and the educational and care systems in an outcome- and target-driven welfare environment, she unwittingly reveals something of the creative and reflective dilemmas that they all have in common.

The whole and the fragments

The embodied critical thinker who is able to use the full range of emotional resources oscillates between different modes of perception and cognition. Much of the psychoanalytical literature on knowing is concerned in one way or another with this alternation which it traces back to sensations of merger and separation in the context of early nurturing. The newborn baby is thought to feel itself 'at one' with the maternal body in a pre-symbolic area of experience where the world seems to be coextensive with itself. The debates as to exactly when and how this illusion of 'oneness' gives way to a multiplicity and separation from the primary caretaker need not concern us here. Common to all strands of psychoanalytic thinking is the importance of the primary, unconscious, pre-discursive process of knowing in which there is as yet no clear boundary or sequence, but instead the immediacy of images which are here or gone – like a dream. The individuation/separation process eventually allows the child to enter a temporal order and develop language, but the images of primary process continue to populate dreaming and fantasizing.

This primary process is rooted in earliest embodied/affective experience and accounts for the irreducible uniqueness of individual consciousness. It suffuses our use of language with a distinctively personal idiom and provides a psychic arena that is partially resistant to socialization (which is why our dreams can be so shocking) and a counterpoint to the 'constructedness' of language. Most psychoanalytic accounts of art, and of personal creativity generally, stress the importance of accessing this material in the creative process. When Milner managed to resist the impulse to immediate representation and allow the picture to emerge, she considered that she was allowing her primary process to guide the work and the outcome then bore her own idiosyncratic imprint. She first invested it with her own vitality, as it were, then she recognized it as an object with a life of its own that existed for others and could be a point of communication and appraisal.

Anton Ehrenzweig (1967) considered these alternating moments of psychological merger and separation in the creative process in the light of Piaget's work on the syncretistic and analytic faculties. The dominant syncretistic mode of perception in young children is libidinally driven until latency, when the more cerebral analytic mode begins to take over. At around age 8, children's creative output tends to change and lose its spontaneity as they begin to match and compare their work to that of others. They typically become more literal-minded and concerned about accuracy of representation and are encouraged in this by educational systems which privilege analytic modes of thought after the early years. Nevertheless, the syncretistic faculty persists and is likely to inform holistic thinking and the creative arts. Syncretistic perception is relatively undifferentiated, taking in complex structures in a single sweep. It involves the scanning of whole objects and their interrelated parts without focusing in on a particular detail or dominant pattern. Whereas analysis breaks up the object into component parts or extracts a gestalt, syncretism takes a global view or perceives the background matrix that produces the figure.

When the practitioner attempts to get a sense of the whole patient or client situation, or when the artist stands back and scans the whole picture, there is a relaxation of focus and a wide-angled vision takes over which is less concerned with accuracy of detail and more concerned with the object in its entirety. The artist in our example uses it when her preoccupation with learning outcomes softens and she suddenly apprehends her disabled students' inner-world and socially situated experience. The syncretistic faculty is by no means confined to visual perception – it manifests itself as absorption by the overall shape or flow of a story, music or poem which at *that* moment is more important for its meaning than any component part. It allows one to see and reconfigure the linkages within a complex structure. In Ehrenzweig's view this is a particularly embodied form of perception in that suspending the deconstructive movement of analysis allows a different relation between self and object in which unconscious associations have free play. As the psychological boundaries of the observer relax, the otherness of the object attenuates and empathic identification can be momentarily established. To arrest the process here would be to abandon oneself to eternal aesthetic contemplation or mysticism. The analytic phase must re-establish distance in order to allow for the reassertion of a sceptical consciousness which reflexively interrogates both the relationship to the object and the object itself.

Conclusion

What is the relevance of all this for health and social care organizations in the current climate? In the Bromley by Bow Centre research we were confronted with an organization that has preserved its artistic heritage (with some difficulty because it is so much at odds with the prevailing culture) but has in many respects gone mainstream. The Centre has had to reckon with the regulatory burdens of a health and welfare environment which imposes targets and time-scales and demands measurability and compliance with outcome-led project design and work processes. In addition, it has had to devise internal systems of accounting and quality assurance in accordance with criteria of value which are often extrinsic to the work it does, or which it perceives as irrelevant or even obstructive.

It was easy enough to identify the resulting difficulties for an organizational culture committed to integrated holistic working. Over the years the Centre had learnt to live and flourish with a high degree of uncertainty and fluctuating resources. It had achieved this by attending to its aesthetic and relational environment and by providing a holding environment for the emergent creativity of its staff and members. Effectively it had provided a space where health and social care practice could be invigorated by a cultural mix of artistic bohemianism, ecumenical nonconformism, liberation theology and Freirean populism, laced with a bracing scepticism towards the centralizing administrative tendencies of the local and national state. Then, with the incorporation of a large health centre, it had shoehorned itself into a restrictive National Health Service framework and a series of major education and welfare service contracts. All of them required service agreements incorporating local and national targets and elaborate processes of regulation and audit. This has substantially reduced scope for the kind of creative risk-taking and rule-bending which allows human and financial resources to be diverted to follow emergent ideas. The very arts activities which have defined the nature of the Centre's cultural environment have become vulnerable without dedicated funding and at the time of writing some of the key creative activities are being curtailed. Nevertheless the organization has remained capable of startling innovation, especially in the field of health promotion. The key to its work – for example in its 'art and asthma projects', or its 'diabetes fairs' (see Froggett *et al.* 2005) – seems to lie in an ability to combine the resources of artists, health professionals, lay staff and volunteers in an approach which recognizes the embodied, social, psychological, spiritual and aesthetic manifestations of health and illness.

The question of how an organization manages to preserve such an approach in the face of current pressures for transparency, determinacy and accountability is clearly of general interest. How, for example, does the Centre help its busy practice nurse 'to link the artist and the scientist' within herself? How does it help its general practitioners to listen to their patients' stories within the managed time constraints of the standard consultation? How can it continue to 'shelter' members of staff who do not conform to received criteria of productivity? How does it manage the processes of accountability within lay–professional working? Given the risks and inevitable failures that attend the constant launching of imaginative projects, how does it avoid falling into the extremes of self-congratulation or despondency? When the research project started, formal procedures were thin on the ground, communication systems were sometimes haphazard, and survival depended on tolerating a great deal of organizational confusion (in this sense staff were a self-selecting group, with a degree of attrition among those who were not prepared to function at the edge of chaos). Although more conventional management systems have since been implemented, the organization is still struggling to hold a line against proceduralization and excessive managerialism.

This chapter has attempted only a partial answer to the question of how this has been possible (for a fuller account, see Froggett *et al.* 2005). It has focused on the forms of reflection sustained in the organization by maintaining embodied awareness and aesthetic sensibility within the critical reflection process. In the end, the research concluded that a key ingredient – or 'protective' factor – lies in a constant movement between analytic and syncretistic perception reflected in a mobility between mental states of fusion/separation, identification/distance, immersion/remote appraisal of the task, and group merger/individuation. This dynamic is reminiscent of the creative processes of artists who are observed to delve into the detail of their work with a concentration which borders on the obsessional, only to stand back again, widen the focus and scan the network of relations which compose the entire product. The Centre has fostered such dynamics through art-based activities but has carried them through into the professional artistry of its health, education and social care projects. The research team concluded that its ability to protect this style of working is supported by diffusion within the organization of artistic forms of perception that facilitate an exploratory openness, empathic identification and the ability to see the whole. Critical reflection helps to sustain these perspectives while working with a highly disadvantaged and culturally and ethnically diverse population and maintaining a commitment to individuated service provision based on interpersonal recognition. Because empathic identification and critical reflection are regarded as complementary, staff and volunteers learn to move fluidly between them in a constant creative rhythm between an embodied 'closeness' to experience and a reflectively critical distance.

Notes

1   Kolb's (1984) learning cycle contrasts the experiential and reflective phases of learning, and Schön's reflection in and on action depicts shifts in professional thinking. My argument here concerns the relationship between the aesthetic, embodied nature of experience and critical reflective faculty.

2   The Bromley by Bow Centre research and evaluation project was funded by Dunhill Medical Trust 2002–5. It was supported by the University of Central Lancashire, the Open University and the Institute of Child Health, University College Hospital.

3   The study employed a mixed methodology which included participant and institutional observation, biographic narrative and semi-structured interviews and a participant action research component, a mapping exercise, 'round table' discussions and visual analysis. Methodological papers have been published on the following topics: psychodynamically informed panel analysis (Froggett and Wengraf 2004); intersection between organizational narratives and personal biography (Froggett and Chamberlayne 2004); and a biographic narrative case study (Buckner 2005). A review of policy implications and a methodological overview are in preparation. The full report (Froggett et al. 2005) is available on the project website: http://www.uclan.ac.uk/facs/health/socialwork/bromleybybow/index.htm.

4   The concept was developed by Winnicott (1965, 1971) to depict the area of illusion where inner and outer reality are perceived as interchangeable and in which 'it is a matter of agreement between us and the baby that we will never ask the question: "did you conceive of this or was it presented to you from without?" The important point is that no decision on this point is expected. The question is not to be formulated'.

5   As a social work educator I sometimes suffer a terrible weight of oppression in reading accounts of anti-oppressive practice. Although the value-base appears impeccable, the results are literally 'deadly' in that the human vitality of the

subject and author are erased. There is no careful observation, thick description, emotional intelligence or reflexive interpretation. There is no space for uncertainty and ambiguity, no sense that the student has 'lived with' the material or been affected by it. In short, there is no sentient embodied response on the one hand, or grounds for intellectual scepticism on the other. Of course, the vocational education system bears responsibility – the students must demonstrate competence and in their performance anxiety may move too quickly to a formulaic response (the ubiquitous and ill-digested 'empowerment-speak' is a particularly unfortunate example).

6   This often quoted concept originates with John Keats who, in a letter to George and Thomas Keats (21 December 1817), writes of the quality which 'Shakespeare possessed so enormously' – 'Negative Capability, that is when a man is capable of being in uncertainties, Mysteries, doubts without any irritable reaching after fact & reason' (http://en.wikipedia.org/wiki/ Negative_Capability, accessed 24 January 2006).

7 Recasting individual practice through reflection on narratives

Sue Frost

Contemporary practice increasingly locates professional development within a reflective paradigm. Guided reflection is widely held to be a core process through which practice is reviewed, challenged and repositioned. Johns (1999), Freshwater (2002), Hall (1997) and Benner (1994), amongst others, have developed new approaches to understanding through critical reflection of our own practice narratives. Writers such as Nelson (2004) comment critically that narrative use has become commonplace in fields such as nursing, often unquestioningly. Johns (2000: 202) argues that 'The narrative is a structured clinical reflection that integrates assessment, evaluation, planning and intervention within an unfolding clinical situation'.

This chapter will explore some of the storied traditions of practice and consider how practitioners can reflect in ways that recast their roles as co-authors, both of their own practice and in partnership with patients and clients. The chapter draws on elements of narrative theory to explore how critical reflection helps to get nearer to understanding the point of the story. In particular, the chapter argues that narrative approaches support critical reflection in building a dialogical approach to practice.

Using narrative in practice

Professional practice is largely undertaken through relationships with others. Understanding how we operate in a dialogical environment is potentially explored through reflecting on day-to-day stories. It involves rehearsing the plot, co-authoring futures and considering 'why' and 'what if . . .?'. The development of phenomenological approaches to understanding health and social care is potentially part of the praxis that distinguishes such practice from more traditional medical approaches which have been dominant in some areas of professional practice. In narrative-based practice, the approach to knowledge construction uses interpretative, naturalistic and participative methodologies.

Hall (1997: 6), for example, suggests in terms of social work that narrative is available in all aspects of social work communication – written and verbal, description and explanation, everyday and theoretical. In health and social care practice, narratives are part of day-to-day practice, and this situates reflection within the storied contexts of real activity.

Many health and social care practitioners associate learning with acquiring wisdom that involves knowing the right thing to do. This takes a position that identifies learning as an outcome where the practitioner gains knowledge and understanding that serves as a foundation for professional 'knowing'.

Learning is both an action and an outcome. It could be argued that the active process of learning is one of the defining characteristics of professional practice, a continuum of developing knowledge and understanding, building skill through solving problems. Critical reflection in practice is an approach to learning that builds on the process elements of our actions as well as the outcomes. It draws on what Marton *et al.* (1997) refer to as 'deep learning', which means seeking deeper explanations that construct alternatives, explore possibilities and test ideas. For practitioners, this means engaging in deeper thinking about practice in ways that transfer to a number of applications. Arguably reflective practitioners learn through thinking laterally, finding a range of solutions, exploring choices and rejecting inappropriate practice.

Narrative approaches are being used to reflect on practice learning. Melnyk and Fineout-Overholt (2005: 175) argues that 'Narratives about experiential learning reveal moral agency and . . . reveal shifts in styles of practice'. Uses of narrative in practice are diverse, and one of the most rapidly growing areas is in the use of narrative inquiry. Seeking to understand the experience of the practitioner and the patient/client through narrative is a powerful device that is in keeping with the storied traditions in creating nursing knowledge. Exploring our storied accounts is an embedded part of reflecting on and in practice. In this way practitioners uncover new practice and explore how to improve and develop.

Storied traditions in professional practice

Practitioners tell stories of their working lives every day. Kim Walker (2000: 87) comments of nursing, for example:

> As nurses, we compile in a life of practice an incredible chronicle of experience that comes to expression in the everyday stories we share over the dinner table, in the wee small hours of night duty . . . have you ever mused what it might be like to capture something of that vast and messy thing called practice . . . for reflection, analysing, theorising – a sort of record of the present as history?

Health and social care practice has strong oral traditions, most practitioners gaining much of their day-to-day information from what is said rather from what is written. They also co-author stories, scripting what should happen, how things should work, what is acceptable, what is rejected. For many the relationships they build with patients, arguably a core element of caring, are mediated, determined, and developed through the stories they share of the patient journey. The sharing of experiences creates a sense of belonging to the same story – being part of 'this club'. Rolfe (2000: 83) argues that

> Narrativity. . . . enables us to ask critical questions of the significant and (seemingly) inconsequential moments of our histories and of the ways those histories inform and inflect our individual and collective understandings as nurses

Judith's story

In this chapter small sections of two stories from health services are shared. The purpose is to use these to help to illustrate the way in which exploring stories assists us in reflecting on things that happen, helps us to understand different perspectives and consider in what alternative ways the story could have been plotted.

The first story is that of Judith (pseudonym), who was a participant in a study of British Pakistani women's experience of health care (Frost and Cliff 2003). Judith is a 28-year-old student nurse, who has a partner and a son aged 5. Before coming into nursing she worked as a filing clerk in an engineering factory. She has just started the second year of her nursing course and is sharing an account of her practice. Consider this fragment from Judith's story of her experience as a student nurse working in a medical ward:

> It was on the medical ward here and it was an old Asian chap who was very poorly and his family came in and they were talking away. The doctor had been in that morning and they asked – the son came back to the nurses' station and the staff nurse was dealing with something and he asked me what the doctor had said about his dad that morning. I said 'hang on I'll get his notes' and he said 'is the doctor available to talk to me?' I said 'yes, but I can tell you what he said – basically carry on the treatment but there's not much progression, he's not responding to the antibiotics'. I just happened to say that – he was in this bay, in a far bay and we couldn't see him, and I wanted to get him onto an air mattress.

Although he was very thin and frail he wasn't moving at all. And I happened to say 'we're going to change his bed and move him onto a different mattress'. He said, 'has the doctor said that he has to'. I said, 'no, no, it's just something that we'll do'. 'I'd rather speak to the doctor about it.' I said, 'well we're only going to move him so that he's near the nurses' station, into a high observation bed basically'.

And they felt very closed off, very polite and very apologetic and very understanding but still didn't want to know. It was a case of I don't believe it, you know nothing and walked away.

I spoke to the staff nurse and the staff nurse went back and she said – 'he won't let us change the bed'. I said 'I've explained this to him, but he's said no'. The chap died that night. I felt that if I'd have been a male he might have paid a bit more attention to me.

Judith is not simply recounting a series of events, she is telling us a story of her world. Think of all of the questions the account generates and what we may be finding out about Judith. The relative wants to talk to the doctor but Judith is competent to give an answer. Her answer was rejected – the family was resistant: 'And they felt very closed off, very polite and very apologetic and very understanding but still didn't want to know. It was a case of I don't believe it, you know nothing and walked away.' Exploring the story involves asking questions, trying to think deeply about what is going on. What do you think is happening here? If you were Judith, what could you learn about yourself, about your practice from exploring this story? Answers to these questions may vary depending on your own experiences, perceptions and expectations. For example, think about the patient's relative for a moment. His father is dying, the nurse wants to move the bed and change the linen. He resists the nurse in moving his father. Judith chooses to explain this resistance by drawing on an explanation – that of the gender differences. The relative may have simply been resisting what he thought would be more uncomfortable for his father. Understanding Judith's story may help to explore why she chose the explanation about gender and the implications for her future practice.

Narrative approaches are concerned not only with collecting facts but also, more importantly, with helping the practitioner to reflect on how she constructs her role and how she practises. Judith's story is telling us about 'how things are done here' – the professional discourse is dominant, which is perhaps why she is puzzled when her explanations are challenged by the relative. Whether Judith's explanation is correct or not is less important, perhaps, than the unspoken assumptions, disconnected explanations and coherence in understanding why Judith acted in the way she did.

Langellier's (1985) scrutiny of the literature on narrative suggests a number of positions commonly emerging as the function of narratives. Narrative can be understood as *story text* in explaining events, helping the listener to know what happened. People tell their stories in various ways because they are a *performance* for a certain audience and are concerned with how their audience responds. Theorists such as Fine and Speer (1977) argue that the shift from text to performance helps to move into the social and cultural context of the story. This more complex approach considers the process of storytelling as well as the textual and linguistic constructions. Arguably this function is highly relevant to the element of performance within the context of clinical relationships between practitioner and client/patient. Judith is not telling her story in a vacuum. She is constructing her story with an audience – her supervisor. The story is not about this patient dying, it is about 'the rules', how things are done around here, what conversation could follow (think of the interaction with the supervisor), what is important, what is unsaid, who is the central actor here, where could the plot take us . . .?

Stories may also serve as a *conversation* in which two actors co-construct meaning in terms of an ongoing stream of talk. Paraphrasing Polanyi (1985: 207), we can say that stories can have as their point 'only culturally salient material' that is generally agreed on by members of that culture to be important and true. This is particularly important in understanding narrative functions in nursing. In this function, narrative can provide a basis for co-authoring a story between practitioner and client/patient and can contextualize the natural rhythm and interaction of clinical practice.

Narratives also emerge as a *social process* where stories are told over time in many situations. They are tested, defined and co-authored through a wide range of interactive performance and conversation. Indeed, the origin of the story may be lost but the story itself remembered as real. For example, how many of us have stories of very early childhood that may have more to do with what we have been told than what we recall? These stories become part of our lived experience, whether or not they really happened. Stories pick up the threads of other stories and are woven into the stories we will tell in the future. Narratives do not just tell of the present, they allow a glimpse at the past and hint at futures. These types of narrative functions build a collective history of practice that helps to define who we are and how we interpret our daily experience.

Much work has been done to demonstrate the function of stories in transmitting values. Some of the earliest work on fairy stories by Bettelheim (1976) explains the transmission of culture and values through storytelling. There cannot be a trained nurse, for example, who has never heard a version of the story of the novice who was asked to go to a department for a 'long stand'. The professional myth frequently extends the length of the stand to a number of hours and the novice is always taken in by the joke – I was such a novice who complied with the request! These myths reinforce the notion of belonging of not being an outsider who is taken in by the joke. Practitioners have a collective set of stories that send strong messages about what is considered to be legitimate to be a member of that professional group, they determine *political praxis*. Sometimes these are heroic – standing up to authority – challenging the doctor, manager or supervisor. Others are about facing adversity – times when things seem hopeless but patients get better, clients solve complex problems, strange remedies work, and an error is made that turns out to be fortuitously effective.

In Judith's story she is building a world where the authoritative discourse is that of the professional: 'He said, "has the doctor said that he has to". I said, "no, no, it's just something that we'll do". . . . And they felt very closed off, very polite and very apologetic and very understanding'. This is a story about a patient's relative who is resisting, not complying with the hidden rule that he should accept the nurse's instruction. There are several explanations that could be drawn on to describe why this scenario occurs in this way. Judith draws on a professional expectation of compliance so seeks to explain the event by drawing on a different power discourse, that of her gender. Perhaps she has previously encountered being subordinated because of her gender. Perhaps she is resisting the implied idea in her story – that the doctor knows best because he is male.

Narratives help practitioners to understand the routine and rhythm of the incoherent and the unstable. In this way understanding the function of stories can help to provide closer links between the unstable world of practice and the seemingly logical and coherent world of theory. Health and social care practitioners are starting to use in-depth reflection of stories to explore the dialogical nature of practice. The impact of stories varies and can depend on how, when and in what context stories are told. Hall (1997: 150) explains the position taken by Bakhtin (1986: 121):

> Dialogue is treated in the widest sense that social existence cannot be separated from communication. . . . It is not dialogue in the sense of turn taking, but the complex interplay of speakers, hearers, occasions of speaking and the many potential voices that can be invoked in relation to a topic.

In this sense professional practice is undertaken 'in relation to' people, contexts and problems that are identified. In this sense health and social care practice is becoming dialogic. It is moving away from the traditional monological approach where the expert takes data to make a diagnosis and then prescribes a solution.

Reflective learning demands a self-critical approach from Judith. She draws on particular explanations because she can – it absolves her of any fault, takes away her responsibility for the resistance. Whether or not her explanation is correct is not the point of this analysis. The purpose of reflection on her story is to explore the alternative explanations and think how things might have been enacted differently.

In Judith's story there are interesting contradictions, unexpected connections and underlying beliefs and values. Rehearsing alternative scenarios, different explanations and plotting a new ending may give Judith practical tools that enable her to reposition herself in this scenario, recast the actors and imagine different outcomes. Helping Judith to reflect on her story is challenging. It will take time to explore how Judith reached her explanations, reconstruct what could have happened, explore how the resistance of the relative compared with the expectation of compliance that the nurses experience of patients. Additionally the story generates issues about the experience of dying. Perhaps this is the first dying person that Judith has encountered. She may be reflecting that she wanted to help this family but was not able to do so. There are many elements to discuss and learn from, it is not solely about events and doing nursing. The story offers an opportunity to explore with Judith what is like to be a nurse.

Recasting practice

The expectations and actions of practitioners are orchestrated through a discourse that represents the social and moral world. Narratives are personal constructions that enable us to explore how these relationships work in ways that help to understand how we, as professionals, understand and explain what we do. This approach sees the role of the practitioner emerging in dialogue with (in relation to) 'others'. In reflecting on practice we accept that the words that we use in this dialogue are not neutral, not something that we use for the first time, therefore the professional discourse cannot be separated out from personal understandings and experience. We react, reply and assimilate (internalize – make our own) the previous words of others and thus have a continued story of our experience on which to draw as we face each new encounter. In one sense this reflects what Mattingly (1998: 8) asserts when she reminds us that narratives are not only 'event-centred' but also 'experience-centred'. The function of narrative as a reflective device supports a search to understand our practice and the ways in which we can learn from our experience.

Reflection in/on practice may be undertaken either jointly or alone. Stories may be shared orally or written down and reflected on at a distance. Gibbs (2003) suggests that we think about what we write in a way that is different from what we say. Oral accounts may be a stream of unedited consciousness and used in different ways from written accounts that enable us to explore the detail of what is written and expose the discourse underlying the narrative. Health and social care professional practice tends to draw on an oral tradition in storytelling, but increasingly the practice of deeper reflection is calling for a more thoughtful and considered analysis of experience that is aided by reflective diaries and contemporary notes.

Rozina's story

The real value of storied approaches is partly derived form the notion that they occur naturally in practice, they exploit the normal interactions and sharing of experience that typify practice environments. We can also learn from the stories of others, the patients and clients with whom we work.

The story of Rozina was collected as part of a study of Asian women's narratives undertaken by Frost and Horrocks (2004). Rozina tells her story as part of a long narrative interview. Rozina describes herself as 'British-Pakistani' in that her parents were born in Pakistan but she was born in England. The clinical record describes Rozina as 'Pakistani'. Her first child was 8 years old and her second child was stillborn 4 years previously. Rozina tells the story of the birth of her third child:

It come to midnight on Valentine's day . . . and uhm I were like thinking, am I gonna have this kid today or not! I was in the delivery suite when they said . . . right you got to go back up (to the ward) because uhm . . . you know the baby is not gonna come today.

But I was . . . I was in a lot of pain . . . and I was trying explain this to this midwife . . . she was just going in and out . . . there was *nobody* in the room at the time with me. I was trying to explain to her that I *AM* in a lot of pain and there is something happening . . . you know it's your body you can tell . . .

But in a way I'm not saying . . . I'm not blaming 'em . . . I could tell . . . coz like she was doing internals and she was saying well there's not much happening . . .

. . . but the problem was, when they took me up it was like she made me walk up, and you know, I couldn't even stand up, never mind walk up, – an then she gives me this massive bag of my own . . . you know which I brought in for the baby, to carry, and I'm thinking hang on a minute I'm in *EXTREME* pain here you know . . . I'm having a baby, and you're asking me to walk up . . .

Riessman (2000) suggests that first readings often fit in with 'precommitments'. She is suggesting that stories are told with a purpose. Rozina's story can be seen as an account that tells of a potential error where an uncaring health service did not treat her with the care she believed that she deserved. Rozina is outraged because she has a story that is a continuing narrative – her first baby dies. Rozina can see that she is vulnerable, at risk – she cannot understand why the experts cannot see what she believes to be self-evident.

In this story we can see how Rozina is marginalized, less powerful, compliant even when she is seemingly outraged by the treatment she receives. Frost and Horrocks (2004) explain that while Rozina's story cites many positive encounters with health practitioners, there are many elements that convey such marginality and compliance. Frank (1995) suggests that when seeking medical care we engage in a tacit agreement to follow professional regimes that require our compliance, the surrender of our choices. Indeed, throughout her story Rozina seems reluctant to firmly apportion blame for the events that occurred. She continues:

> Anyway I did what she said and we went up to the ward – then suddenly I just had this pain . . . and I said I just need to lie down . . . I just can't believe . . . I mean I was really scared coz there was blood . . . then I think the midwife panicked as well who was up at the ward . . . so she just rung down to emergency and said look your gonna have to have her straight down coz obviously the baby's about to come
>
> We got back down there – an' the midwife who was there with me in the delivery suite said what happened? I just said to her, you tell me what happened *you know*, I was really angry, I was really . . .
>
> Ok I don't say this to blame them all the time but they shouldn't of rushed me up, they should've waited another 15 minutes say after 12 just to see . . . say well let's see if this is what she's saying *maybe it is true*.
>
> After I asked them . . . I said er the midwife did say to me that they needed the room . . . the delivery suite an' obviously he [the doctor] did come to me and he told me the truth which was nice because some doctors obviously stick together don't they? He said to me you're the only person who's had a baby this morning the whole rooms are empty.
>
> That made me feel terrible because I was like you know . . . Why did she say they needed the room? Coz you can take that into consideration if there's an emergency case coming, – you have to go to the ward then, . . . I've got to go obviously coz there could be somebody who could be in a worse position than I was.

Frost and Horrocks (2004) argue that stories do not simply describe what someone does in the world but what the world does to that someone. Rozina's experience is not happening in a social vacuum, the events are part of the relationship between Rozina and the nursing staff. Rozina seems reluctant to blame, but can this be located in being marginalized and might this also be related to her acceptance of the powerful position of the professional? Bakhtin would argue that this is part of a monological discourse where the professional practitioners do not permit Rozina to negotiate her position. Frost and Horrocks (2004) explain that Rozina is cast in the role of patient. They argue that she must comply or be marginalized, criticized or even penalized for resisting. What does that imply for the way in which 'patient-centred practice' operates? What does the practitioner learn from this?

In the story, Rozina's baby was about to be born with potential serious complications in the light of her clinical history. Rozina also has a previous story where she experiences conflict between her expectation as a woman and that as a patient. Therefore Rozina is resistant to apportioning blame, challenging the authority of the professional, while at the same time speaking in a voice that is outraged. Frost and Horrocks (2004) explain how Rozina is able to cast and then recast health professionals as *both* expert and incompetent. Rozina is multi-voiced as woman, mother, patient and complainer. Frank argues that health-care practitioners tend to be monologic in their relationships casting single roles for themselves and patients, failing to understand that one can be compliant and resistant at the same time. Thinking about 'in relation to' in this way helps us to engage in guided reflection through which practice is reviewed, challenged and repositioned.

Reflecting on Rozina's story causes us to consider that the story does not exist in a separate space – it emerges in dialogue with practitioners. Frost and Horrocks (2004) assert while Rozina's explanation might be challenged with regard to its 'correctness', what cannot be challenged is that her participation in a social and moral world enables her to make such evaluations. Rozina makes interpretations about what happens because she is able to do so. Using the stories of others helps us to reflect through a process of acknowledging the ways in which we are actors in the story of others as well as our own. Like Judith, Rozina makes assumptions at the end of the story. The last thing that Rozina shares is 'perhaps it's because I'm Asian?'. Is she right? Whether it is true perhaps does not matter in one sense; Rozina, like Judith, uses the explanations available to her. Within her social and moral world, for Rozina it is race that is the explanation, for Judith it is about her gender.

Do stories matter in practice?

Stories matter because they can accommodate contradictions, connections and discontinuities in our everyday practice. Through reflection we can start to get a deeper understanding of our practice by exploring these elements of our storied lives. Giorgi (1985) suggests that narratives are useful because they can accommodate contradictory experience and respond to the contexts in which they are shared. Giorgi essentially offers a view that stories matter because they are a reflective device that can be shared, challenged and reconstructed in ways that transform practice. Stories matter because they have the capacity to tell the 'inside' story. Stories help by giving voice to experience in ways that create an intimacy between explanation and action, between theory and practice, between the outside and inside world of experience.

Final thoughts

Judith and Rozina are not telling stories about neutral events. They are talking about relationships, about intersubjectivity in the power of relationships they experience. Moreover, they are seeking a response from the listener, a contribution in one sense that helps to create the context and the atmosphere of their experiences.

There are many ways in which to seek explanation of our day-to-day practice. This chapter has suggested that the storied accounts of our daily lives enable us to reflect more deeply on the way in which we use ourselves in relation to others. Judith's story gives us glimpses into a world where assumptions are made. The authority and position we take means that these assumptions are unspoken and unquestioned. These assumptions are built and reinforced in a lifetime of practice and inform how we act. Judith has a set of assumptions about how Asian men relate to women and the consequences for the family. Challenging these tacit assumptions enables us to think of different explanations and foster a more compassionate approach to practice.

Rozina's story is an example of how using patients' narrative accounts can give different explanations, and different perspectives. Rozina reminds us that her role is not solely that of patient, but that she is also a woman with a voice of her own. She is also a patient with a story that needs to be understood and heard if the care is to be effective. Rozina gives us a different set of insights and assumptions that help to understand how to provide more sensitive and thoughtful care. We are better for knowing these stories because they re-create the world in ways that make us want to practise differently from those in the story. We are better for knowing our own story in different ways, through different lenses and in ways that make us think of how we want our story to be. We want to be the object as well as the subject of our story. Walker (2000: 89) paraphrases Lyotard:

> The knowledge transmitted by these narrations is in no way limited to the functions of annunciation; it determines in a single stroke what one must say in order to be heard, what one must listen to in order to speak, and what role one must play . . . to be the object of a narrative.

8 Disrupting dominant discourse: critical reflection and code-switching in Maltese social work

Marceline Naudi

This chapter presents findings from a study of social work in Malta. Although social work, like all other professions, is situated within 'a complex of social and cultural arrangements and understandings' (Blagg *et al.* 1989), many of these arrangements, understandings or knowledges are part of the taken-for-granted background and hence practitioners may not be self-consciously aware of them.

This study aims to render explicit these implicit taken-for-granted background and rationalities that form an essential part of social work assessments of clients and clients' situations in Malta. It argues that the dominant discourse, with the effect of the Catholic Church heavily marked, is reflected and reproduced in the way that social workers in Malta categorize and define the service users. The aim is that, by 'making the usual strange', I will be providing social workers in Malta with the space to reconsider 'the acts, gestures, discourses which up until then had seemed to go without saying' (Foucault 1981: 12). Being myself Maltese, the study also acted as an exercise in critical self-reflection, part of the effect of which is considered in an epilogue at the end of the chapter.

Case discussions during tutor visits to social work students on placement were audiotaped and the transcribed texts analysed using critical discourse analysis within a Foucauldian perspective. Critical discourse analysis gives researchers 'permission' to 'take sides' and 'actively participate in order to uncover, demystify or otherwise challenge dominance' (van Dijk 1997: 22). The ultimate goal is not only scientific, but also social and political, namely change through critical understanding. Hence the relation of this study as an aid to critical reflection, which is seen to first question and then disrupt dominant structures and relations, thereby laying the ground for change (Fook 2002). I would acknowledge this as my own perspective.

During the analysis it became clear that participants' use of code-switching, that is, the changes from Maltese to English and vice versa, was a particularly important feature of the case discussions. Looking at the code-switching in the verbatim transcripts helped to deepen the critical understanding of the way that we reflect and reproduce the dominant discourses, often without conscious intention, and provided further evidence for the existence of underlying assumptions about social categories. As Fook (2002) states, the primary purpose of critical reflection is to unearth how we ourselves participate in discourses which shape existing power relations. Greater awareness of this would therefore aid practitioners in critical reflection on their own practice. This means that practitioners will be subjecting their own knowledge claims and practices to scrutiny as a topic in its own right (Taylor and White 2000).

During the tutor visits the student, the fieldwork teacher (professional social worker employed by the agency to whom the student is accountable during placement) and the university tutor discuss cases allocated to the student. The specific case discussed below touches on the issue of homosexuality.

Malta

Since this study is concerned with the processes of case formulation associated with social work in a Maltese context, it is of import briefly to lay out the Maltese cultural context. Rather than just 'taking the text to the audience', this contributes to 'taking the audience to the text' (Bassnett and Trivedi 1999).

The Maltese archipelago has a total area of 316 square kilometres holding a population of just under 400,000 people. The population density is one of the highest in the world, with several communities having the highest population density in all of Europe (O'Reilly Mizzi 1994), helping to produce a high degree of social visibility. Knowledge that elsewhere would normally be private or unavailable is easily obtained, even inadvertently, and is rapidly transformed into a public consumer good via the exchange of information and gossip.

Historically, Malta has been fought over and ruled by various powers due to its strategic position in the middle of the Mediterranean. For almost half a millennium prior to independence (1964), however, we only had two major 'rulers': the Knights of the Order of St John, often referred to as the Knights of Malta (1530–1798), and the British (1800–1964), with a short spell under the French in between (1798–1800). It is therefore the effects of these colonizations that are mostly still felt.

One such effect is the strong position of the Catholic Church in Malta. It was during the period when Malta was administered by the Knights of St John, who were a religious order, that the powers and privileges of the Church in Malta proliferated. The Church had 250 years to grow in wealth, importance and power. When the British took over, they were interested in the national affairs and left local affairs to the Church. This further consolidated the Church's influence over the people (Sultana and Baldacchino 1994), and, as noted by Fox (1991), the Church was long the guardian of morals, manners and learning in Malta.

As a result, the context of welfare generally in Malta is different from that of the UK. Since the Church 'looked after' the local population, it also stepped into the breach to see to the 'needy'. Most residential services, whether for children, the elderly, the disabled or women subject to domestic violence, are to this day run by the Church. Only very recently have some residential services started to be provided by the state and, even more recently, by private organizations. Apart from residential service provision, the Church also acted as a 'social work' agency, in that whatever the problem, people would turn to the clergy in their parish for help. Whilst we now have mainly state social work agencies, the effect of the Church is still felt.

Several experienced practitioners in the field are likely to have had little or no training in anti-oppressive practice since social work education in Malta has only included a taught anti-oppressive practice element since 1995. Hence, they may well have a limited awareness of the issues involved. Most social work agencies do not operate an equal opportunities policy within their agency both generally and specifically with regard to service delivery, although this is beginning to change. With Malta being a strongly Catholic and traditional society, some of the issues within equal opportunities and anti-oppressive practice are considered controversial, and as such have not been mainstreamed, with the result that there is limited general awareness of them. Homosexuality is one of these.

Issues of sexual 'morality'

Abela (1994a) argues that by European standards the Maltese have retained an extremely strict sexual and moral code. The upkeep of this stringent sexual and family morality is strongly related to the activity of the Church and its corresponding support by the people.

Part of this stringent sexual morality relates to homosexuality. Cole (1994) states that Maltese society operates with an assumption of heterosexuality. Homophobia looms large. Gay men and lesbians are generally seen as challenging the family and the existing relationships of power and authority. The reaction to this challenge would be expected to be particularly strong in Malta which, compared to other European countries, scores higher on traditionality (Abela 1994a). The strength and primacy of the family as a social institution in Malta give further basis for the buttressing of traditional values and the reduced likelihood of the emergence of homosexuality as a social force. Opposition to homosexuality is closely bound up with the nature of our

Judeo-Christian heritage. The official position of the Catholic Church on homosexuality refers to it as a 'moral disorder' that cannot be promoted in a Christian society (Babuscio 1988). This means that the act of homosexuality has been condemned as morally wrong or sinful, but that the homosexual is welcome to remain in the Church so long as s/he observes chastity. With studies in the sociology of religion having observed an incapacity of the official church to recognize the injustices committed against people with unconventional lifestyles and sexual orientations, including homosexuals (Abela 1998), change in this regard is unlikely to be swift. This is confirmed by the document written in June 2003 by the 'Congregation for the Doctrine of the Faith' and published in July of the same year, by order of the Pope, reiterating this same position, and exhorting Catholic politicians to strongly resist state policies running counter to it.

Notwithstanding that homosexuality was decriminalized in Malta about 30 years ago, the dominant Catholic discourse still prevails. Sexually active homosexuals tend to be viewed as either bad ('*moral* disorder'), and therefore to be converted or ostracized, or mad ('moral *disorder*'), and therefore to be cured or ostracized (and maybe pitied). Generally, therefore, homosexuals are still socially stigmatized and rejected. It is noteworthy that Abela (1994a, 1994b, 1994c, 1998, 2000) found in his various studies that between 40% and 47% of the Maltese do not want a homosexual as a neighbour; 67% think that it is right for the Church to speak out against homosexuality; and 73% would never justify homosexuality (as compared to an average of 40% for Europe as a whole).

A survey on sexual orientation discrimination carried out by the recently established Malta Gay Rights Movement (2003) starts by stating that 'homophobia and intolerance still prevail in Maltese society'. The survey found that more than one in ten respondents claimed that they had been subjected to some form of violence due to their sexual orientation and that half of the respondents claimed that they had experienced some sort of harassment. The majority of reported incidents of violence and harassment were at the hands of strangers, reflecting the general homophobia found in Maltese society. Disturbingly, however, in some cases the perpetrators were family members, Church authorities, work colleagues or members of the police corps. A considerable number of cases involving bullying in schools were also reported. Furthermore, notwithstanding that the sample is biased towards respondents who are relatively 'out', the majority of respondents take measures, to different degrees, to conceal their sexual orientation in order to avoid harassment and violence.

The above forms part of the general dominant discourse within which social workers in Malta work, often without conscious awareness of the effect of this discourse on their practice. The effect of this 'homosexuality' discourse on the assessment of the client (and client system) and the resultant recommended intervention is encountered in the following case discussion.

The analysis is based on extracts of a verbatim transcription of two tutor visits to a young BA (Hons) social work student on placement within an educational setting. Present at both meetings are the university tutor (TUT), who is also the researcher, the social worker from the agency acting as fieldwork teacher (FWT) to the student on placement, and the student (ST). All three are female. The client (M) is a 12-year-old girl referred to the social work unit because of absenteeism. Her mother is a single parent, and officially lives in her parents' household, together with her sister and her daughter, M.

Analysis of case discussion

Most Maltese people are at least bilingual (Maltese/English) and tend to use a mixture of languages when speaking. Gumperz (1982b) points out that many residents of the ex-colonial countries freely alternate between their own language and that of the ex-colonizing power. Hence, the case discussion analysed during this study was conducted in a mixture of Maltese and English. It was during the process of analysis that I became aware that the constant code-switching could possibly form an important part of the analysis. Conversational code-switching can be defined as the juxtaposition within the same speech exchange of passages of speech belonging to two different grammatical systems or subsystems. Apart from the alternation itself, the passages have all the earmarks of ordinary conversations in a single language, with the code-switching offering an extra resource or tool in communication at the disposition of bilinguals and allowing for greater nuances of expression (Dolitsky and Bensimon-Choukron 2000; Gumperz 1982b). Code-switching is 'automatic', with the participants often unaware of which language is used at any one time, and is based on tacit shared understanding, with the speakers building on their own and their hearers' abstract understanding of situational norms (Gumperz 1982b: 61). Code-switching is also seen to link up with larger facts about the speaker's life world (Auer 1998: 5). Looking at the code-switching in the case discussion therefore allowed me to access a deeper level of analysis, as is seen below, resulting in greater possible awareness and therefore more scope for critical reflection. Since I was also a participant in the discussion (TUT), it also allowed me to look at my own 'automatic' code-switching.

When M's case is first discussed, the student explains to the tutor that during a home visit, where she met with the maternal grandmother and M, part of the problem identified was that M was being bullied by a group of eight other girls in her class. The main content of the bullying centres around M's mother being 'like a man, because her hair is short and she's flat chested'. This is the first time the mother is discussed and we are straight away introduced to her as being 'man-like'. It is also hinted at in this tutor visit that the mother is not always around since the grandmother is reported as saying that she tends to care for M. This is taken up again at the following tutor visit (approximately 4 weeks later).

The student tells us that the mother was hard to find at home, further building the picture that the mother is not often around. She also tells us that the mother did, however, come into the agency, accompanied by a female friend. This turns out to be an important part of the picture.

The student goes on to say that when she first saw the mother she 'literally' thought she was a man, emphasizing the extent of the masculine image presented by the mother. The student continues building this picture: it is not just short hair, it is the way she dresses; and later, it is also the way she sits and moves. And it 'really sticks out'.

Following on from the description of the mother in the case discussion, the student considers the possibility that she may be a lesbian. There is a certain amount of hesitancy to actually state this:

> I also have . . . I mean I think too . . . we were discussing it with FWT . . . I don't know whether she is a homosexual or not, like.

She appears to be very careful not to 'judge' the mother by her appearance. Her use of the word 'judge' may suggest implied wrongdoing of some sort, that is, that being a homosexual is a bad thing. Her hesitance too may be heard to suggest this. She does not seem to want to be seen as 'accusing' the mother of potential wrongdoing unless she is certain of it. In fact she then uses a counter-argument, 'maybe it's just something she likes to wear and that's it', and then immediately stresses the masculine non-verbals, so the work being done in reality is to dismiss or discredit this counter- argument. She ends the turn, again, being very careful not to be seen to be jumping to conclusions: 'I don't know though. It is still hypothetical y'know.'

The above is presented as showing us the student's internal thoughts. It builds the picture bit by bit, making a case for the mother being a lesbian, while appearing to counter-argue at the same time. The mother is never at home (is she maybe living with her 'female friend'?). She comes into the agency accompanied by her 'female friend' (is this her lover?). She is *very* masculine looking, both in the way she chooses to dress and wear her hair, and in the way she moves, sits, and so on. However, since the mother did not actually state 'I am a lesbian', the student stresses that this is 'still hypothetical'. The last few turns in this extract from the case discussion, however, once more further reinforce the 'hypothesis': the female friend is 'very feminine, on the other hand', fitting in with stereotypes of lesbian femme and butch; she furthermore clearly shows an interest in the girl, which impresses the student. This latter point could be heard to suggest that she might be more than just a 'friend'. Although each separate segment of information may not amount to much on its own, they derive significance from the context, that is, by being contexted as they are in the accounted sequence of events (Wattam 1989).

The following extract, which occurs shortly after the above part of the case discussion, attempts to shift the focus away from the mother and the lesbian hypothesis, and back to the girl. The issue of lesbianism, however, is still central.

The first four turns and the first part of the fifth work at putting the focus back on M and away from the issue of homosexuality. Let us look at the bilingual version of those turns (bold text in bilingual transcript indicates words spoken in English):

1 ST: . . . biss meta iddiskutejnieha *(but when we discussed it)* **sort of** . . .
2 FWT: **It's irrelevant**, iktar pjuttost it-tifla . . . *(it's more the girl)*
3 ST: it-tifla . . . *(the girl)*
4 FWT: tajjeb li tkun tafha, imma it-tifla, kif *(it's good to know, but the girl, how)*
5 ST: dik *(that's it)*. Mhux qed ngħid *(I'm not saying)* . . . **I'm not really interested in the mother's personal life, I mean**, iktar kif taffetwa it-tifla *(more how it affects the girl)*

It is noteworthy that the sections where the participants are fielding off any potential accusations of maybe placing too much emphasis on the mother's sexual orientation, are in English (FWT: It's irrelevant (turn 2); ST: I'm not really interested in the mother's personal life (turn 5)). The bits which put the focus on the girl, on the other hand, are in Maltese (FWT: iktar pjuttost it-tifla . . . *(it's more the girl)* (turn 2); ST: it-tifla . . . *(the girl)* (turn 3); FWT: imma it-tifla, *(but the girl)* (turn 4); ST: iktar kif taffetwa it-tifla *(more how it affects the girl)* (turn 5)).

One possible interpretation of this is connected to the overall discourses. The macro level, as Gardner-Chloro *et al.* (2000: 1309) state, needs to be taken into account together with the micro level in order to discover the underlying meaning of individual code-switches. Homosexuality in Malta is still a strong taboo subject, and not one that would be generally discussed in the course of the average day. Their use of English might be precisely reflecting this. In other words, since it is not part of the Maltese discourse to discuss homosexuality openly, it would be more acceptable to do so in English, as doing so puts a certain distance between them and the taboo subject. Lawson and Sachdev (2000: 1352) found that the use of a specific language tended to vary according to the topic of conversation, in that topics are seen to reflect their language environment. It would then make perfect sense to use Maltese in relation to the girl. The primacy of the family in Malta has been previously referred to: children and (conventional) family form a very large part of our dominant discourse (Tabone 1995). Focusing on the daughter therefore is to do with the Maltese 'life world', or, as Sultana and Baldacchino (1994) put it, with local customs, traditional beliefs and values, thereby resulting in Maltese being used, since this 'realm' is characterized by the Maltese language.

A further interpretation would relate to the more specific local context, that is, university tutor on placement visit. Although the participants are Maltese, and as such would have been 'normalized' into the dominant culture, they are also social workers, and therefore aware of the possible accusation of being generally 'judgmental'. The potential accusation would come from the university tutor who is there to assess the student. Sultana and Baldacchino (1994: 20) claim that the English language tends to represent the official, documented, public dimension in Malta. The official formal language would therefore be English, and so those bits can be seen to be specifically targeted at the tutor who is there in an official capacity. Gumperz (1982b) lists 'addressee specification' as one of the functions of code-switching. The parts spoken in English actually reflect what they would expect the tutor to want to hear ('it's irrelevant'; 'I'm not really interested in the mother's personal life'). When focusing on the girl, they are on safer ground, and so can code-switch back to Maltese.

Throughout the case discussion we see examples of homosexuality/ lesbianism being considered a 'sensitive' issue, which is in keeping with the dominant taboo discourse. If we pick up in the middle of turn 5 again, we can see a similar bilingual configuration:

> 5 ST: [. . .] għax peres li shaba qed jitfgħula il-botti u hekk, *(because since her mates are throwing barbs and so on)* **maybe she hasn't yet dealt with it, maybe she hasn't yet realized** . . . qed tifhem *(know what I mean).* U anki għaliha speċi iktar . . . *(and even for her sort of, it's more . . .)*

The student switches back to English to talk about 'it' ('maybe she hasn't yet dealt with it, maybe she hasn't yet realized'), and then back to Maltese to put the emphasis back on the girl (U anki għaliha speċi iktar . . . *(and even for her sort of, it's more . . .)*).

In fact, the student seems to be trying to avoid using the 'sensitive' words 'homosexuality' and 'lesbianism'. It is only when pressed for clarification by the tutor in turn 6, that she resorts to saying 'if it's as I'm thinking, that maybe her mother's homosexual' ('homosexual' being the only English word used in that phrase in the bilingual version, as opposed to the Maltese words 'homo-sesswali' or 'lesbjana'). In the following turn, the fieldwork teacher follows a similar pattern by putting the stress on the girl accepting that this is what her mother *looks* like. The emphasis is placed on looks, not sexuality, although we know that both the student and the fieldwork teacher had already previously established a definite link between the mother's masculine image and her hypothetical lesbian sexuality.

In turn 12 the student once more demonstrates the sensitivity of the subject:

> But it wasn't mentioned, when I spoke to the mother, the subject didn't come up. And since I had only just met her for the first time, I didn't risk . . . 'cos I thought, I don't want her to think . . . something, I don't know, maybe think badly, that sort of I've interpreted it . . .

Her hesitancy, her wording and rewording, is available to be heard as discomfort with the issue. If we pick up the bilingual version from there, we once more find a similar configuration to above:

12   ST: Qisni ħallejt l-**issues** jiżvolġu waħedhom, peres li kien l-ewwel **meeting**, *(I sort of let the* issues *evolve on their own, since it was the first* meeting) mbagħad qisni, għedt lil FWT b'kollox u hekk, *(then I sort of, I told the FWT about everything and so on)* **to keep it in mind**, biex jekk il-quddiem ikun hemm bżonn jiżvolġu fuqhom *(so if in the future they need to go deeper into it)* . . .

13   TUT: ħassejtek ma kontx bnejt relazjoni biżżejjed biex titakilja l-**issues** *(you felt that you hadn't built enough of a relationship to tackle the* issues*)*

14   ST: eżatt *(exactly)*. Għax *(because)* **it was quite a sensitive issue** naħseb *(I think)*.

The words 'issues' and 'meeting' can be seen as loan words, since they are widely used in certain contexts in Maltese, such as this one. However, 'to keep it in mind', used in the middle of turn 12, is available to be seen as once more referring to 'it', that is, the issue of possible homosexuality, and therefore the code-switch to English would be in keeping with the above interpretation. Similarly, the code-switch in turn 14, 'it was quite a sensitive issue', reflects the use of English to refer to the 'sensitive' issues of homosexuality and masculine image, which appear to have been clearly conflated by this point in the discussion.

It is interesting that in the following turn the fieldwork teacher, whilst still emphasizing the 'sensitivity' of the issue, feels obliged to separate once more the masculine image from lesbianism:

> I think even today, she's feeling that it's a sensitive issue to discuss with the girl. I got that feeling at least. I think that the only way it could be handled is through the girl's school counsellor and guidance teacher. Not the issue of . . . lesbianism I mean . . . the fact that the mother, she is that way and you accept her that way, and no matter what others say . . .

The effect of the hesitancy can be seen to be displaying unwillingness, almost embarrassment, around the use of the word 'lesbianism' (this being the only time she uses the word). The whole issue is deemed to be so sensitive that it can only be handled by the school counsellor. The need to clarify that she is referring to the mother's appearance, as opposed to the mother's sexual orientation, is be available to be heard in two different ways. Firstly, it may be heard as in keeping with the dominant taboo, therefore clarifying that she is not referring to the subject which must not be mentioned, thereby reflecting her normalization into the dominant culture, and displaying being a 'good' person within that. Alternatively, it can be read as above, displaying her unwillingness to be seen to be making assumptions or to be seen as 'judgemental', reflecting her socialization within the profession. Either way, it does the work of clearly marking the dominant taboo.

Overall, in relation to the 'sensitivity' of the taboo subject of homosexuality, when referred to, or inferred, it tends to be with the use of the English code, which serves to emphasize the 'foreignness' of the homosexual discourse. One of the uses of code-switching is that it signals the degree of speaker involvement in, or distance from, a message (Gumperz 1982b). One can also note the apparent unwillingness to use the actual terms 'homosexual/ity' or 'lesbian/ism'. The main extract used in this analysis contains three uses of these words (once each by ST, FWT, and TUT) and at least 15 other references to homosexuality as 'it' or the 'issue'.

In another turn in the discussion the student once more refers to the mother as follows: 'Ehmm, also, when I spoke with her mother – she was very nice you know, she's very concerned for her daughter I mean'. It is of interest that the student feels the need to get this message across. The rhetorical effect could be heard to indicate that notwithstanding the hypothetical lesbianism, she was actually very nice, and even more importantly, very concerned for her daughter's well-being. Although at no point in the case discussion is it stated that someone being ascribed the category 'lesbian' would be an indication of her being not nice, or not concerned for her daughter, the rhetorical effect of the student's remarks suggests just that, by stressing the opposite.

There could be, once more, two ways of hearing this. The student may have been assuming that others will think this (in keeping with the dominant discourse that would be 'lesbian equals bad'), and so goes out of her way to explain that it was not so. Alternatively, it may have been what she herself had thought (again in keeping with the discourses into which she was normalized), but found it not to be the case, and so worthy of comment. Either way, it once more reflects and clearly lays out the dominant discourse on homosexuality in Malta.

Conclusion

During this case discussion the prevalent discourse on homosexuality as being a taboo subject, and a 'bad' thing, though not overtly stated, is clearly demonstrated. Gumperz (1982b) suggests that the communicative resources found in code-switching enable the conveying of messages that only those who share our background, and are thus likely to be sympathetic, can understand. They also allow us to suggest inferences, as has been seen above, without actually putting ourselves on record and risking loss of face. It is highly unlikely that any of the participants would have actually said what was in fact implied, but the meaning is conveyed nevertheless. Code-switching, as previously stated, provides evidence for the existence of underlying assumptions about social categories. Gumperz further finds that the shared 'conventions' enable individuals to build on shared understandings which eliminate the need for lengthy explanations, as also demonstrated above.

However, whilst 'normalization' into mainstream Maltese culture may result in the rejection of the lesbian mother, these specific participants have also been 'normalized' into the social work profession which, even without the benefit of anti-discriminatory training, is quite clear on the essentiality of a non-judgemental attitude and acceptance of the client. Hence, within the context of the tutor's visit, in some aspects of the above case discussion, it may have been attempted to give priority to the latter 'discourse'.

Nevertheless, the recommended disposal route, or intervention, resulting from the assessment of the client and the client situation in this narrative is that the client, M, should be referred to the educational counselling services to be helped with dealing with the *specific* type of bullying she is experiencing. This is because the whole 'issue' of the 'hypothetical' lesbianism of the mother is considered too 'sensitive' to be dealt with by the social work unit. A possible consequence of this is the reinforcing of the 'taboo' around homosexuality and giving the message to M and her mother that this whole issue (the mother's masculine appearance and/or lesbianism) is a very serious and worrying one, maybe even 'bad', and therefore requires specialized handling.

Clearly there were alternative ways this case could have been handled. The intervention could have been focused mainly on the eight girls in M's class who were perpetrating the bullying. This would have given the message that the problem lay with them and not with M or her mother. At no point in the case discussion was it suggested to do work with the perpetrators to have them address their behaviour towards the client. The problem was seen as located within M (or her 'maybe lesbian' mother), that is, within the client system, rather than within the 'environment'. Any resultant intervention therefore would automatically be targeted at the client, rather than at the classmates or the school.

Hence, the disposal route chosen, as a result of the assessment made reflecting the dominant discourse, works to maintain and constitute that same discourse. The effect of the Catholic Church in producing, maintaining and normalizing this discourse in Malta cannot be underestimated. The full strength of this effect was brought home to me as a result of my overall study.

Greater awareness of the taken-for-granted background and the part it plays in assessments of clients is necessary to allow for critical reflection on our work in the profession of social work, and, as has been demonstrated, analysis of code-switching patterns helps to increase this awareness. We have seen that the knowledges used include not only professional criteria (e.g. non-judgemental attitude) but also the everyday knowledge that we have gathered as part of our socialization into our specific culture (e.g. homosexuality is morally wrong). White (1997) emphasizes the direct relevance to practice of such analyses. By rendering manifest everyday 'talk', activities and rhetorical constructions, as I have attempted to do, it often becomes extremely difficult for people to continue to reproduce behaviour previously considered as part of the 'natural attitude'. Greater awareness not only gives us more conscious control of the criteria we use in our professional work, but also makes it possible for us to question them. This in itself may act as a 'call to action', and result in 'change'.

Whilst I am clear that I am aiming to 'describe' rather than 'prescribe', as van Dijk (1997: 23) reminds us, critical scholars of discourse do not merely observe linkages between discourse and societal structures, but aim to be agents of change, and do so in solidarity with those who need such change. A personal observation is that although I was a participant (TUT) in the case discussion, and one in a position of relative power, and therefore able to challenge, it is only as a result of the code-switching analysis that I became fully conscious of the inferences being made. This study results in raised consciousness on my part in future student placement visits. Sharing of this study in classroom situations with social work students similarly results in helping them to reflect critically on their underlying assumptions and the part they may play in client assessments and suggested intervention routes.

Epilogue

I would like to end this piece by reflecting on the impact this study had upon me as a Maltese woman social work academic. The doing of this study resulted in personal feelings of ambivalence, which I should like to explain. As a member of an ex-British colony I am very aware that I am exposing myself and my country to the gaze of the ex-colonizers. All through colonization, our experience was of the English being presented as superior in every way to the Maltese. Various personal experiences during my school years in a convent school run by English nuns suggested to me that we were constructed as 'other', almost as the 'natives' or 'savages' of the British Empire. As a relatively young adult I lived and worked in England for several years. I always felt 'different', and somehow I could never belong. Although I had very good spoken English, better than many around me, although my non-English accent was but a trace, although my physical appearance 'blended' with those around me, I nevertheless felt 'other' – different, and somehow not quite 'right'. My country was seen as 'exotic', 'quaint', a holiday destination, as opposed to the 'normal' Britain.

In this study I am translating and transposing texts from one culture to another. Bassnett (1991) warns about being aware of the ideological implications inherent in this. The act of translation always involves much more than language. It is not an innocent, transparent activity but it is highly charged with significance at every stage; it rarely, if ever, involves a relationship of equality between texts, authors or systems. Translations are always embedded in cultural and political systems, and in history (Bassnett and Trivedi 1999). This raised various questions for me. By translating and transposing Maltese texts into English, am I giving more power to the already powerful? Am I, by translating and generally exposing Maltese social work practice to the ex-colonizer, giving them more power to define me yet again as the 'other'? Even worse, am I exposing my trusting and co-operative colleagues to this scrutiny? Will we once more be seen as the 'savages'?

There is, of course, yet another issue. I will be using the colonial language to do so. Pennycook (1998: 191) asks:

> To what extent *is* English an unencumbered medium of communication available to its users, and to what extent is it, by contrast, a language that comes laden with meanings, a language still weighed down with colonial discourses that have come to adhere to the language?

By using English am I furthering the colonial discourses that have given me, and my Maltese colleagues, the identification of 'other', with all that that category entails? Bassnett and Trivedi (1999: 15) point out that Western cultures 'translate' non-Western cultures into Western categories, imposing their own grids (conceptual and textual) regardless.

Pennycook (1998), however, gives some tentative hope. Writing by indigenous people (which would include me) in English, he tells us, may also help to break apart some of these discourses, dislodge them from their adherence to English. Postcolonial writing can be a way of narrating different realities in English about the nation concerned, as a nation in its own right, and not just an ex-colony. Bassnett and Trivedi (1999) further add that in translation, a decision is always made between whether to take a text to an audience, or an audience to a text, and the same distinction applies also to postcolonial writing. I am clear that I am taking the audience to the text.

As Professor Oliver Friggieri, a leading Maltese academic, states (*Sunday Circle* 2002):

> The Maltese are no longer under the rule of the English, the French, the Knights – they are now a sovereign state. We are who we are because we have survived. . . . For several centuries we have been on the receiving end . . . But once we received something we were able to adapt it and reshape it. The Arabs introduced the language but we created Maltese out of it. St Paul gave us Christianity, but we made our own version of it. . . . being Maltese means we are small, but complete and equal.

PART III
Research

9 Rationalities, reflection and research

Andy Bilson

This chapter will consider the implications of using research for reflection if we start from a point of view that suggests that whatever we see and do is shaped by our jointly held and often unexamined assumptions. Research into teams in social care (e.g. Pithouse 1987; Hall 1997; White 1998), medicine (e.g. Bloor 1976) and nursing (e.g. Latimer 2000) shows how cultures develop locally and can sustain the practices of occupations, organizations and teams. These cultures and the practice that is supported by them are based on tacitly held assumptions generated and maintained by ongoing interactions within the team or organization. The assumptions are relatively invisible and can lead to resistance to change or learning new practices. At the same time these local groups and teams can be the source of creativity and new learning. I will consider how to tap into this creativity using research to promote critical reflection in teams and organizations.

In order to do this I will consider the use of research to develop conversations that reflect on the nature of a problem identified in a team or organization and to help participants to reflect on the often tacitly held assumptions that shape their work and maintain the problem. Although I will consider this using the biological concepts developed by Humberto Maturana, the issues raised are similar for other theoretical frameworks that acknowledge a dynamic and negotiated reality. I will illustrate this with examples of my work in using research to aid reform in teams and organizations. The approach I use is participative, aimed at developing new conversations that reflect on the network of conversations about the problem in the team or organization. However, I will also argue that engaging people in reflection cannot be based purely on rational argument but requires dealing with our emotions (e.g. Taylor 2001) and can be achieved through what Maturana (1980: 58) has called 'aesthetic seduction.' It is this focus on emotion that differentiates the approach from most forms of participative action research, though others have commented on the need for an emotional dimension in critical reflection (see for example, Bolton 2001: 16–17, Brockbank and McGill 1998: 45–8).

Before going on to consider examples of the use of research in reflection, I will first comment on the underpinning concepts that led me to my point of view.

Underpinning concepts

One starting point for considering Maturana's position is the nature of reality. Many different sociological and philosophical conceptions conclude that we do not experience a single stable reality but what Maturana (1988) has termed the multiverse – the idea that there are many realities each experienced as real with real consequences for our actions. Thus, he says:

> Science, a political doctrine, a particular religion, and many, many other creations that appear as particular cultural systems, constitute such domains. . . . we can observe that in each cognitive domain we, and all living systems with us, operate as if in a domain of objective (absolute) reality whose relativity can only be asserted if we step out and [reflect on it].
>
> (Maturana 1988:46)

According to von Glasersfeld (1997):

> This position is by no means new. One can find it in Vico, Kant, Schopenhauer, and recently in Richard Rorty. . . . If one takes this interpretation as working hypothesis, it has far-reaching consequences for our conceptual relation to the experiential world.

This chapter will suggest that taking this viewpoint can help us to reconsider the application of research and the nature of critical reflection to give a powerful tool for new forms of co-operative action. Rather than leading to the 'kiss of death' (Swoyer 2003) of an anything-goes philosophy as characterized by critics of relativism, I will stress how it leads to the centrality of responsibility and the importance of reflection. However, reflection in this framework does not reveal truths in any fixed sense, rather it acknowledges and works with the self-referential nature of our experience. That is, it reveals the part we play in constructing the realities we live, and reveals the choices of new ways of living that reflection makes possible.

Maturana builds his viewpoint on the basis of a range of studies of biology, including the study of colour vision. He suggests that the reality we experience is mutually specified by our bodily structure and the history of our interactions with our environment. In particular, he builds a theory of language starting with linguistic behaviours. These consist of behaviours through which an observer sees participants co-ordinate their actions. Animals and humans alike participate in linguistic behaviour, but a new domain occurs when linguistic behaviour can reflect on itself. With this reflection a new, second-order linguistic domain is brought forth, which is language. Maturana suggests that language is central to the manner of living that human beings have developed. He stresses that language is not limited to speech acts but covers a whole range of behaviours and that it is an ongoing process. Maturana and Varela (1998: 26) thus point out that 'Every reflection . . . invariably takes place in language, which is our distinctive way of being humanly active'.

Maturana talks about a 'conversation', which he defines as a flow of co-ordinations of language and emotions taking place in recurrent interactions in language between human beings (Maturana 1988: 50). It is in conversations that we bring forth different domains of reality:

It is our emotioning that determines how we move in our conversations through different domains of co-ordinations of actions. At the same time, due to the consensual braiding of our emotioning with our languaging, our conversations determine the flow of our emotioning. . . . [so] human life is always an inextricably braided flow of emotioning and rationality through which we bring forth different domains of reality. And we live our different domains of reality in our interactions with others . . . according to the flow of our emotioning.

(Maturana 1988: 50)

This idea of living in conversations is also found in cybernetics (e.g. Pask 1975), and similar conclusions can be found in postmodernism (e.g. Hassard and Parker 1993), social constructionism (e.g. Gergen 1985), social constructivism (e.g. Vygotsky 1978) and discourse analysis (e.g. Foucault 1972). Maturana's view that a human being lives in conversations has considerable consequences. Living in conversations means that we live in a continuously changing domain of descriptions that we generate in a series of recursive interactions within this domain. Maturana (1988: 43) summarizes some realizations of accepting our living in conversations. These realizations are profound and impact on all that we do as professionals (and in fact as humans) in any arena. His first point is that we do not have access to an independent reality. This is similar to the claim of Kant that we cannot know the thing in itself (*ding an sich*), but whilst for Kant the *ding an sich* is an ultimate point of reference Maturana says that it is meaningless to even talk about the thing itself, because 'all that we can say about it is dependent on our personalities and perceptions' (Maturana and Poerksen 2004: 118). He goes on to say that in conversations our rationality is based on premises chosen, not rationally, but out of preference (emotionally) – although we tend to claim that *our* premises are rational and that it is only those of our opponents that are irrational.

These premises 'bring forth' a rational domain or domain of reality (for example, a Melanesian cargo cult is brought about by premises about how at the millennium the spirits of the dead will return and bring with them cargoes of modern goods). This explains how people can share an experienced reality, which can appear totally different to an observer who does not share the same premises. From this it follows that if someone is operating on the basis of different premises they will not accept an argument as valid, since it is not valid in the rational domain they live. Thus accepting the rationality of an argument requires the adoption of the premises on which it is based. Finally, if premises are chosen through preference, not through rational decisions (even if within the rational domain we appear to be able rationally to defend them), then to accept an argument requires triggering an emotional shift to accept the new premises – or, as Maturana terms it, *seduction*.

If we accept this we see that there is no privileged access to reality or truth and that our claim to certainty has no greater foundation than any other. But this does not mean that because all the realities we are able to live are valid, they are all equal. The implications of all this for ethics can be seen in two contrasting areas that are central to many ethical dilemmas. If we work from this biological position we are both respectful and responsible: respectful because we recognize that the realities that others constitute in their networks of conversations are as valid and as ungrounded as our own; responsible because we are aware when we dislike the actions of others or experience them as abusive to others or ourselves and we are also aware that our awareness about what we do has consequences for what we do (i.e. our awareness and ability to reflect on what we and others do, generate choices in what we do, and with choice comes responsibility for our choices)

Maturana also considers the nature of science itself. He claims that scientists produce scientific explanations of their experience that are acceptable to the scientific community. In this view a scientific explanation is one that proposes a mechanism that would create the experience. Thus science is a rational domain different from others only in that it applies the rules of science to observation and explanation.

Preparing for reflection

The above discussion will make it clear that research within this framework cannot provide a picture of a reality existing independently of the researcher's actions. The research described here is based on the assumptions about science given above. It assumes that people working in organizations participate in a network of conversations based on tacitly held and often unexamined assumptions. The rational domain created in this network of conversations shapes how any problem might be constructed, along with the responses that are considered to be possible. This is illustrated in a study of referrals of older people to a social work department. A colleague and I were asked to help the department consider the need for reorganization of services. In a file study of referrals to various services we found that social aspects of old people's care were rarely mentioned. This is well illustrated by the comments found in a case file at the point of closure of a case leaving the couple with little support. The case concerned a bedfast woman whose husband was worried about his continuing ability to care for his spouse, exacerbated by living in a third-floor apartment with restricted access:

> Mrs. Y is a very poorly lady all of her needs are met by her husband (he will not accept help). . . . issues raised were around housing issues. Mr. and Mrs. Y have been waiting for ground floor accommodation for a long time. I have liased with housing re my concerns.

The extract shows what we saw as the tacit assumption of the worker, and the first-line manager who closed the case: that their role was to provide packages of physical care and that social aspects of the problems such as inappropriate housing were not part of the team's responsibility. Note the bold statement is made that 'he will not accept help' despite the file making it clear that he would have valued emotional support and advocacy to help secure rehousing. The help that he turned down consisted of packages of home care, and he made it clear that this was not the support he needed. The statement that 'the issues raised were around housing' shows how social problems such as inappropriate accommodation were not considered to be the responsibility of this social work team. Mrs Y and her husband were not alone in suffering from what appeared to be a wholesale approach to the nature of social work that left the social dimensions of their problems unaddressed. Similar comments were found in the whole range of files we studied.

Within this approach, reading files or interviewing is important as a way of proposing a mechanism for what is observed, in this case the assumptions of the participant(s) shaping the possible solutions to the problems of older people. A further assumption is that in most cases the teams and organizations have the ability to make a difference to the problems they identify. So from this point of view research is not aimed at gaining an independent viewpoint from an objective position. Rather the aim is to engage participants in a conversation in which new possibilities for consensual co-ordination of actions become possible. To do this I have developed a framework which I find helps with this process of enabling people in an organization or team to engage in the research process, to draw new distinctions aimed at increasing possibilities for beneficial action, and to consider any changes they might make. This framework has mainly been applied to health, education and social work fields – in older people's services (Bilson 1997, forthcoming), in child protection (Bilson 2002), in a range of social work settings (Bilson and Ross 1999), in governance in health (Bilson and White 2004), in developing new approaches to evidence-based practice (Bilson 2005; Lawler and Bilson 2004) and in social work education (Bilson 1995a; Bilson and Ross 1999) – but its applicability is far wider than these areas.

My starting point, following discussion with those who identify the problem, is to find a way to listen to the network of conversations in the team or organization(s) around the problem. I recognize that a problem is defined in a social context and may not exist, or be viewed differently outside that context, and this is the very reason for focusing on conceptions of what the problem is. In this I am trying to hear the implicit assumptions which shape the social construction of the problem. This is not to deny the reality of the problem to those who perceive it, as it is real in the rational domain created by those in conversation about the problem. This listening can take a number of forms, including interviews; reading secondary sources such as files or other records; simply talking to people and observing what they do; or doing formal ethnomethodological studies.[1] The aim is to orient myself towards the team or group with whom I am working.

In social work, files and official records such as reports to court are a very helpful source of this information as they often contain arguments or descriptions intended to justify a particular course of action. The clues to the assumptions in these conversations come from the creation of patterns, including those from quantitative data (Bateson 1980; Bilson and Ross 1999); from identifying differences (Bateson 1980); from the words and images used; and from reflecting on my own emotional responses to what I see and hear.

Reflective conversations

Throughout this listening to the network of conversations I engage with people and share ideas and thoughts about what I am seeing. My aim is not to be neutral and objective but to engage and learn. This is often followed by a more formal conversation with members of the organization or team, often at a seminar or workshop.

In these seminars or workshops I follow the approach of Atkinson and Heath who suggest that, to encourage reflection, research needs to enable the consumers of research 'to be more open to the research process' (Atkinson and Heath 1987: 15), stressing the need not only to give direct access to the research 'data' but also to demonstrate how the researcher constructs their results from them and the premises they use. The researcher can then offer the opportunity to see what happens if participants construct a new view based on the conversation in the seminar. A pattern I commonly use is to start from my thoughts, findings and sharing my emotional responses to what I have seen and heard. If possible, I then discuss alternative ways of viewing the problem and the premises on which these alternative views are based. I illustrate this with stories taken from my research, often about service users, and may also involve service users who have the opportunity to talk about their own situations and feelings.

Following some discussion of a presentation such as this, I then ask participants to look at data (frequently files or records) themselves and invite them to construct their own patterns from them. Following this, we discuss what has been discovered, anything that might be changed and what the possibilities are for change.

My approach in these seminars needs to be both passionate to convey my emotions about what I have seen, and at the same time open to change through attending to the views and emotions of participants. My aim is to achieve a situation that Maturana (Maturana and Poerksen 2004: 52) describes as being 'naked and unprotected' and having 'no discrepancy between what is said and what is done'.

For example, in recent work in eastern Europe it became clear that a key issue in the lack of support for families with young children was the invisibility of parents from Roma minorities. People would repeatedly say things like 'their parents don't care' or 'they are all young girls and prostitutes who don't want their children'. Research carried out by Roma women showed these issues were not accurate. The parents were mainly in their mid- to late twenties having a third or fourth child and were living in serious poverty (Bilson and Markova, 2005; Bilson 2004). In seminars aimed at promoting critical reflection and making these parents visible, I presented this research and told the stories of some of the families I had interviewed who had been helped to keep their children by the provision of family support. I presented pictures and quotations such as the following from the father of a little girl who had been homeless and destitute when his wife gave birth:

> God praise that project we had no other people close to us . . . no one else helped us. We had no place to live, we had no money, nothing. Everything was very complicated. . . . I would have murdered someone just to find a warm place for her.

This and similar stories, along with a picture of the clearly proud parents, had a powerful effect on participants who became much more open to the idea that parents may simply need help.

The impact of seminars such as these is, on occasion, dramatic. Following research into the reasons why children were sentenced to care or detention for offending, a seminar on the lines described above was held for managers in social work and probation. Only two children were sentenced to care orders in the 6 months following the seminar, compared with 88 in the previous year, and sentences to detention fell by a third (Bilson 1995b). Similarly, following work on child protection investigations in an agency having substantial numbers of unfounded investigations, the number of unfounded investigations fell by 84% and these families instead received support (Bilson 2002). Other similar changes occurred in the areas of older people's services (Bilson 1997, forthcoming); increasing contact between children in care and their families (Bilson and White 2004; Bilson and Barker 1998); and preventing admissions of children to care (Bilson and Ross 1999; Bilson and Thorpe 1988). In all these cases the critical reflection was followed by rapid changes in practice and the development of new approaches and services.

Implications for professional development

The approach to reflection discussed here suggests that professionals develop a rational domain that shapes the way they construct their day-to-day work. The task of reflection is to create a space in which the assumptions behind this rational domain become the subject of reflection. I have provided a framework that I have found helpful for working with teams and organizations that have a problem. It promotes critical reflection that uses research as a means to trigger a conversation that enables participants to try out new assumptions if they wish. This approach contrasts with current rationalistic managerial approaches that increasingly attempt to proceduralize and control professional practice. The approach here values the competence of professionals. Because it is based on respect for the realities lived by others, it avoids blame and encourages ongoing reflection on practice. This also provides an approach to the use of research which is different from and complementary to that found in evidence-based practice and suggests the need for a broader framework for thinking about the nature and use of research in developing and shaping professional practice.

There are a number of implications for professional development, the first being the need to provide greater exposure to one or more relativistic epistemologies in professional training. The emphasis on evidence currently found in professional training needs to be tempered by an understanding of the limitations of positivist approaches, particularly in the field of human interactions.

But, importantly, professionals need to be encouraged to reflect on their own practices and to consider how their day-to-day practice is shaped by often unconsidered assumptions. In my experience this can unleash creativity and learning as people are encouraged to view their work in new ways.

Conclusion

The approach discussed here is built on the idea that within an organization or team there is the capacity to adapt and change, and that the task of the professional faced with a problem is to tap into and encourage this ability. To do this she needs to be aware of the way that current approaches and responses are maintained by the frequently unquestioned and often invisible beliefs and presuppositions, which create the rational domain of the various participants in the organization as well as those in its environment. Whilst a rationalistic approach may bring more predictability and greater conformity, it is my contention that it does little for the professional development of workers in the organization. The development of approaches that encourage reflection on the rational domains that we build together offers the possibility to unleash creativity and encourage new ways of working. In this way professionals can truly continue to develop and grow.

Notes

1   These are sociological studies, based on the theorizing of Garfinkel (1984), which focus on the way people make sense of the world and display their understandings of it.

10 Using critical reflection in research and evaluation

Fiona Gardner

What difference might using a critically reflective approach make to research and evaluation? Critical reflection as a theory and a process unsettles dominant thinking and unquestioned beliefs, which can lead to greater clarity about underlying assumptions and values. For those carrying out research and evaluation, this process can be enlightening, encouraging a focus on useful questioning, clarification of issues and processes to be used, and a balance between process and outcomes. In this chapter, I explore the value of such an approach in my experience of collaborating with a large human service agency on a research project. The focus of the research project was on developing a research culture in the organization; my role as the outside evaluator was to help foster this process and to evaluate the outcomes. What I want to do here is not so much to look at the effectiveness of the project itself, but to explore the influence of critical reflection.

First, I want to define what I mean here by critical reflection. As this book demonstrates, there has been a major increase in interest in critical reflection across a wide number of disciplines. However, how critical reflection is named and what it means vary considerably. Partly, Kember (2001) suggests, this is because, until recently, writers about critical reflection have tended to focus on their own discipline. In a telling example, he talks about looking for books on reflective practice in a library and finding them spread across many areas. The language used often reflects a particular discipline; social workers tend to talk more about critical reflection (Fook 2002; Gould and Baldwin 2004b), reflective practice seems more common in nursing (Johns and Freshwater. 1998; B.J. Taylor 2000), and transformative (Mezirow 1991) or action learning (Cherry 1999) or in adult education. Sometimes it needs careful reading to clarify what is common ground and what is different.

Redmond (2004) compares a number of approaches to reflective learning, demonstrating that there are often common themes in spite of quite different language. She suggests that what Argyris and Schön, for example, call 'tacit knowledge', Mezirow would call 'unresolved dilemmas based on habitual assumptions'; what Mezirow and Habermas would call 'emancipatory learning', Brookfield would call 'development of alternative perspectives'. Kondrat (1999) makes a useful distinction between:

- reflective self-awareness, which she sees as the capacity to be aware of yourself, your own preferences and biases, for example;
- reflexive self-awareness, which is awareness of the impact of our culture and history on how we interact with others; and
- critical reflexivity, where the self and the social structure are seen as linked so that one cannot change without the other responding.

This highlights a significant difference between writers – the degree to which the act of reflecting must take into account an awareness of the influence of broader social structures and a desire to influence them. Clearly all reflective practice encourages thinking about practice. Whatever the process is, it involves analysing practice in the sense of exploring assumptions and values, taking into account feelings and thoughts, and considering how these impact on practice. Being 'critical' adds an expectation of exploring practice in the context of the social system in which it operates, looking, for example, at the influence of social expectations about such issues as gender or age, class or ethnicity. Bolton (2001: 31) points out that:

> We all wear culturally tinted lenses through which we view the world: there is no way we can take off our emerald (or crimson or aquamarine) spectacles and see the world, our actions, and those of others as they really are. . . . [Reflective practice] is an approach in which the learner is encouraged to be as reflexively aware as possible of their own social, political and psychological position, and to question it, as well as their environment.

Fook (1999a: 202) says the 'emancipatory element – the capacity to question and change existing power relations' is central, including the 'capacity to analyse social situations and to transform social relations on the basis of this analysis and to combine this analysis with self reflective knowledge'.

The definition I am using here is the one that we use where I work – at the Centre for Professional Development, Victoria, Australia. Developed by Jan Fook, this definition suggests that the critically reflective practitioner develops the capacity to deconstruct knowledge and assumptions, in order to 'develop (reconstruct) their own practice in inclusive, artistic and intuitive ways which are responsive to the changing (uncertain, unpredictable and fragmented) contexts in which they work; and in ways which can challenge existing power relations and structures (Fook 2002: 41).

This definition comes from an understanding of critical reflection that includes a wide range of background theory from reflective practice, reflexivity, postmodernism and critical social theory. What, then, are the key elements here for thinking about research and evaluation? Underlying this definition are the following:

- the importance of articulating and questioning assumptions;
- acknowledgement of feelings and thoughts, particularly that this can be an unsettling and uncomfortable process;
- awareness of subjectivity – that assumptions may be personally and/or socially determined and are likely to be both;
- affirmation of the value of experiential and tacit knowledge;
- awareness that in any situation there will be a variety of views and perspectives, and commitment to ensuring that the voices of those potentially or actually marginalized are heard;
- understanding of the importance of context and the influence of culture;
- a desire to use awareness to lead to positive socially-just change.

So how, then, does critical reflection relate to research and evaluation? Alongside the development of critical reflection has been the growth of interest in what are often called more participatory forms of research and evaluation, often, but not always, with a preference for qualitative methods. These include collaborative evaluation (Cousins and Earl 1992), empowerment evaluation (Fetterman 2000), evaluative inquiry (Preskill and Torres 1999) and a variety of forms of action research (Wadsworth 1998; Cherry 1999). Some of these approaches more than others see the process of the research or evaluation as achieving change in itself – the process is empowering for those involved. Others have a more clearly articulated link to seeking broader social change. All would recognize that research is not value-free and build in processes for reflection and collaborative work.

Interestingly, some similar language is used across the practice and research domains; some writers on practice see critical reflection as a form of research on practice, carried out by the practitioners involved (Bolton 2001); some researchers see critical reflection as part of their approach to research (Winter and Munn-Giddings 2001). Bolton talks about creating a 'spirit of enquiry' through encouraging students to reflect on experience; Winter (1987:67) about research as 'a form of inquiry located in biographical experience'; Winter and Munn-Giddings (2001:23) about 'creating a "culture of inquiry" in practice settings [i.e.] building in continuous evaluation' supported by a climate including respect, harmony and supportive criticism.

Action research is a typical example of participatory research where the evaluator and participants are jointly involved in a cycle of reflecting, planning, implementing, analysing, reviewing and reflecting. However, as Kemmis (2001: 92) points out, action research comes in many forms. He identifies three main approaches: the first with a focus on effectiveness, the second focusing on process (how change happened), and the third a critically reflective process which 'aims not only at improving outcomes and improving the self-understanding of practitioners, but also at assisting practitioners to arrive at a critique of their social or educational work and work settings. This kind of action research aims at intervening in the cultural, social and historical processes of everyday life to reconstruct not only the practice and the practitioner but also the practice setting. It aims to connect the personal and the political in collaborative research and action aimed at transforming situations to overcome felt dissatisfactions, alienation, ideological distortion, and the injustices of oppression and domination.'

Co-operative inquiry is similar to action-research, in that it too is a participatory approach that works in cycles. What is distinctive about it is the emphasis on the researcher/evaluator and those involved as participants in some way being seen as co-researchers. Heron (1996: 19) stresses that this form of research is

---

with people not *on* them or *about* them. . . . In its most complete form, the inquirers engage fully in both roles, moving in cyclic fashion between phases of reflection as co-researchers and of action as co-subjects. In this way they use reflection and action to refine and deepen each other.

This means that the researcher must be interested in the issue in a way that means they can participate directly, rather than only guiding the process for other people. However, while Heron's preference is that researchers are fully involved in the experience, he acknowledges that at times researchers may be fully involved in sharing decision-making about the research questions, but not as much in the experience of the research.

The research project

St Luke's was interested in a collaborative partnership with the Social Work Department at La Trobe University's Bendigo campus in Victoria, Australia, to carry out a research project exploring how to develop a research culture in a human service organization. St Luke's is a large voluntary agency which offers a wide variety of services, including community-based support for adults with a psychiatric disability, services for young people not able to live at home, work with families and community development. The agency had carried out a range of research and evaluation projects over the years and now wanted to develop a research culture across the agency, that is, a culture of inquiry, questioning how things were done and why, as well as what worked.

The agency and I (representing the Social Work Department) formed a Reference Group, which met to talk about how this could be done. We successfully applied for a grant to research how such a process might work and used it for part-funding of a research officer. St Luke's wanted a form of research that fitted with their general philosophy – a solution-focused, competency-based approach. We agreed on an action research method with a focus on working in collaborative or participatory ways where staff would be actively involved in the process and using a critically reflective approach. The Reference Group decided to ask for expressions of interest from teams or small groups of staff in carrying out some kind of research or evaluation project. The aim was that staff would primarily do the research but be supported by a combination of the research worker and/or other members of the Reference Group and/or me as the outside evaluator of the process. Two teams were selected: the youth team which wanted to work on funding services for young sexual offenders, and one of the mental health teams which wanted to evaluate some tools being used with people with a mental illness.

Before the teams started, the research officer, a Reference Group member and I met with each team separately for a training session. This session mainly used a sheet called 'Useful questions to think about for effective research' (see Box 10.1). It had a series of questions that related to a critically reflective approach, and these were used to present ideas about research and then to link these to the particular projects staff were interested in. In the training session, these were used to generate discussion about how to carry out the project. This sheet continued to be used in some other sessions with the teams.

Each team then met to work on their project, sometimes on their own and sometimes with the research officer and/or a member of the Reference Group and me. By the end of the project each team had made progress on their project. Evaluation interviews were held with individuals, each team and a focus group made up of interested workers, and asked questions about the processes of the project as well as the outcomes. I have used these to explore how the aspects of critical reflection described above related to the participants and to some extent the organization's experience of the project.

- The importance of articulating and questioning assumptions. We spent a considerable amount of time initially both in the training session and in subsequent meetings exploring the assumptions that participants had made. These often related to assuming a specific outcome – for example, the development of a service – but also to a particular way of looking at the issue. Both groups identified that an important part of the process was developing clarity about the aim of

---

Box 10.1 Useful questions to think about for effective research

What is the issue to be explored?

How is it constructed as a problem?

- Who sees it as a problem?
- What variety of views are there?
- What specifically do people want to consider?
- What are the underlying assumptions and values?
- Why has it come up as an issue now?
- What is the history of this issue?
- Is there a range of views about the background? What impact does that have on how the issue is now being seen?

Has the issue been thought about by other people? Who, where, what? What did they think? What conclusions did they come to? What questions did they raise?

Why are workers interested in this issue?

- What range of views is there?
- What do workers hope will happen?
- What do workers know from their experience?
- What do workers assume from their experience?

What needs to be asked/explored? What kind of information is needed? What is it that you want to know? For example, specific questions or general questions and prompts, factual information, views, ideas, beliefs?

What voices need to be heard about this issue?

- Are there particular voices likely to be harder to access?

How will people be involved? What ways of asking people for information are likely to work with these groups, particularly people experiencing the issue?

What resources are needed? What are the timelines?

---

the project: What was it, for example, that they wanted to do and why? What assumptions had they made? How had they reached this point? Using the questions related to history and background were particularly useful for this. One team felt that it was helpful at this stage to have people outside the staff group to contribute, providing outsider views with different viewpoints and preventing staff from becoming enmeshed in the issue. Part of this was encouraging staff to question and explore the issue more fully, articulating and assessing their assumptions. Some staff also identified assumptions about how to do research and how to work in general that they felt came from their different training as professionals. Again it was useful to have these differences articulated, so that they could be explored further.

- Acknowledgement of thoughts and feelings: that this can be an unsettling and uncomfortable process. This questioning of assumptions was experienced by some participants as a frustrating part of the process, especially in the beginning. It seemed that rather than making progress, things were going backwards; the team had started with clarity about a desired outcome and now was back to debating the issue. This was particularly so for the youth team who had started with the aim of having a service already available in another regional area also offered to their clients on a local basis. They had already done some work on this, talking to key people in the community and gathering information about services. Given busy workloads, talking yet again about the complexity of the issues sometimes made it feel 'too complex to grasp and get going'.

  In many ways, for me as the evaluator, this felt like a 'normal' stage of a research process, particularly in a field with no clear answers. What seems like a clear question or hypothesis to begin with often turns into a complicated set of possibilities. With the teams, sometimes the sense of frustration with the process was in relation to this complexity: the emerging of such difficult and unanswerable questions as 'what is normal anyway?' and 'is it only normal in our current context?'. This related to the next aspect:

- Awareness of subjectivity: that assumptions may be personally and/or socially constructed and are likely to be both. Workers already had some consciousness of the structural implications of their issues for themselves and their clients. Both were working in socially sensitive areas – one group with young people believed to be sexual offenders, and the other with people with psychiatric disabilities. Both groups were very conscious of the stereotyped views and assumptions in the community towards both these groups: in a sense, this was taken as a given that had to be worked with. Wanting to have a service for young people believed to be sex offenders, for example, was known to be of concern to some other agencies and to the local community. What did perhaps start to happen more was that workers could see more clearly the dangers of becoming so enculturated to those attitudes that they no longer saw them as needing to be part of the work. Over time, the tension between educating the community about the complexity of these issues and wanting to focus on providing services became clearer. Workers wanted to make sure that they too were not just reacting to the concerns of families and communities with the 'quick fix' of a service or overly simple evaluation tool, but looking more closely at some of the assumptions that were made about sexual responsibility, psychiatric disability and community reactions.

- Affirmation of the value of experiential and tacit knowledge. The critically reflective process did affirm the value of workers' practice knowledge. The questioning process helped reinforce that workers were the people who had the expertise in this area. The research officer and I had not worked in either field directly. While we had some relevant knowledge, which helped us focus and/or extend discussion, the team clearly had significant knowledge which partly emerged during the process. They could give pertinent examples that illuminated the points they were making and which helped determine direction. Their knowledge also indicated the complexity of the issues involved which related to:

- Awareness that in any situation there will be a variety of views and perspectives. The need to be aware of a range of views quickly became clear in both groups. Within each team there were various perspectives on the project itself, what was important to notice and what action would be most effective as well as the value of spending time on research. Discussion demonstrated that people also had different beliefs and assumptions about central issues, and this led to helpful debates about what approach to take. The importance of views outside the team was also raised. Client views were often represented through stories and examples and the possibility of talking directly to clients about their experiences was raised. This had previously been done in the mental health team in the development of the tool to be evaluated, so there was a greater awareness of the possibility of talking to clients and their families. This previous project had concluded that one tool would not be likely to suit all clients, so this all reinforced the need to check for a variety of perspectives. However, there was some concern from workers about what it would mean to more actively seek other perspectives from clients: partly because for workers this felt like a time-consuming and therefore daunting prospect, partly because of potential ethical issues about interviewing young people and people with a psychiatric disability. The discussion at least affirmed the need to be conscious that there were people whose views were important but had not been included: family members, for example, who might well have ideas and views.

- An understanding of the importance of context and the influence of culture. Another source of 'other voices' was the local community, and again this was seen as an important source of information particularly for the youth team. Both teams reflected on the importance of the context; at an immediate level, the influence of being in a rural community where clients were often more visible. Community attitudes were seen as important in the development and delivery of services. Thinking about the wider context also meant the political and economic climate: the need to justify how services are delivered and what benefits they generate. The mental health team, for example, articulated the tension between finding tools that clients found helpful and tools that sufficiently demonstrated the agency's effectiveness for continued funding. Finally, both teams were acutely aware of the mixed and often negative attitudes of the local and broader community to their client group. Some young people accused of sexual offences had been removed from their families usually because of perceived danger to younger children. Even if they maintained their innocence and were not prosecuted so not convicted, they were not allowed to return home. This was seen as reflecting the attitudes of the local community, but also prevailing social norms. This offended team members' sense of justice for these young people and was a major source of frustration.

- A desire to use awareness to lead to constructive socially-just change. In spite of the initial frustration of the research process, workers maintained a sense that overall the process was worthwhile and would lead to change in terms of a better and fairer deal for their clients. Both teams became clearer about what they wanted to do and why. They were both able to use students doing work experience to carry out some work for them: in one team, the student generated a useful literature review; in the other team, the student interviewed workers about their experiences and wrote up the results. Becoming clearer about the complexities of the issues in the long run was felt to be helpful in developing more appropriate plans for action.

Implications of the research

What does this mean for using critical reflection in research and practice in organizations?

First, critical reflection is a useful approach for practitioners interested in research and evaluation. It encourages workers to assess potential projects more critically, developing awareness of assumptions and values that may lead them in unhelpful directions. Using a critical reflection approach reminds workers to ensure that their chosen research or evaluation methods are compatible with their practice values. It was important to St Luke's as an organization to have approaches and methods that fitted their general values and assumptions. Using a critical reflection framework helped articulate what this would mean and to ensure that the research approach and methods fitted with the organization's philosophy. Hopefully, this will mean that the 'culture of inquiry' will be sustained. What this will mean in practice will depend on the particular project. It might mean, for example, asking whose views need to be heard, whose views are less likely to be heard and how can they be included. Workers using critical reflection do ask questions about social attitudes and values, the impact of the community and cultural context on their research projects.

Feedback from workers, the teams and the focus group was generally positive about the experience, valuing the impetus of having outsiders to the team help them think critically about the issues. However, they were also clearer about the amount of time and energy required for research and evaluation and able to make suggestions to the agency about the need to be adequately resourced.

Second, this experience suggests that using critical reflection enables workers to see connections between research and practice. The kinds of questions generated by a critically reflective approach in research are clearly relevant to practice. This can help create a culture of 'inquiring about' or researching practice, asking questions about what is happening at a deeper level and what this might mean for processes and outcomes. The project did seem to influence practitioners to explore their practice in more depth – to generate their own 'spirit of enquiry', in Bolton's (2001) terms, or research their own experience of practice. In this way research can become an 'on the ground' activity rather than an activity done by workers designated as separate researchers. In early meetings, the Reference Group talked about developing a research culture being epitomized by a greater 'spirit of enquiry' or 'sense of curiosity' in the organization. This was evident in the findings, with the teams saying that there was a greater sense of stopping to 'think, question, ask what happens and why'. The change was partly that it 'starts to agenda this is as part of what we do'.

Some participants gave examples of when members of their team had taken time to investigate and explore a particular issue instead of continuing to accept a situation or complaining about it. However, it is fair to say that some staff valued the expectation of reflecting critically more than others. While some made comments suggesting there had been a 'change from seeing evaluation/research as extra work to seeing it as helping reflection and in the long term meaning more time with clients', others said 'some people have a sense of having to do this rather than being enthusiastic'. For some it was also a matter of timing: 'it's a wave with the implication it hasn't reached everyone yet'.

Third, using critical reflection in research may provide a way for professionals from different disciplines to connect – the concepts are familiar even if the language may be different, as Redmond (2004) suggests. Participants in this process were able to acknowledge their different training and professional backgrounds. In Kondrat's (1999) terms, some were more familiar with the idea of reflexive self-awareness than critical reflexivity. However, the framework of critical reflection and the links to the structural fitted with their experiential knowledge. As part of using critical reflection, they could then explore what these differences could mean, what extra insights or useful knowledge there could be from different approaches, as well as articulating what was similar. The use of critically reflective questions that can fit across disciplines is important in this process.

The general approaches to research and evaluation – action research and collaborative inquiry, as well as the specific research methods of individual and group interviews and the focus groups – would also be used across disciplines and were familiar to most of those engaged in the project. Using the critical reflection framework helped to sharpen why these fitted for this particular project

This relates to the fourth point, that critical reflection as a process and theory is congruent with a range of research approaches and methods. In this project, critical reflection reinforced and complemented a collaborative, action research approach. The dimensions – critical reflection and research – overlapped here and both highlighted potential or actual gaps. Heron, for example, from a collaborative inquiry perspective, might have advocated more strongly including clients or families in the research group. A critical reflection approach would also ask whose voices are not being heard and encourage looking at why and how this could be overcome. In a situation where the critical reflection and other research approaches are less compatible, critical reflection would enable participants to see the implications of this.

Conclusion

What needs to happen to encourage use of critical reflection in research in organizations? First, there needs to be recognition that such processes take time and need to be adequately resourced. Workers in the project described above valued both the initial training and the ongoing input, particularly if this is to become an embedded part of their practice – developing a 'culture of inquiry' takes time and commitment to a new orientation. Having a collaborative researcher from outside the group was helpful in prompting critical reflection: reminding workers and teams of the value of discussing assumptions and values, looking at broader issues and connections, particularly in a pressured work environment. The commitment of the organizations was also important in taking seriously the issues raised by workers as part of their sense of inquiry.

The experience described in this chapter suggests that critical reflection can be a valuable enabling approach for research and evaluation by workers in human service organizations. Critical reflection provides a framework to prompt considering research and evaluation at a deeper level, articulating underlying assumptions and values and how these might influence the research process. Critical reflection suggests the questions that need to be part of the ongoing discussion of a dynamic research process. It fits well with the values of human service professions and challenges workers to ensure that research and evaluation are compatible with their values.

11 Using reflexivity in a research methods course: bridging the gap between research and practice

Colin Stuart and Elizabeth Whitmore

Since 1997–98, we have taught research and evaluation methods at Carleton University School of Social Work and have designed the course to incorporate a variety of opportunities and tools for reflexivity, including reflexive journals, team-oriented research, adult education methods, and community-based research partnerships. One important purpose of the course is to bridge the well-documented gap between research and practice (Hess and Mullen 1995; Task Force on Social Work Research 1991). In addressing this gap, we intentionally move beyond conceptualizing theory and practice as dichotomous, to explore the role of research, and the interaction between these as a complex, interactive and ever changing process (Harre Hindmarsh, cited in Fook 1996).

In this chapter, we first describe the course, its rationale and underlying philosophical bases in more detail, then examine data from reflexive journals and focus groups held in three successive years with students who had completed the course. In both the journals and the focus groups, students were asked to reflect on their experience in the course and probe more deeply into the connections between research and practice. We have organized these data into seven categories, with direct quotes to illustrate the students' learning. Finally, we put this together into a model, suggesting ways in which the tools and opportunities for reflexivity in research work, emerging from the data, can act to provide a link between partnerships and our goal, the development among students of a research-minded practice and culture.

We build on Fook's earlier conceptualization of reflective and reflexive practice (Fook 1996, 1999a, 1999b; 2002, forthcoming) in examining the degree to which the reflexive process has been a useful tool in helping students make the links between research and practice. *Reflective practice* focuses on raising awareness of our own, often hidden, assumptions and theories (based on what Schön calls 'theories in use') and how these are congruent (or not) with what we believe ('espoused theories'). Do we, simply put, practise what we preach? And if not, we are asked to re-examine this, with the potential to change both our ways of thinking and our actions. *Reflexivity* takes this further, drawing attention to the perspective of the knower and how it influences what is known and how this occurs (Fook 2002: 33). It requires a more complex understanding of the many ways in which one's own presence and perspective influence the knowledge and actions that are created (Fook 2002: 43). We are asked to examine the process of how what we see and understand in a situation is influenced by our own 'subjectivity' – including our embodiment (e.g. race, gender, social position, sexual orientation, ability, age), biography, values, ethics, emotions, cognitive and theoretical constructions (Fook 1999b: 14) – and, in turn, how this influences the very situation in which the research takes place. 'If we recognize ourselves holistically, that we as researchers are whole people, who experience in context, then reflexivity simply becomes the influence of any aspect of ourselves and our context which influences the research' (Fook 1999b; 14).

Building partnerships: A brief overview of the course

In brief, here is what we do in the course. In May we send out a letter inviting local agencies and organizations to submit brief proposals for research or an evaluation that will be useful in their work. In August we screen the proposals for clarity and feasibility (in the 6 months that students have to do their work), and in September students, usually working in small teams, select a project as the centrepiece of their research learning. (There is also the option of initiating their own individual projects, based on their particular interests.) The intent is that each team experience a complete research or evaluation project, from negotiating details with an agency, to designing the study, collecting and analysing data and reporting results. The discussions, stimulated by the wide variety of projects undertaken, offer students the opportunity to address most philosophical, methodological and ethical issues 'covered' in any research text.

A crucial part of our approach to the course is expressed well by Riane Eisler when she discusses partnership systems: 'The core logic of partnership systems is that people relate with mutual regard' (Bradbury 2004: 211) and that 'while *ideas* about equality and mutual regard are well known, they are not as mainstream as *practices*' (Bradbury 2004: 211–12). The course design, including the reflexive journals, used as a course assignment, is intended to bring together the ideas and the practices, the thinking and doing.

Partnerships are embedded in another key element of the course design which draws on the experience and literature of community-based research (CBR). CBR unites the three academic missions – research, teaching and service (Cordes 1998; Stoecker 2001, 2003) – and involves the collaboration of community members and university researchers to address community-identified needs and student learning as well as fostering social and institutional change (Stoecker 2002). 'Its most important characteristic is that the impetus for an influence over the research comes from the community, not the academic' (Stoecker 2001: 2). CBR is not really a new idea, and has many sources inside and outside of academia (B. Hall, 1992; Stoecker, 2001).[1]

As part of their assignment, we ask students to submit two reflexive journals, one at the end of each semester. Our intention is that, in the process of conducting actual research and reflecting upon the experience, students will find connections to practice that they did not see before and that they will become, in Everett *et al.*'s (1992) terms, more 'research-minded practitioners'. In the autumn we pose a series of questions to help them think about their experience and tease out the lessons learned. In the winter we again pose questions to assist them in deconstructing and then reconstructing their experience (Fook 1999b).

What is particularly innovative about our experience with this course is that we have attempted to construct a way of teaching research that relies on developing partnerships with community-based organizations. Most university research courses continue to use a deductive, hierarchical, top-down approach to teaching and to doing research. While there are many research courses that draw on community examples to illustrate certain concepts, few actually attempt to put Eisler's partnership system into practice in this way. Even fewer use reflexive journals as a key learning tool. None that we know of has held focus groups sometime later to probe this further, using reflexivity as a guiding framework.

Reflexive journals and focus groups as learning tools

In writing this chapter, we have used two sources of data. The first is the reflexive journals that students have written over the years. The second is transcriptions from focus groups held with students from three successive cohorts (2002, 2003 and 2004). Two to three months after completion of the course, we drew together a focus group of eight to ten course participants to reflect on the utility and learning from the course in light of the work they were doing professionally, either as part of a mentored placement in the social work programme, or as already hired employees of an organization in the community.

These focus groups were exceptionally rich for us as instructors. The time lag of 2–3 months after the course was completed and grades assigned was an opportunity for students to express themselves outside power relations between professor and student, and with some sense of distance from the academic milieu. We owe a debt to the students for their participation in the focus groups. They provided an opportunity for us to think critically and reflexively in dialogue, about what we were teaching and how we were teaching.

We organized the focus groups as a dialogue centred on the relationship between research and practice. We asked them to reflect on their current experience in their practice, and whether research or evaluation was relevant to what they are doing. We also asked them to discuss whether the placement agency or organization was conducting any research or evaluation. Finally, we posed questions about their attitudes towards research and what role, if any, the course played in their thinking. The conversations ranged far and wide, with a great deal of very rich reflexivity emerging as they considered their own thoughts and listened to others.

We have organized the learning discussed by students into seven categories.

Confronting one's own habits and biases

From the experience of preparing and completing a research or evaluation project in collaboration with a community-based organization, the students often gained a more nuanced appreciation of what reflexivity means and how it can challenge one's own biases and habits:

> The really challenging thing about research is that sometimes you find out stuff you don't want to know.

Many students come to the course with the idea that research is too complex, something only 'experts' do. Reflecting at the end of the course, one student noted in her journal:

> To be quite honest, in September, I was dreading taking this course. I believed that research was not practical and did not particularly pertain to my future work. When I thought of the word 'researcher', I never associated this with myself. I believed researchers were strange individuals who dealt with insignificant problems and who were out of touch with the real world. . . . After completing the applied research study, I am glad that these prior assumptions were incorrect and exaggerated. The research process is not a mysterious event that graduate students should fear. To the contrary, I would assert that the research process is a useful tool, which every professional should have access to. In fact, it is the very basis by which professionals make competent decisions.

A number of students come with a background in other disciplines that focus almost entirely on quantitative research methods, and the positivist assumptions underlying them. It takes them a while to recognize the legitimacy of other approaches.

> What I've learned is that research doesn't need to be big and full of testable data to be worthwhile and valid.

The complexity of research and its link to practice is emphasized in this journal entry:

> In addition, the complexity of the work we engage in with clients can be obscured by the overemphasis on logic models and focus on measurable outcomes.

This same student concluded that:

> I have learned through this research experience that imposing order too soon, or in an inflexible way, limits discovery . . . Being flexible enough to allow for a little 'chaos', revision and uncertainty will lead to a richer, more valid picture in the end. It is interesting that this approach to research (which I initially resisted) actually reflects how I try to work with clients. The fact that I did not see a parallel between these two activities, reveals my assumption that social work research and practice are separate and distinct spheres.

Still others recognize that they have particular ways of working, and that conducting research with community organizations challenged the need for predictability:

> The project with [agency] has not been an easy one for me . . . I am the type of person who needs to have everything moving along smoothly with very few bumps in the road. I do not deal particularly well with the unexpected, and . . . a number of unexpected, yet revealing, events occurred [with our project]. . . . Rather than be disappointed [with having chosen this project], I will take this experience and learn from it.

Expectations vary and are often challenged:

I learned about the many contradictions of research: objective research is viewed as the most legitimate form of research and yet it most likely does not exist; the process of research is meant to be straightforward and yet there are many bumps in the road. . . . Indeed, the most valuable thing I have learned through this process is to never expect what is coming and to be flexible with whatever comes to you.

Issues of power – their own and others – were explored. One student reflected on her expectations of respondents' attitudes to her as a researcher:

One of the major concerns I had about interviewing homeless persons with additional issues was how they would perceive our roles as researchers. Initially, I thought our position of privileged students would strongly impact our ability to interact with this population. I anticipated that the majority of individuals participating would be somewhat aggressive towards us and uncooperative . . . However, I could not have been more wrong. I was surprised that all the participants in the focus groups were quite respectful and eager to share their insights . . .

What she did not do, however, was probe further into her thinking about her own, and others' attitudes and behaviours. Why would she assume that less privileged participants would behave aggressively? What was it about this that made her uneasy? This could have taken her reflections to a deeper level, what Foucault refers to as 'critical subjectivity' (Heron, 2005).

A student who conducted an extensive literature review realized the power inherent in research.

We had the power, to pick apart and reformulate the literature to serve a particular purpose. It really reinforces the bias in everything I read and how I need to be a critical reader, something that I struggle with because I tend to take information at face value.

Referring to questions around effectiveness of her work and tracking 'measurable' outcomes, a student observed:

These questions are reflective of a shift in my own thinking about the provision of child welfare services in this province. It was also the most important shift for me because I am beginning to recognize many of the inadequacies of the current system . . .

Finally, students working in groups have varying experiences. Some work very well as a team; others do not. All bring some prior experience, which tends to influence their expectations, and their experience in this course often serves to confirm them. Students who probe this more deeply take lessons away that will help them in future teamwork.

I have learned so much about the importance of respect and honesty within a group and the impact that these values have on mindful, sensitive research.

Another student, concluded:

I realize that there are some individuals that I will not be able to work with . . . I learned about my level of tolerance and 'non-negotiables' when working in a partnership.

The importance of keeping logs and journals

Logging and journalling are critical and some, though not all, students recognized this:

People want tangible evidence that you've done your research, here are the findings of your research; everything you say is backed up by evidence . . . In fact, I am so glad to have learned about the research journal. At the beginning I did not see the importance of it.

This from an older student who was also employed by a national disaster reporting agency to assist in establishing practical definitions of disaster. Her experience points to the very basics in research: in this case the importance of recording evidence. We stressed in the course the crucial habits of keeping logs and journals, and using these as a foundation and point of departure for reflexivity. As instructors with field experience and practice, we often take the habits of logging and journalling for granted.

Another student was involved in a study that became highly politicized, with the possibility of media involvement, or that he might someday be asked to testify in a legal hearing. His comment reflects the good will and often naivety of social workers.

> Prior to coming into the program, record keeping was an area of research that all members of my group tended to neglect. For me, I had never really understood the importance of it as I had always been taught to trust people and 'to take them at their word' . . . When this project started, I never thought that one of the most critical lessons that I would learn would be the value of keeping records.

Building confidence and skills

A course which embeds students in the real world of research as it is done within an agency and community, and at the same time provides class-room teaching, accomplishes at least two interrelated objectives: it builds professional research confidence and develops new skills.

> The placement that I am doing right now is at a cancer centre . . . it turns out that the social workers there are doing an incredible amount of research and I am able to be involved with it . . . I would not have known any of that information or any of those skills had I not taken the course.

Another commented:

> It gave me an amazing basis, you know . . . having done the focus groups, having designed the questions that we've asked, and recruiting and sort of the fine details that I would not have thought of beforehand.

Still another observed that:

> we have been very much involved in the [research] design. We have actually felt really respected. So that is nice. It renews some hope.

The confidence expressed in these quotations is based on experience gained by students during the course. At the beginning, student apprehension is high: they realize that the process will include both accountability to an agency or client for research outcomes as well as acquisition of theory and skills in research methodology and methods. As instructors, we too are apprehensive: more so than for any other course we teach. We know that the unexpected will happen within a research project and that the students and ourselves will be engaged in the task of revising or redesigning the project and maintaining or mending relationships with a community group or agency. It is in responding to these challenges that students gain both the confidence and professional competence to undertake research in social work.

As instructors we have to make classroom time available not only for the necessary lectures and presentations, but also for reflection on the problems encountered in projects. It sounds a little trite, but without trust among those in the classroom there can be no critical reflection: it has been our responsibility to ensure that this trust is built. We use a number of processes, all based on adult education models drawn in large measure from Freirean concepts and methods (Freire 1970; Whitmore and Stuart 2001).

Promoting individual and organizational change

Engaging in the research process, from beginning to completion, can result in both organizational and individual change. Such change hinges on the researchers and members of the organization being reflexive. It does not occur in every research project, or even in most, but it is immensely rewarding for both students and instructors when it does occur, and demonstrates, as little else can, the importance in social work of binding research to practice:

> the other thing that was really interesting about that [research] process is how it changed us as an organization . . . we had to stop thinking of ourselves as the people who can provide the solution to the problem . . . We started to have to really think about how we practice social work and that was as valuable as learning how we needed to practice differently . . . There was all this kind of challenging stuff that was going on that was . . . a by-product of this research that we had done. In fact, it kind of let the lid off.

Individual change is reflected in this comment:

> Research renews; it reminds us that our work is never done . . . it provides the outlet for creativity and change, even if it only breaks up the stress in my own job initially.

Another student, in her journal, connects the agency mandate to how workers practise, but with a different focus. She notes the obstacles of under-staffing, lack of resources and time to implement well-designed evaluations:

> There appears to be external pressures placed on the worker to put emphasis on the investigative part of the job . . . it seems that no one is measuring the quality of the services consistently throughout the province through tracking intervention outcomes.

Those students doing evaluation research[2] come to recognize the political nature of this work. One group conducted an evaluation of a drop in center. 'People are protective of their spaces', as one student reflected, in her journal, on the fact that participants were saying only positive things, in order not to jeopardize the centre's funding. She also explored the issue of the evaluators as outsiders:

> If you are worried about watching your funding evaporate, protecting your space becomes a political act . . . we were the ones (as evaluators) that would construct the space that other outsiders would see, evaluate and critique. Our evaluation would be the lens through which funders viewed a space that wasn't ours.

Later, she recognizes the potential power of evaluators to be helpful, providing tools for improvement, or to be damaging. She realizes that how a report is worded is key, and thus the importance of language, what and how something is said. Another student from that same group observed, in light of evident internal conflicts, that:

> The evaluation served as a vehicle through which disagreements [in the agency] were being played out.

Barriers to reflexivity

As part of the reflexive process itself, students and instructors learn that there are barriers to reflexivity inherent in the research context.

There is, within the world of social work practice, especially in larger institutions, the risk of self-censorship inimical to reflexivity and critique in research. In the experience of one student, working with well-paid social workers in a large health institution tended to inhibit critical change-oriented research:

> I had some fabulous non-profit jobs where I could pretty well say anything and we did amazing research and people did listen, but I always made under $30,000 a year ... These hospital social workers, they are getting paid in the $60,000 [range]. That is a lot of money. They are not willing to go there [to cutting edge research].

Other students in the focus group, who were also working in medical contexts, including hospitals, commented that much hinges on the quality of the particular medical team the worker is involved with. Another student working within government cited an incident where the publication of a mildly critical book chapter on personal services was subject to approval by a deputy minister and publication was prevented.

Students made a sharp distinction between front-line and policy-oriented social work. The intensity of work on the front line poses special problems for the research-minded practitioner, particularly in documenting their work; some felt this was not entirely unintentional, that it had a clear political dimension:

> One of the big gaps is people on the front-lines are the ones who know what's going on and they don't document it, they don't research it, and they don't write about it ... because it is political, I mean, so much of that is political. The reason why social workers don't document is that we don't have the time ... it is a way of keeping us quiet. We are too busy putting out fires.

In general, one of the most important lessons students draw from their course experience is the significance of institutional constraints on research and critical reflection and how to negotiate the conflicts and contradictions that ensue. An important part of in-class reflection, and our individual consultations with students, leads students to a critical perspective on the agencies or groups they work with. A lesson learned by us as instructors is that this critical reflection or 'critical coaching' with students cannot be simply deconstructive in a haphazard or negative manner. It must simultaneously be both critical and 'reconstructive' because the next day the student must go back to his or her agency or group, to the 'real world' of research, and negotiate an alternative path that does not compromise the research task or individual ethics. There have been situations where negotiation did not succeed, and students, with support from us, withdrew from a research project.

Contributing to a research-minded culture

Teaching a community- and agency-based research course, centred on research-in-practice, may over time contribute to a research-minded culture in the social services and social advocacy sector of a relatively large community. In the most recent focus group of nine participants we realized that all but one were involved in research. This group was in part self-selected, of course, so a bias is evident. Nonetheless, based on 8 years of experience, this is a change from when we first started teaching the course. We asked the participants if they felt that the assumption underlying the course – that social workers were insufficiently research-minded and needed a course that would both theoretically and practically link research and practice in a 'real-world' context – was still valid. At least one response offered a clue:

> Some of my colleagues at work have been in your classes in the last few years, and I really wonder if over the last 6 or 7 years they have taken it with them. They certainly remember you and the course.

In some sense, over time, perceptions of what constitutes research have changed:

> When we would start a new program we would research it and evaluate it while we did it. I think, looking back, I never would have called that research. I think the course kind of demystified the term, what you realized research is.

It would be presumptuous to overstate the influence of this particular course in the community; there are many other variables at work, including funders' insistence on a more evidence-based approach. However, it would also be wrong to ignore or diminish the contribution the course has made to a much wider acceptance and capacity within the voluntary and social services sector to undertake research and evaluation. Certainly having roughly 400 graduates from the course, many of whom continue to work in Ottawa, where it takes place, is bound to have some impact on the way research is used and perceived in the sector. Specifically, as a direct consequence of the course, a community-based research network, based in the community, was established in the late 1990s.[3]

Research ethics review

Critical reflection on research ethics is, or should be, ongoing, but a one-time formal review process can strengthen and reinforce ongoing critical reflection.

Students take responsibility for ensuring that their research is ethically sound and in conformity with university and national guidelines – in Canada these are referred to as the Tri-Council Policy Statement or TCPS (Canadian Institutes of Health Research *et al.* 2005). Their proposals must undergo an independent university ethics review process which, with its institutional formality, plays a part in developing students' reflexivity. Its 'once-only' formality and almost rules-based approach impose a critical discipline on students which serves paradoxically to reinforce what we say in class: that ethical reflection should be ongoing and constant as one moves through the various stages of research; that changes in the institutional or social context of the research will require ongoing ethical reflection, and that the ground for this ongoing reflection is respect for the integrity of persons.

One student reflects on the power invested in her group, as outside evaluators. The group was conducting an evaluation of a drop-in centre program, and were concerned about possible negative repercussions on a respondent if they used her information in their report.

> Much of the intentionality for actions is rendered moot . . . the researcher is accountable for rights and wrongs rendered. This approach necessitates reflexivity and constant questioning of the historical processes that let the researcher and participant [evaluate] the moment in question. . . . The impetus for action comes from within, not without; while respectful of TCPS guidelines, I consider them to be more of a compass than the actual steering mechanism for my research.

This same student questions the assumptions inherent in the guidelines:

> research is conducted under the aegis of trust, and the [Tri-Council guidelines] imply a mistrust of the researcher.

Social workers tend, first and foremost, to care about those they work with. While the formal ethics review process brings specific criteria or rules to a proposal, students (and practitioners) usually go well beyond this. One student reflects on the power invested in her group as (outside) evaluators:

We need not have been concerned with the outcome of using this woman's data, as she had already signed the consent form. We could have walked away from the situation . . . and have been able to find support within our ethics process to legitimize such action. However, it seems to me that this 'power' is not legitimate and our role as social workers is directly implicated in our handling of the situation. I learned that as researchers and social workers we can be supportive, open and still construct valid and rich research projects; a gap that is too often neglected . . . we attempted to illustrate that we did care how she felt, that we were concerned for her safety within the Centre and that her contribution was extremely important to us.

If one sees reflexivity as an ethical imperative, then the definition of research ethics goes well beyond the categories required by standard ethics review procedures. It demands moral autonomy, an understanding that one must act in a conscious and intentional way, and take responsibility for what occurs. Ethics also involves genuine caring for participants, that responsibility goes beyond seeing them as merely 'providers of data' to be extracted and used for our own purposes.

The question of moral autonomy is probed more deeply and linked directly to practice by another student:

Moral autonomy is the worker's saviour and destroyer. It reminds me that I have agency to 'work', to contemplate and then 'do'. Yet acknowledgement of moral autonomy over standardized ethical frameworks requires an examination of one's conscience; the constant questioning of whether or not I am researching for the right reasons. I cannot simply punch in/out of work if I am genuinely concerned about the job I am doing. For this reason, workers who actually care come up against burnout, for their conscience often rubs organizational ethical frameworks the wrong way.

Not all students are truly reflexive in their journals; indeed, moving beyond description and probing more fully into what their 'subjectivity' means can be a challenge for some. This takes time, training and an ability and willingness to engage in a process of examining one's own deeply held beliefs and actions – not an easy process. To help students be more deeply reflexive, we may need to discuss what we mean more fully in class, and perhaps include some exercises and case examples. The inevitable power dynamics of the classroom and certainly the grading system make it more difficult for some students to feel comfortable in being fully candid in class discussions and even in their journals (which are confidential in that they are shared only with us, as instructors). Those who do use the opportunity learn, in a profound way, about the interrelationship between research, theory and practice, and about themselves, in ways that contribute significantly to their growth, professionally and personally.

Conclusion: Towards a research-minded practice and culture

Our course provides a variety of opportunities and tools through which reflexivity is possible. What are the links between partnership (in Eisler's sense of mutual regard), the opportunities and tools, reflexivity and our stated goal of helping practitioners link research to practice? Our effort to bring the pieces together is illustrated in Figure 11.1.

We begin with a deep commitment to developing partnership relationships and attempt to build 'mutual regard' into all facets of our work. This is done primarily through two mechanisms, one external and one internal. Externally, we establish research partnerships with groups and organizations in the community that offer useful information for their purposes, while also providing grounded learning opportunities for students. Internally, in addition to encouraging students to work in teams, we spend considerable time building mutual trust and a culture of shared leadership in the class as a whole. Once students look beyond the professors as the only 'experts', and recognize the value of their peers' experience and wisdom, they feel more comfortable sharing their questions, dilemmas and learning.

The opportunities and tools include exposure to a broad range of methodologies, and direct experience with the unavoidable politics one encounters in

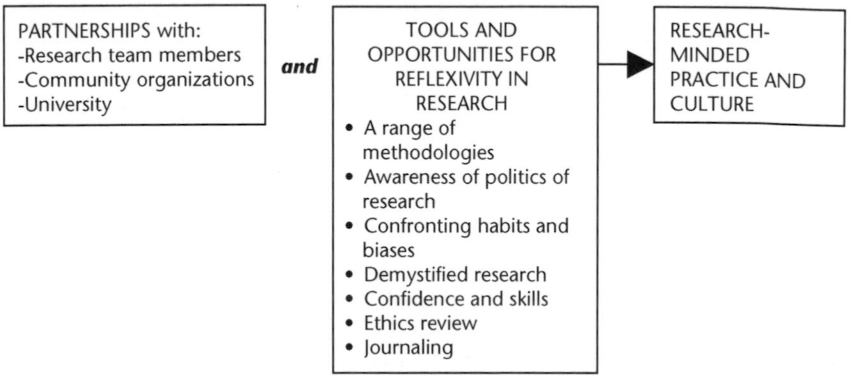

| PARTNERSHIPS with:
-Research team members
-Community organizations
-University | **and** | TOOLS AND
OPPORTUNITIES FOR
REFLEXIVITY IN
RESEARCH
• A range of
  methodologies
• Awareness of politics of
  research
• Confronting habits and
  biases
• Demystified research
• Confidence and skills
• Ethics review
• Journaling | → | RESEARCH-
MINDED
PRACTICE AND
CULTURE |

Figure 11.1 Reflexivity in research

any research or evaluation project no matter what methods one might choose. It is almost inevitable that conducting research will bring to the surface and hopefully challenge students' habitual ways of doing things, as well as their biases about research, about participants, about what constitutes truth and how one decides this. In the process, we certainly hope to demystify research, so that students recognize that it is something they can, in fact, do. This, in turn, builds their confidence, as well as their skills. Exposure to ethical concerns is built in through formal review procedures, but at the same time it gives us an opportunity to raise broader debates around what constitutes ethical research. The journals form one of the major tools for reflexivity, in addition to class discussions in which all of these issues are raised.

Hopefully, these elements contribute to students individually becoming more research-minded practitioners, and also to the development of a broader culture of research among community-based organizations.

Where do we go from here, for this is not a static, 'one off' process? Rather, the course is constantly changing, as we reflect on what occurs and adjust the content and process accordingly. Indeed, one of the joys of teaching this way is the continual challenge of working with the unanticipated, for this is how we learn.

Engagement in partnerships with diverse groups and organizations in the community imposes a welcome degree of interdisciplinary research or evaluation in the course. In the future we would like to expand this emergent interdisciplinarity on a more structured and systematic basis. The cultural comfort of having only social work peers to work with in the classroom needs to be challenged, since professional diversity is something graduates will normally encounter in their professional work. At the same time, there are many community organizations that have a broad range of tasks and needs that require greater interdisciplinary collaboration (e.g. law, architecture, computer science, geography, psychology, health professions, business). This would certainly complicate the process, but also enormously enrich the potential for reflexivity.

Notes

1   See also the Highlander Research and Education Center website at http://www.highlandercenter.org.
2   About half of the projects submitted by community organizations are evaluations. This usually reflects funder pressure on them to evaluate their projects, though it is important to note that most agencies do evaluate their programmes, though perhaps less formally (Hall *et al.* 2003).
3   See the Community-Based Research Network of Ottawa website at http://www.spcottawa.on.ca/CBRNO_website/home_cbrno.htm.

12 Research for and as practice: educating practitioners in inquiry skills for changing cultural contexts

Fran Crawford

> Experience is at once always already an interpretation and in need of an interpretation.
>
> (Scott 1992: 37)

Reflected experience: Researching for and as practice

The boxed quotes up until the end of the first one on p. 181 are the author's narrative of a reflected experience of 33 years ago. During a 500-kilometre drive with a government medical officer in outback Australia, she happened upon more than 300 Aboriginal people evicted from surrounding cattle stations. This experience formed part of a growing consciousness of research for and as practice.

Being the wet season it was hot and humid. Crocodiles, lizards like crocodiles, flocks of red-tailed black cockatoos, waterholes fringed with green: these are a few of the memories of that morning. It was January 1973 and back from the obligatory working-holiday trip 'home' to London, I was filling in time before starting a professional degree. Raised in Perth, the capital city of the million square mile state of Western Australia, I had seen nothing like this tropical Kimberley exotica along the highway from Derby heading for Fitzroy Crossing. Driving the government air-conditioned four-wheel drive was Sam, a young doctor with the Health Department.

Sam pulled up at what he called Middle Camp en route to lunch. It was raining steadily. It took time to decipher the scene ahead. The landscape was gray, flat and desolate in contrast to the green elsewhere. Shades within the gray

---

became children, women and men. With their dogs they were huddling out of the rain against corrugated iron draped with scraps of hessian. Soaked debris of food packaging and muddied cloth lay on the ground. The windscreen wipers framed my view. It was like watching a documentary of third world conditions but my guts said this was here and now.

The story above serves as a starting point in relating the development of an interpretive research unit in a professional programme over the past 15 years. The described sense of disorientation and disruption to my taken-for-granted world stayed with me for many years. I came to question the framing of social and health professionals as 'applied practices' – applying knowledge generated elsewhere. Instead I came to use reflected field-based practice to generate ways of practising differently. This led to educating student practitioners in research skills suited to understanding the specific contextual and cultural dimensions of any practice. Many of these skills came from the ethnographic practices covered in my undergraduate degree in anthropology. The narrative/interpretive/linguistic turn in social theory of the 1980s and 1990s added other approaches. Identifying some of the key social theorists influencing my thinking, I detail how I endeavoured to use a research unit to develop critical reflexivity in students. The interactivity of students with the development and teaching of the unit is described, as is how this development was connected to the quantitative research unit and to the four-year social work degree as a whole.

There has been a complexity of learning barriers, teaching dilemmas and learning moments across almost two decades of curriculum development. The case study concludes by recounting comments from graduate practitioners on how they use research skills in current practice across a diversity of settings.

The definition of critical reflection used in this chapter is an organic one growing out of an increasingly shared practitioner need to deal with difference in ways that stay with the purpose of the practice being enacted (whether that be nursing, social work, medicine or teaching) while being responsive to the actual site of practice and the 'natives' of that place. Time and place shape the human condition, but humans always have the potential of critical reflection in this. Foucault (1980, 1997) has argued that, as human beings, we can never autonomously shape ourselves. We are always shaped by our positioning in the world. In critically reflecting on this positioning, global truths may well be useful, but they carry the danger of stultifying the development of the independence required for being effective in your setting, your time and place. Foucault, in establishing the possibility of such critical reflection, does not deny the existence of norms and normative frameworks. Rather, he denies normative claims to acultural, ahistorical universal social truths. His persuasive logic on these points leads to a rethinking of the theory–practice relationship dominating the Western knowledge industry. In the prevailing culture, a 'universal intellectual' tells the truth to those unable to see or say it. With a privileged view from the mountaintop of science or ideology, such a figure is able to produce totalizing theory on the basis of which practice becomes possible. From within this modernist understanding the practitioner learns to apply expert knowledge developed elsewhere.

Foucault argues for the development of a culture that honours the 'specific intellectual' who works hard at critically thinking to ethical/political ends at a site located in time and place. This chapter looks at one example of supporting practitioners to develop the skills for critically and reflectively researching in and for practice: to be able to ask what is happening here for these people and what that means for my practice.

Seeking an education for practice

Sam did not get out of the car or stop the engine. He spoke through the window to two of the elder men. His task was to check what the community was doing to control the spread of hookworm. With 350 people at the camp and only one tap, Sam explained that the wet season was always worse for the Health Department. The people had no toilets, no showers, no laundries, no telephone and no vehicle. It was at least a mile across the flats to any of the Fitzroy Crossing government offices or food store. Because so few of the people spoke English it was hard for nurses to convey health instructions.

Like many of us educated to a normative understanding of our profession, Sam was ready to apply his expertise – it was just that the setting and the people made this problematic. Hoping to be part of providing better services in such settings, I started a master's in social work in Perth in 1974. As part of this degree I completed an ethnographic study of a remote Aboriginal community (Crawford 1976), but not without having to justify taking this interpretive approach over the expected measuring of 'Aboriginal problems'. The dominance of structural-functional social theories meant a default framing of 'fixing' the deficits of the different (Howe 1987). The social work discipline was itself caught in this logic. It often reacted to being judged as 'soft and unscientific' by taking a position that doing 'real' research with hypotheses and statistics would fix this marginalization.

Key texts in shaping my research were *The Social Construction of Reality* (Berger and Luckmann 1966) and *Interpretation of Cultures* (Geertz 1973). The community residents placed faith in me as being able to 'get the word out' for them with governments in Canberra and Perth. Both they and I believed it was just governmental 'not knowing' holding up the delivery of services that the rest of the country took for granted. Thirty years later their clear requests for responsive educational, health and policing services remain often unheard.

Practitioner learnings

On the radio driving out we heard the newly formed Federal Aboriginal Affairs Department being attacked by State politicians. Previously Aboriginal people had been 'protected' by the State government. The local radio report suggested that Aboriginal people were now being kept in unnecessary luxury because of the ignorance of Canberra based politicians.

Variance between local and centralized knowledge is the stuff of power and politics. The dynamics of this are not always transparent to those involved. On graduation I was posted to Broome in the West Kimberley. The population was then 3000, with over 50% being of Aboriginal descent. Life was very different from the urban modernity of Perth. The State Welfare Department I worked for was charged with the responsibility for protecting children. For 7 years I worked to this end with indigenous people and practitioners from many disciplines. There was widespread local practitioner agreement that targeting negligent parents was futile if there was no simultaneous development of communities as safe places to raise children. This led to ongoing tensions with various Perth-based authorities keen to see centrally planned programmes implemented locally in a standardized manner.

Returning to Perth in the early 1980s, I was conscious that few practitioners working with Aboriginal people had any preparation for this work. I set down some of the complexities in working with remote Aboriginal communities out of reflected experience (Crawford 1989), stressing that effective practice could not just be about drawing on technico-rational knowledge but required critical reflection from the practitioner as to what they were doing with whom (Schön 1983). Denzin (1989) has described this as interpretive interaction in which the practitioner as investigator situates themselves and interacting others within a given historical moment and works to develop understanding of the interacting subjectivities. In this listening, curiosity and a 'not knowing' stance were important as regards understanding both self and others.

In 1984 I became a social work educator. I discovered colleagues similarly enthused about developing a curriculum informed by practice experiences. People were working with ideas of feminism, consumer rights, multiculturalism and welfare rights. Over many collaborative discussions a recurring theme emerged. When it came to knowledge that counted, only knowledge developed through the traditional scientific method approach had standing. How could new ways of thinking become integrated in the discipline if they were not quantifiable through traditional research methods?

The case of an undergraduate interpretive research unit

In the sober question and answer time following our departure I learned the Middle Camp site was developed for a population of ten people by the State Native Welfare Department. There were now hundreds of extra residents. After the introduction of the Australian 1968 Equal Pay Award for pastoral workers, Kimberley pastoralists, refusing to pay their resident workers equal pay, had evicted them and hired in contract labour.

(Hawke and Gallagher 1989)

It shocks me now to think how little I was prepared as a practitioner to understand the impact of colonizing processes on people. Smith (2005: 91) argues that 'negotiating and transforming institutional practices and research frameworks is as significant as the carrying out of actual research programs' if research is to make a difference in the lives of people marginalized and silenced by traditional research approaches. Such work is necessarily political in nature and can be perceived as destabilizing and threatening to the existing order (Kuhn 1970). At a macro level it can be argued that the practice of social work has been, as Howe (1994b) suggests, a child of modernity. It has successfully demonstrated across many settings the productive union of scientific objectivity and politico-economic rationality. The creation of the welfare state in Britain, Australia and other places, concomitant with the industrial revolution of the nineteenth century, attests to the success of such centralized and standardized planning.

Yet social work as a practice discipline has also been a mediating force working between what is and what should be at the local level. Often this has compromised the power of the discipline to 'know' in the objective and generalizable ways acceptable as scientific. Working with Aboriginal people, I was used to fellow practitioners and educators dismissing this as a marginal area of practice, in which saying 'Oh but they are different' was considered sufficient to explain why core theories of the discipline did not work. It was affirming, then, to join with educator/practitioners keen on making working with diversity and working in diverse ways part of the knowing for practice.

At least half the faculty collaborated on a dream of widening the ways of knowing that could count as research. This led to a formal decision by 1990 to design and implement a new research unit – one called 'research inquiry' to complement the existing 'research methods'. These names signalled the scope and focus of both units. A growing number of social theory approaches and ways of framing practice had consequences as to what could be known and how it could be known (Hartman 1990). The proposed unit set out to explore and understand some of the research implications attached to these different ways of thinking about social reality and the differing ways this could be known. The focus was to be on preparing students with hands-on skills in doing some of the emerging qualitative and interpretive ways of knowing for practice.

Considerable differences had to be negotiated to ensure that the two research units sat alongside each other in meaningful dialogue as to the relationship of research to practice. Those involved with the existing research unit were bemused and increasingly bewildered by the push for change. Deaf to the idea of bringing to the fore silenced voices, an academic suggested at one of many planning meetings that 'research methods' be renamed 'rational research'. This reflected his taken-for-granted binary thinking that this left those of us pushing for change only the possibility of irrational research.

What happened for us locally was similarly happening in professional courses around the English-speaking world. Higher education at the local level was being shaped by extra local forces as it became increasingly obvious that in a postmodern world of multiple coexisting cultures and changing contexts the modernist image of the practitioner as one who applies knowledge developed by researchers was not adequate (Smith 1987). Practitioner knowledge was more than knowledge that could be generalized, standardized and commodified as 'best practice'. It was necessarily responsive to context. In their classic text *Naturalistic Inquiry*, evaluators Yvonna Lincoln and Egon Guba (1985) spelt out axioms of traditional positivistic knowing (research on) and contrasted these with the understandings guiding action in natural settings of people interacting with purpose (research with).

In Canada, Smith (1987: 154) argued that social relations organizing the world 'knit local lives and local settings to national and international social, economic and political processes', but not in predetermined ways. Smith advocated researching people's lives from where they 'are at' and for the purpose of improving those lives. While not dismissing the usefulness of quantitative research in this, she argued that the position of the disinterested researcher retaining distance from the researched could no longer be assumed to serve 'science', as indeed science could no longer be presumed to serve human progress. Rather, all humans are, by virtue of their cultural being, meaning-makers, and each of us has some necessarily delimited view of the world and our place in it. Through research with people it is possible to connect out, to move to action for human improvement. Smith's ideas of improving lives through research were an important influence on me in designing the new research unit.

By the early 1990s, the unit was taught to all third-year students alongside the traditional research methods unit. From the beginning there has been an emphasis on the philosophical framing of differing research approaches, especially as regards ontology and epistemology. This links the unit to the social theory and praxis elements of the overall course. The focus has been on narrative, ethnographic and feminist methodologies and methods in researching across cultures and contexts for everyday practice. Assessments centre on students doing research.

A 1989 Canadian publication, *Experience, Research, Social Change: Methods from the Margins*, inspired by Smith's ideas, was of particular use in shaping the curriculum. Authors Sandra Kirby, an activist, and Kate McKenna, an academic, show how if the ends of research are to serve the lives of people and not just the interests of the powerful, 'research must begin to reflect the experience and concerns of people who have traditionally been marginalized by the research process and by what gets counted as knowledge' (Kirby and McKenna 1989: 25). Kirby and McKenna argued for alternative research courses to redress a void in conventional research methods courses. They describe their methods of researching from the margins as two interdependent processes. The first was *intersubjectivity*, in which all participants are respected as equally knowing as to lived experience. The second drawing on Paulo Friere's term was *critical reflection* of lived experience, as involving 'the real, concrete context of facts' (1989: 51).

These ideas stress the importance of embodied knowing being valued by the practitioner both in those they work with and in themselves. In many ways intersubjectivity came easy to those third-year social work students who had gained beginning skills of active listening. The skills of an ethnographer, a feminist researcher and a qualitative researcher inevitably overlap with those of a social work practitioner. Early on in the development of the course I introduced the eight Rs of research inquiry to support students in making conscious links between the content of this unit and what they had covered in other parts of their course, especially communication skills, interviewing skills, group work skills and critical social theorizing. I stressed to students the focus on preparing them to use these research approaches as part of everyday practice as a social work practitioner. Drawing on the work of Reinharz (1992), the eight qualities students were expected to develop were the following:

- *Resonance.* This involves identifying with the topic of research and feeling some concern for the participants or the issues involved in their activity. By not striving for objectivity and neutrality, the researcher is able to identify some connection between topic and own value stance.

- *Risk-taking*. A sense of not being in control is often involved. There is risk in engaging with strangers and opening yourself to engage with 'others'. If you are not protected by status and position, you may well suffer rejection.
- *Realities*. While we all live on the same planet, there are multiple human realities. A researcher strives to make connections between differing realities.
- *Rapport*. This refers to the process of communicating, of active listening.
- *Relationship*. This goes further than rapport and is the active valuing of the mutual encounter.
- *Reflection*. It is essential to reflect on both the research process and the meanings to be made of it.
- *Reflexivity*. This refers to your self in action and your ability to react to circumstances of time and place. It involves awareness of the effect that you have on shaping the process and outcome of interaction and the effect of the process on yourself, and asking what you have learnt about yourself – your strengths and weaknesses   through doing.
- *Rigour*. The planning, action, presentation and reflection of the research process must be thorough and coherent. Although aspects of the research are encouraged to emerge according to participants' interest, this openness must not be confused with an 'anything goes' approach.

The narrative approach that I first learnt from colleagues such as Julie Dickinson became important in shaping the curriculum (Crawford *et al.* 2002). Australian narrative writers such as White and Epston (1990) became an integral part of the course, and it resonated with me that Michael White had arrived at many of his ideas through reflecting on his practitioner experiences with the South Australian State Welfare Department. The word 'narrate' is derived from the Latin *narrare*, to know. Narrative approaches connect to a poststructuralist understanding of language as constitutive of the social. They are part of a larger turn to language and interpretation in social theory. Social work has always dealt in talk and interaction but has not always been comfortable in theorizing this. Yet who speaks, who listens, who is heard and who is passed over in silence are questions central to effective practice. These questions are not necessarily answered by active listening skills alone nor by drawing on fixed theoretical models of understanding human complexity. The research unit sought to support students in learning to interweave theory, practice and reflection.

What do students do?

Did the chaos of Middle Camp come about because a progressive national legal move to ensure equality between workers had unintended local consequences? The economic development of the Kimberleys in Western terms was less than a hundred years old. In that time Aboriginal groups had made adaptations to the colonial presence. A system had evolved enabling clans to continue living on their homelands. While working cattle or sheep for the 'boss', people sustained interconnected activities such as caring for the land, collecting food, performing initiation rituals and generally keeping their 'country' alive. In changed circumstances station owners of the Fitzroy River Valley rid themselves of any continuing responsibility for their station 'mobs' by loading everybody on trucks and depositing them in the nearest town.

Interpretive research activities designed to develop students as self-directed, reflexive learners have been the key assignments since the unit started. I ask students to write in the first person, not to write an academic essay, and to display a conscious use of the eight Rs in their research. Students are assessed on the way they explore differing understandings of what can be known about the social and how it can be known. Students are asked to question the common understanding that method is the driving force of research. Rather, the unit inquires into the processes of research and how in practice these are shaped by the particular purpose of a project. Ethical and value issues of research are considered as integral to the research process itself and not necessarily ensured by 'scientific methods' and externally governed set of standards.

There are three main forms of research undertaken by students. One is a participant observation in a student-selected site with the proviso that the site is not one which involves students consciously looking at clients. In the write-up students have to be able to position themselves in the participant–observer continuum of possibilities while thickly describing the actors and activities in the chosen scene (Bodgewic 1992). The exercise aims to develop skills at being able to observe the everyday.

This individually completed task is usually followed by pairs organizing a co-operative inquiry (Heron and Reason 1997). The co-operative inquiry focuses on developing skills at researching intersubjectivity and critical reflection. Student pairs have to engage with three to five peers in researching a shared experience. They actively seek to explore the different ways of knowing the same experience and work to build shared understandings. Many of the projects, such as researching the experience of being a male in the social work course, living on government benefits or being an international student, result in the group moving into participatory action research (Wadsworth 1992).

The third exercise developed over the life of the unit in collaboration with colleagues teaching in the unit. In part this was a conscious move to explicitly integrate the unit with student placement experiences. Students are asked to write a 600-word narrative describing a 'learning moment' from their first placement (Crawford *et al.*, 2002). Students are asked not to identify the learning but rather show it by richly and complexly describing what happened, with whom, where and how. In this description no language of social science is to be used. Students are asked to hone and rehone their writing on the idea that writing is research (Richardson 2000). These cameos of student experience are powerful insights into what is happening for students on placement. With student permission, they are a tool, allowing for ongoing reflexive dialogue between field supervisors, students and educators.

Interacting with student feedback

> At the local level there was little capacity to halt this economically rational move. Fitzroy Crossing, a service town of less than a hundred white residents at the time, provided few resources to respond to an influx of refugees.

A key resource lacking in regard to Middle Camp was a quality of responsiveness in practitioners and the services they represented. In keeping with my aim of equipping students to be responsive and open to researching an uncertain, ambiguous and complex world, it has been important to actively value student feedback in the ongoing honing of the unit. Reviewing more than a decade of qualitative feedback on the unit, there are six themes that consistently appear as to the perceived weaknesses and strengths of the course: exclusionary language, alien concepts and dense reading were frequently identified as what students experienced negatively. This was balanced by an expressed valuing of learning by doing, connecting to lived experience and seeing the world from a new perspective. The following sample of comments gives a flavour of how students experienced the unit:

> Language is power – exclusion!
> Readings were not easy going and required a lot of time to extract the relevant information.
> I particularly enjoyed the participant observation exercise. Good for really reflecting on your own reality and trying to look through the eyes of others.
> The narrative assignment was very enjoyable for me.

> The assignments seemed initially overwhelming but in practice were attainable and a large part of the learning experience.
>
> Most invaluable experiential learning especially through participant observation and cooperative inquiry. Gave one the opportunity of seeing the world from a new perspective.
>
> Great to have the freedom to explore issues and values in relation to your own experience and to be credited for sharing your own views.
>
> Not as dry as just reading and writing as able to give own opinions and feelings.
>
> It was a long time before I knew what was going on but I learned heaps from the assignments.

Language being experienced as exclusionary is a consistent and strong theme in feedback from students. This has led to many class discussions on the use of language by social workers. Many students are firmly of the belief that social workers should use only ordinary words understandable by their clients. Other students recognize a need to be multilingual and interpreters in practice. Drawing on her hospital placement experience, a student found being able to speak the same language as the client (whether that be a language of class, gender or ethnicity) is not enough when you are on the oncology ward and the client asks what the doctor just said.

Various ways have been tried to support students in gaining familiarity with the language of qualitative research. We have used tests on the meanings of key words, glossaries developed both by students and staff, and there has been a conscious focus on talking about language as core to the interpretive research in ways analogous to measurement and numbers in quantitative research. Over time more and more resources have become available in addressing this issue. Laurel Richardson's (1990) *Writing Strategies* has always been a helpful short text to support students in moving away from an understanding that language was as straightforward as calling a spade a spade.

The assessments have consistently been identified as bringing the unit content to life. I have consciously crafted this learning through doing to allow students to draw on their developing identities as practitioners. So interviewing skills, group facilitation skills, active listening skills and observing in context are consciously brought into their tasks as developing researchers for and of practice.

As so much of the reading, especially in the early history of this unit, has been dense and abstract, consistent efforts are made to ground ideas in particular sites and settings. Four videos were made in the university's media centre to bring to life different methodological approaches (Crawford and Gacik 1998). All made with practitioners' support, they were designed to reinforce the idea that research is practice. The first video featured participant observation and was made with workers in an inner-city mental health service who consciously chose to work in territory chosen by the client. The other videos highlighted feminist research, participatory action research and co-operative inquiry.

Over time the unit has assumed a more comfortable fit with the rest of the course as the concepts of reflexivity, narrative and postmodern thinking are addressed across all years of the course. Students have used interpretive research approaches for honours and higher-degree projects. I have been gratified to also consistently hear practitioners speaking on how they use skills and ideas gained in their research units to help them ask critically reflective questions as to what is going on in everyday practice. Recent such feedback indicates how research in and for practice happens:

> Research experience has allowed me to conceptualise. I have been encouraged to explore, question and inquire. I have learned to question assumptions and not necessarily go on models that already exist.
>
> Research has created a space for me where ideas may be useful but can't be accepted as universal truth especially with indigenous people and other marginalized groups.
>
> I use all the interpretive approaches such as participant observation and narrative when I work, not just with clients but with organizations and systems
>
> It has helped immensely my own understanding of the connections between theory and practice. I am able to work with a diversity of audiences and I have learned a lot more about myself.
>
> Language is *huge* – that was a gift from Research Inquiry – that unit has had such an impact on me. It was a different way of thinking, engaging with a different language to make meaning. And I think it is a language that transcends the supposed borders between research and practice. The dominant language of more traditional scientific research doesn't engage clients, practitioners, and service delivery people who are often not interested in research and think it has nothing to do with what is happening on the ground. This Research Inquiry language works in the spaces-in-between more meaningfully and engages better with complexities of working with people about people
>
> Being able to travel the research continuum has debunked a lot of myths around what research is all about.
>
> I have developed a lot of skills in sitting the two – quantitative and qualitative – alongside each other. I have done a lot of that in my work. It is so important for social workers to be able to have these skills – without them they are just not in the conversation to influence policy agendas, funding, service development, understanding social issues and how 'we' as a nation are responding to them.
>
> It has given me an awareness going into any situation where the culture is different; you go in more humble now. The more you learn the more you know you don't know.
>
> Because I did narrative I guess that rolled on very easily into doing counselling.

Australian social work, like many related human services, developed at a time of great faith in the promise of social science. This led to an unexamined assumption that the knowledge these modern approaches produced would be universal. Early curricula were shaped by texts imported from both the United Kingdom and the United States and practitioners and students expected to apply this knowledge out in the field. It is only recently that a specific litera-ture of Australian practice has developed based on local research. Negotiating difference and diversity are increasingly issues for all human service workers in their everyday practice.

As Jan Fook (2003: 93) observes:

> I think this is the gift of postmodernism to social work – that we value and include the voice of the practitioners and their own contribution in theorizing from their own practice experience. It is our responsibility to the profession that we enable and create culture and environments in which this can happen.

Conclusion

This case study of the design and implementation of one interpretive research unit in Perth, Western Australia, is an attempt to textualize some of what too often in the practice disciplines is left untextualized. It is not a singular tale, as any quick literature search reveals (see Donnelly 2002; Pyett 2002). It docu-ments one case of the ongoing theorizing and researching as the doing of any practice discipline.

Practitioners of human services will continue to be served by knowledge that meets the rigid epistemological cannons met by the randomized experi-ment. There is also no doubt that human practitioners will continue to find themselves in dynamic social contexts where what works will need to be made, not found. This chapter has argued that in this work of seeking truth in action there are useful research tools to support the development of critical reflection.

PART IV
Education

13 Ethnographers of their own affairs

Gerhard Riemann

Doing professional case analyses while being 'entangled' in work with clients is a complex epistemic process, which cannot be misconstrued as the mere top-down application of technical knowledge and higher-order scientific abstractions. This was demonstrated – under the influence of John Dewey – by Donald Schön (1983) whose work on the 'reflective practitioner' has given the strongest impulse to the spread of 'critical reflection' in the professions in Anglo-Saxon countries and Scandinavia. As is shown in the contributions to this book, there have been many interesting attempts to develop social arrangements for fostering the development of skills of 'critical reflection' in and for professional practice.

My own work with students of social work[1] is based on the idea that if future social workers become familiar with different approaches and procedures in qualitative or interpretative social research and if they are encouraged to do their own supervised qualitative field studies, they will acquire helpful competencies for their work with clients. When social workers have to engage in demanding, risky and consequential case analyses in their work with clients 'here and now', a familiarity with biographical research, narrative analysis and other qualitative procedures can serve as an important resource for a self-reflective, self-critical and responsible practice (Schütze 1994). This applies to the work of other professionals (teachers, health professionals, etc.) as well.

I would like to present one element of my work, which consists of encouraging students to look at their own work experiences (in the context of practice placements) and the practice of institutions and professionals that they encounter as ethnographers of their own affairs.[2] Elsewhere I have written about the basic premises of this endeavour and the work and social arrangements of encouraging students 'to make their practice strange' (Riemann 2005a, 2005b). I have chosen a different starting point in this chapter in order to make parts of this work visible: I present fieldnotes of a student and summarize some of the reflections which emerged during a seminar with students in which this material was discussed. The example which I select derives from an early phase of this kind of work. At that time thinking about the opportunities and limits of working with this data was useful for me in refining 'my way of doing things with students'. Because the fieldnotes will be made accessible in this chapter readers can analyse them by themselves and thereby enter into a critical dialogue with the student writer, the participants of this seminar and myself. My short summary should not be taken as the 'philosopher's stone', but as an unassuming interim report of something which could continue. We only had about one and a half hours for talking about this data.

Student fieldnotes – an example

The following fieldnotes were written by a male student of social work (in his early twenties) while spending 40 weeks in a practice placement in a family counselling centre (in a small southern German town) which belongs to one of the large Church-affiliated German welfare associations. The services are free of charge. Students in my department have to spend the fourth and fifth semesters of their undergraduate training in practice placement.[3] He was a member of a group of ten students who met with me four times during this period in order to share and reflect about their experiences in their respective settings of social work practice. Each time we got together for a week-long seminar. While students had the chance to spontaneously and extensively narrate their experiences during the first week, so all of them could get a sense of what happened to everyone else, we spent the second and third week discussing fieldnotes which the students had prepared for the seminar. The following fieldnotes were discussed during our third week (in October 1998).

I had told the students to focus on certain events and processes in their work environment which they found especially interesting and to write fieldnotes on these occurrences which revealed 'how everything had developed'. Notice that this recommendation was rather vague. I did not provide them with any categories of a strict observational framework, but just stressed sequentiality ('how everything had developed'), the need to wonder aloud about things which were more or less taken for granted in the routines of their workplace, and the necessity to explicate how one was personally involved in these events and how one experienced them. My recommendations became somewhat more precise later on (see below) after learning more about the limits and possibilities of working with such fieldnotes: I found out that some fieldnotes turned out to be more fertile ground for reflecting and 'grounded theorizing' (Glaser and Strauss 1967) than others. But such guidelines should not become a Procrustean bed stifling students' creativity and personal expression.

Students selected different foci. Some of them, for example, decided to reconstruct how their relationship with a certain client had developed over a period of time, while others described a working day in their institution or concentrated on types of action or speech events which were typical of their institution. The writer of the following fieldnotes chose the latter variant.

In presenting the following fieldnotes I definitely do not mean to give the impression that I regard them as a model of 'perfect work'. I choose them because I can still remember how the students and I discussed these fieldnotes and because this discussion which I will summarize somewhat later helped me to reflect about my work with the students and to learn about what is involved in doing 'ethnograpies of one's own affairs'.[4]

I did not change anything in the text which the student gave to us, only translating the fieldnotes from German into English. You will notice that once in a while the student used italics in order to mark some of his inner states and retrospective reflections or background information. Michael, the counsellor whom he mentions, is a psychologist.[5] There are social workers as well as psychologists working in this centre.

It is Friday, 17 July 1998, around 1 p.m. When I look at the big diary at the reception desk in which all workers usually write down their appointments I discover a 'blue' first session with the Olschewski family which is set up for 2 p.m. Every worker uses a pen with a different colour, blue is Michael's colour. Since I try to participate in as many counselling sessions as possible (besides my own sessions which are mostly filled with play therapy and different forms of training) I ask Michael if I may take part in this session. Since it is a first session – joining an ongoing counselling process would be irritating for clients, therefore this is not possible at this centre – and since I probably don't know the people Michael has no objections. (Since my home village is in the same county it could happen that new clients and I know each other. I can understand that such an encounter would be unpleasant for most people.) But he says that he needs the consent of the family. – I spend the time until the session at the reception desk answering the telephone, since the receptionist has gone already.

The Olschewskis arrive ten minutes early. Therefore I send them to the waiting area before entering Michael's room right away in order to get him. He asks me how many persons have arrived so we can put the right number of chairs in a circle. I tell him that a boy, a woman and two men are waiting, one of them around 40 years old and the other one about 20 years older. We don't know if the older one belongs to the family or what his relationship is with the family. There are only scant entries on the registration sheet (the information is filled in during an initial contact, mostly on the phone), which means that this time Michael does not give a short explanation of the family situation and how he plans to proceed, as he does in other situations. *Of course this does not mean that the information on the registration sheet is used to plan the encounter in detail, but sometimes one* can develop assumptions about its possible direction; sometimes a new situation can develop for the counsellor on the basis of new insights deriving from the conversation, so that he has to rearrange things more or less.

We walk over to where they are waiting, Michael introduces himself. Then he introduces me as a 'trainee and future colleague' before asking the four persons to follow him into his room.

Having entered the room, the older man, Mr. Mueller, takes the floor. He presents himself as a neighbour who supports the Polish Olschewski family in their contact with the authorities. He says that he has been asked by Mr. Olschewski to arrange the appointment and to accompany them, in order to describe the family situation. He would like to do so now. He says that he regards this as his civic duty, since he believes that the family has been treated worse because of their origin than would have been the case with a German family if the same incidents had occurred there. *Mr. Mueller speaks very elaborately (it emerges during the conversation that he had been an independent merchant in earlier days), but at first I cannot clearly understand on the basis of his statement why exactly they had shown up in the counselling centre.*

He says that they have arrived because of Agnieszka, the daughter of the Olschweskis, almost 16 years old. Even though he had seen her seldom he had always perceived her as 'very decent' and 'very eloquent'. He says that there had been no problems at school, she had been a good student and that it is sad that things have developed like that.

After five minutes I still don't know what's the issue.

Mr. Mueller says that he cannot imagine why she had done that, since she had received from her parents what she needed. He says that her father is good at helping him in his garden.

I tell myself that she probably has stolen something somewhere.

He continues that her parents had been surprised when they had been summoned to appear before the family court and when finally their right to custody of her had been revoked.

Bam! I am puzzled when I learn about the sudden revocation of a right to custody. This information is buried in a subordinate clause after he has talked about eloquent Agnieszka for ten minutes. It seems to me that Michael feels the same since he now tries to structure the information.

He asks and writes down who belongs to the family, what the parents are doing for a living, how they had come to Germany. He is told: The Olschewskis have two sons besides Agnieszka, Marek who is 14 years old (he is present) and Lech who is 5. Mr. Olschewski is unemployed and the mother occasionally works as a waitress. He has been living in Germany for eight years, his family had joined him two years later. Agnieszka was caught shoplifting in a department store, therefore she had got into contact with the youth welfare office where she had apparently confided to an employee. Finally, the parents had been summoned to appear before the court, they had only been given a short hearing and in the end their daughter had been 'stolen' from them (to quote Mr. Olschewski). Mr. Olschewski has the court order with him. Michael asks him if he may read and photocopy it. The parents give their consent to his reading the paper, he gives it to me and I take it to the copy machine which is placed in the corridor. I take a look at the pages and discover some serious charges against Mr. Olschewski, e.g., that he would consume alcohol 'to excess', that he would beat the mother, that he would lock Agnieszka in the basement and would also beat her, once even when a worker of the youth welfare office was present.

When I return to the room together with the photocopies Mr. Olschewski complains about German law while gesticulating in a lively manner: The children are allowed everything, his Agnieszka is allowed to smoke, to dye her hair and to go to discos, while her parents have no rights. It is different in Poland, his daughter had been stolen from him, he had not seen her since March. He says that he had demanded the address of the foster family, but has not received it. – Michael concedes that some unhappy circumstances during the contact with the court had led to an aggravation of the situation. He says that, e.g., there had been no interpreter during the hearing of Mrs. Olschewski who does not speak much German, and Agnieszka was only willing to talk to her mother in German. He says that the situation had escalated in a way that Mrs. Olschewski had almost suffered a nervous breakdown and security people had to intervene. At the same time Michael points out that it is not so easy in Germany to take the right to custody away from parents and that there had been some things in Mr. Olschewski's behaviour which were wrong.

Michael wants to know what the family expects from him now. Mr. Mueller responds that the family would like to have a talk with Agnieszka to clear things up and to give Mr. Olschewski a chance to apologize to Agnieszka.

Now Michael draws a genogram of the family on a flip chart and writes down how he perceives the relationship between the family members. He says that he can see the worries of the father, but also the uncertainty as to how the father should behave with his daughter and how the daughter should behave with her father. Michael explains that he could only accept the father as a whole person, his positive as well as his negative sides. He appreciates the father's worries as positive and explains that many parents who are prone to violence often really regret having hurt their children, but have little clue as to how else to bring them up. Michael goes on to say that quite a few violent fathers tend to find a 'false friend' in alcohol, so that it becomes totally impossible for them to develop adequate methods for bringing up their children. He believes that this is also the case with him, Mr. Olschewski, and I notice that Mrs. Olschewski agrees with Michael (by slightly nodding her head).

Mr. Olschewski, whose face looks bloated and slightly red, says that he does not have a problem with alcohol, but during the course of the conversation he had already mentioned that the doctor of his former firm had sent him to hospital because of high blood pressure. Michael offers to talk to him during the next session about how he might act if his daughter returns to the family, and he promises to contact the youth welfare office.

After the family and Mr. Mueller have left the room Michael talks to me about the case. We agree that Mr. Olschewski's attempts to play things down (he had mentioned that he sometimes drinks a little or that Agnieszka really needs a little discipline) seem at odds with reality. Of course it is possible that Agnieszka's account doesn't exactly mirror the truth, but it is a fact that Mr. Olschewski had beaten Agnieszka in the presence of a youth welfare office worker. Michael says that he regards it as a starting point to get the father's alcohol problem under control. He actually regards him as an amiable person, and as someone who only sees violence as a way to solve problems when he is under the influence of alcohol. Michael says that he could not tell him this right away, but could only proceed one step at a time: from the family as a whole over the relationships of the family members to the father with the different components of his personality.

The telephone call with the youth welfare office confirms the charges against Mr. Olschewski which are reported in the court order. Michael contacts the addiction counselling centre and arranges the date for a session to which he wants to go with Mr. Olschewski if he agrees (during the next session at the family counselling centre).

Thursday, 30 July 1998

This time Mr. and Mrs. Olschewski are alone [when they arrive at the centre]. Michael quickly tells me that he wants to suggest to Mr. Olschewski that he go to addiction counselling together with him.

Mr. Olschewski is not very enthusiastic about this suggestion. He says that he does not have a problem when he drinks a beer once in a while. Mr. Olschewski wants to have his 'stolen' daughter back and asks who is Mrs. Seiffert anyway (the family judge who is responsible for this case) who does not know Agnieszka at all but may take his daughter away from him. *I think that the constellation with exclusively female office-holders is difficult for an eastern European male with regard to the acceptance of authority. The behaviour of Mr. Olschewski before the court (uncooperative and aggressive) becomes more understandable if you take this into account.*

Mr. Olschewski asks if it is right if his daughter smokes and children in Germany have more power than their parents. Michael asks in reply how he would react if Agnieszka returns but still smokes and dyes her hair. Mr. Olschewski ignores this question and the conversation more or less goes round in circles. Mr. Olschewski finally threatens to return to Poland together with his family if he does not get his daughter back. Michael offers to continue working with Mr. Olschewski, but only if he goes to addiction counselling at the same time. Mr. Olschewski does not respond to this, the session ends without arrangement of a new appointment.

> One day later Mr. Olschewski calls again. I ask Michael if there is anything new, but he says no.'
> Addendum three months later
> . . . He [Michael] says that Mr. Mueller had called a short time ago and had mentioned that Agnieszka had returned to her family again.

Our discussion

I cannot go into the details of our seminar discussion after the students had become familiar with these fieldnotes, but can only give a short summary which might raise doubts and questions among readers. My aim, in making the fieldnotes accessible to readers and in summarizing some of the issues and commentaries which emerged during our seminar, is to invite readers to join in and continue a critical dialogue.[6] I encouraged the students to freely share and discuss their impressions. Their various remarks referred to (a) the features of the material itself, (b) what one could learn about the events depicted, especially the work of the professional, and (c) the writer himself. While he did not participate in the first round of statements when the rest of the students took turns to say what was on their mind, he stepped in after some time to provide more descriptive detail and actively engaged in the unfolding discussion which led to more generative questions (Strauss 1987: 82–108) about, and insights into, the problems of professional work.

The material[7]

While all students in the seminar agreed that the fieldnotes were dense, had 'drawn' them into the events described, and revealed a lot about their fellow student's experiences and attitude, there was a host of questions which referred to what the other participants regarded as gaps or vague sequences in the material. Some of the gaps could be filled by the writer's recollections, others had to remain empty because he could no longer remember the details (three months had passed) or because it had not been possible for him to pay attention to the phenomena in question. It is much better to recognize and to stick to the limits of perception, comprehension and memory than to create artefacts for the sake of producing a dense and lively text. But of course the limits can be widened, otherwise there would be no point in a critical discussion. The students' comments can be summarized as follows:

- Is there a discrepancy in the text or in the events themselves? According to the fieldnotes the psychologist had announced that he wanted to ask the clients if they consented to the participation of the student, but it is not mentioned if he really did.

- There are blurred references to the beginning, transition or ending of certain activities. For example, how is the floor offered to Mr. Mueller at the beginning of the counselling session? At what point and how does Mr. Olschewski begin to take part in the presentation of the problem? Whom does the counsellor address when he 'wants to know what the family expects from him now'? (It is noticeable that Mr. Mueller responds on behalf of the family.) How does the counselling session come to a close and what do the participants agree upon in the end? (One learns that the couple returns about two weeks later.)
- The fieldnotes do not sufficiently focus on the presence and perspectives of certain participants (Mrs. Olschewski and Marek). What did the observer learn about them?
- There is not enough consideration of the intercultural dimension of this encounter. Mr. Mueller has come along as a 'representative' and mediator, but apparently it is 'somehow' possible to communicate with each other without his presence (e.g. during the second encounter). The 'somehow' does not become a topic at all. What about the problems of understanding and misunderstanding in such circumstances?
- What is involved in the performance of certain 'insider' activities is not sufficiently explicated and marked as an interesting phenomenon for an outsider (e.g. 'drawing a genogram').

Such a critical collection does not serve to denigrate the student's observational abilities but to create an awareness of the complexities of communicative interaction and how professionals are involved in the unfolding of events. Even if a specific question about gaps or vague references cannot be answered, it can lead to a self-reflective and self-critical discussion of relevant and more general issues of professional practice and communication.[8]

The counselling work and session – critical observations

The students' overall attitude towards the professional work as it appeared in this data was critical. These were the main points:

- A general criticism was that the counsellor did not sufficiently attempt to develop a relationship of trust with Mr. and Mrs. Olschewski and to allow time for a genuine counselling process to unfold. They had the impression that he did 'counselling in a hurry'. At this point the student writer offered some interesting background information: because of the many persons who sought help at this counselling centre and because the professionals did not want to create waiting lists they had agreed among themselves to work in a 'solution-focused' style, that is, to limit the number of sessions reserved for individuals, couples or families. He mentioned that in his opinion the speeding up of the counselling process and the lack of a patient inquiry into the problem had to do with these structural constraints.[9]

- The students felt that the counselling space was not sufficiently protected when the family's 'representative' remained present during the discussion of the Olschewskis' family life, even though the clients (the Olschewskis) and the psychologist could 'somehow' communicate with each other in the German language. The focus of the counselling process remained blurred: when Mr. Mueller answered Michael's question about 'what the family expects from him now' instead of Mr. and Mrs. Olschewski, it is possible that his answer deviated from how Agnieszka's mother and father (and possibly brother) defined the situation of seeking help.

- The students were critical that the counsellor did not take time for a careful (narrative) inquiry into the experiences of the family members: their experiences of a migrant trajectory which Mr. Olschewski referred to in his complaints about a society (and its institutions and representatives) which he does not understand, in which he feels strange and claims to be treated without due respect. Instead, the psychologist ostensibly used an official document (the court order) as a resource for discrediting and discouraging a different version. The document itself apparently gives testimony to grave problems of understanding and possibly misunderstanding in the proceedings (as in the reference to Mrs. Olschweski's loss of control) and the exclusion of perspectives (the absence of an interpreter). Mr. Olschewski seemed to look to the counselling centre as a possible ally in the dispute over his daughter. The professional did not have to distance himself from the family court or the youth welfare office, but there was also no need to become their coalition partner and to support the established 'hierarchy of credibility' (Becker 1967) right away.

- Even if Mr. Olschewski had a drinking problem and was prone to violence the empirical basis for this dominant definition and categorization ('alcoholic') was shaky. The psychologist prevented the development of a trust relationship by forcing the category upon him. He expected him 'to surrender' and to give in to this dominant definition, which the client (at this point in time) saw as loss of face and refused. A counselling relationship with Mr. and Mrs. Olschewski could possibly have developed if the couple had had the chance to speak freely about the problems with their daughter and to mention how they were entangled in this process. Under such circumstances Mr. Olschewski might have become more receptive to critical comments about himself and his contribution to the mess.

The student writer

The fieldnotes show that the student is eager to learn something from the professional: he wants to participate in and to observe an event which he regards as important for his professional socialization and he is quite careful in noting what the psychologist does and how he interprets the situation. I think it is important that university teachers respect students' loyalty and identification with practitioners at their workplace and avoid a debunking style of criticism.

These fieldnotes (in contrast to fieldnotes of other students) do not contain any doubts and (self-)critical reflections. When the other students developed such a critical line in the seminar the student writer was very open and did not react defensively. It was important that all of this was part of a friendly and egalitarian discourse and that no one expected the student writer to don sackcloth and ashes because he had revealed that he had not been sufficiently 'enlightened'. If students were shamed, denigrated or made fun of such a discussion would be in vain or turn into an isolating and humiliating exam (instead of encouraging him to search for critical feedback from other members of his profession). The fact that the student writer had reconstructed his experiences and inner states in a lively and open manner meant that he had provided valuable data on professional work, its problems and possible mistakes and undesirable developments.

These were the main points in the discussion:

- The members of the seminar criticized the fact that their fellow student had privileged the perspective of the professional and the processing institutions, whereas the perspective of Mr. Olschewski was put into doubt (as in the writer's remarks on the 'truth').
- The student became aware of how he had taken on the professional's viewpoint and how his own observations had been shaped by his early categorization of Mr. Olschewski as an 'alcoholic' (his suspicion-driven description of the client's face and his reference to his high blood pressure as evidence of his alcohol problem).
- When the other students focused on his ethnic stereotype of an 'eastern European' male (which he had verbalized in a commentary which was probably introduced in retrospect, but might already have been on his mind during the scene which he witnessed) he admitted that such a typification was problematic and derived from his cultural distance from people whom he did not know much about. In other cases he could have used the term 'Turkish', 'African' etc. in reference

to a stranger. In using this category he drew upon a stock of collective categorizations which has been shaped by European history and the cold war.

- Beyond that it is possible that the members of the 'Polish family' do not identify themselves as Polish at all, but as German, and are just categorized as 'Polish' by the natives (a collective experience of *Spätaussiedler* from central and eastern European countries who see themselves as 'returning' to 'their' country or the country which their ancestors had left a long time ago).

Features of student fieldnotes: some recommendations

In critically reflecting about what one can – and sometimes cannot – learn from such fieldnotes and how they could be used in the training of future social workers as ethnographers of their own affairs, I have developed a number of recommendations which students should keep in mind when writing down their observations during practice placements. They are advised:

- to write notes for sympathetic readers who they assume are not familiar with either the specific field of practice or the history of their work placement and want to learn more about them as actors in the respective field and as writers who are retrospectively making sense of their experiences and reflecting on them.
- to overcome the tendency to take things for granted.
- to write in the first person and to clearly differentiate between the 'first persons' at different times (in the situation described, later on and during the 'inscription' and reflection of their own experience).
- to avoid the tendency to 'self-absorption' (as in a private diary) and to focus on the discovery of social processes in a professional field of practice to which they belong as an actors.
- to focus on sequences for the sake of discovering the order, but also the disorder of social processes. The disorder could consist in the violation of interactional reciprocity and in breaches and irritations of sequences of action and communication (Riemann 2005d).
- to take into account and to differentiate the perspectives of different actors without privileging certain powerful and established perspectives as natural, authoritative and normal.
- to differentiate the language of the field from their own observational language.
- to present social processes, situations, organizational contexts, inner states and reflections in such a way that it is possible for outside readers to analyse the text by themselves.

I have developed a type of student training during the last years in which excerpts from field notes on practice placements are used in 'practice analysis seminars'. These are settings in which students take turns to present and discuss their material (cf. Riemann 2005a: 95–97) and use the feedback of others to write their final research reports in which parts of their data are integrated and discussed.

Conclusion

This has been an exercise in remembering and describing what happened a couple of years ago when I met with students of social work to discuss the fieldnotes which one of them had written down and given to me. My own memory of the meeting in which 'we did something with his notes' is rather vague. I remember the good humour and the intensity of our discussion, although I cannot reconstruct the details of our interaction.

I remember, though, that one student's initial reaction was rather reserved when the lively discussion became critical of the counsellor's practice. I wrote down what he said: 'He is a psychologist. He knows what he is doing.' As a future social worker he was very respectful of a member of a profession which he regarded as more prestigious (Hughes 1984). I told him that it does not matter which profession the counsellor belongs to, but that it is important what he does and does not do. Michael could just as easily have been a social worker. No professional practice should be immune to critique or self-critique.[10]

Perhaps some readers will find the students overly biased – that 'real' ethnographers should act in a more neutral and disinterested manner and should just focus on what is going on in the encounter observed and how the participants accomplish their meeting. When I reflected on my own research and in discussing it with Fritz Schütze I also discovered that a critical component was woven into my kind of analysis (Riemann 2005d: 408): that there are implicit criteria for my critical and case-specific analyses of the work of professionals which are grounded in the sequential order as well as in the interactive reciprocity of the processes of interaction, communication, action and work. The students relied on such criteria, too, when they sensed that things 'went wrong' in the counselling work and that there had been a lack of fairness. In arriving at such an assessment they did not need a prior explicit model of what constitutes good professional work. They learned to discover and consider alternatives of action in focusing on their own and fellow students' data.

This way of discussing fieldnotes could foster a self-critical and egalitarian discourse among practitioners on their own work, its paradoxes and mistakes (Schütze 1992; Riemann 2000, 2005d). Beyond that the ethnographic project of making one's own practice strange may be essential for the development of professional competencies which serve as a basis for practical case analyses.

Such a project entails different tasks, for example, the need to look very closely at oneself and the situations in which one participates and to learn the descriptive skills of writing ethnographic fieldnotes (Sanjek 1990; Emerson *et al.* 1995), especially notes which stress self-reflection. Developing such skills is a special way of appropriating one's own work, of gaining new insights and of making it visible for collegial discourse. If (future) social workers get drawn into such projects they can make important contributions to developing grounded theories (Glaser and Strauss 1967) based on their own experiences – in contrast to primarily applying prestigious 'received theories' to their practice in order to assure, legitimize and 'ennoble' their expertise.

Notes

1 My style of working with students of social work has evolved during a long collaboration with Fritz Schütze, especially while we were at the Department of Social Work at the University of Kassel. In Kassel we started to work with students in 'research workshops' (Riemann and Schütze 1987; Riemann 2005c) in which their qualitative empirical research, quite often based on autobiographical narrative interviews, was supervised. We have continued to organize 'research workshops' in our respective academic environments at the universities of Magdeburg and Bamberg. (The work which is presented in this chapter is not done in the context of 'research workshops' but in a somewhat different setting.) Since 1997 I have been working at the Department of Social Work at the University of Bamberg. An important resource for my research and teaching has been the work of the late Anselm Strauss and the tradition of Chicago interactionism.

2 I see some similarities with Taylor's and White's (2000) project of 'practising reflexivity in health and welfare'.

3 This is also the case in the other social work courses in Bavaria. Such an extended period of exposure to social work practice as a student will soon vanish because of the wholesale introduction of bachelor courses.

4 I cordially wish to thank the student for allowing me to use these fieldnotes. He would like to remain anonymous.

5 His name was changed by the author of the fieldnotes (as were the names of all persons who appear in them).

6 See Riemann (2003) for a similar attempt in the context of doing biographical research based on an autobiographical narrative interview.

7 The use of such data meets with a lot of criticism from social scientists who regard it as 'technologically outdated'. The German sociologist Ulrich Oevermann criticizes ethnographic fieldnotes as inevitably tarnished because of their methodological deficit of a 'circular intertwining of data collection and interpretation' – in contrast to the use of audio and video recordings and films

(Oevermann 2001: 85). Of course this data does not lend itself to analytical procedures which can be performed on the transcription of an audio-recording of a counselling session, for example, the fine-grained analysis of its structure of turn-taking, of the transitions between different phases or of the production of tensions and misunderstandings. Nevertheless, (good) fieldnotes reveal a lot of the order or potential disorder of the interaction and lend themselves to critical questions and insights with regard to the practice observed and professional work in general (beyond the particularities of the depicted scenes). A special virtue of this material consists of the quality of revealing the inner states of the writer – her or his experiences and perspectives during and after the event. Fieldnotes and off-the-cuff narratives are the best material for learning something about the writer's experiences and reflections (Riemann 2005b).

8 A selective reading of studies in the tradition of ethnography of communication (Keating 2001) or conversation analysis (ten Have 1999) could help students to become more astute observers and writers of fieldnotes. Note, for example, that the gaps mentioned above can often be described as incomplete references to 'adjacency pairs', as they are called in conversational analysis (cf. Schegloff and Sacks 1973). The term refers to a single sequence of utterances by different speakers, in which the first utterance (the 'first pair part') constrains the second utterance (the 'second pair part') in some way, that is, it makes a certain type of response expectable. A reading of studies by ethnographers of communication (cf. Gumperz 1982a) can be especially sensitizing with regard to the fragility of intercultural and interethnic communication.

9 I find it interesting that the term 'solution-focused' which has become influential in the context of 'solution-focused therapy' (e.g. George *et al.* 1999) is used in this way and serves to legitimize a practice.

10 As a matter of fact, this psychologist was informed by the student in placement that he had used his fieldnotes on this particular encounter for the seminar discussion. The psychologist wanted to learn about the criticism of the seminar and he agreed with the main points. It is important that such criticism is constructive and detached and cannot be taken as an attack *ad hominem*.

14 Telling stories . . . and the pursuit of critical reflection

Jennifer Lehmann

Educators, professional staff and managers in the human services industry have always had high expectations, one of these being to ensure that effective, professional responses will be provided to those seeking assistance. However, contemporary trends in the human services sector have led to clearer articulation of the expectations of professional practice, with concomitant development in the documentation of codes of ethics, practice standards, accountability processes and quality assurance regimes (Australian Association of Social Workers 1999, 2003; Lehmann 2003a). A wide range of competencies is now expected of new graduates and established professional practitioners alike, and there is an increasing emphasis on continuing education in most human service disciplines in order to ensure high standards of practice are achieved.

One aspect of continuous learning that has emerged in the current context of service delivery and professional education is the ability to critically reflect on professional practice in a way that integrates information, theory and experience. This is significant because, as Merizow (1990: 13) states, 'By far the most significant learning experiences in adulthood involve critical self-reflection – reassessing the way we have posed problems and reassessing our own orientation to perceiving, knowing, believing, feeling and acting'. Cameron (2003: 362) has commented that 'work settings are characterised by far too rare opportunities for feedback and by contested spaces for reflection', concurring with Marsick's (1990: 23) comment more than a decade earlier that 'Workplaces are not typically associated with reflection or critical self-reflection'; nevertheless, reflective practice has been a focus of interest across a number of professional disciplines for many years. It has become perhaps even more of an imperative, given that the work of human service professionals takes place within a dynamic social, political and economic climate of uncertainty (Edwards *et al.* 2002; Pierson 1998) and confronts busy practitioners with complex choices on a daily basis. At the same time there is ongoing pressure for speedy responses that remain within the bounds of established policies and procedures, all of which lead to the tendency to maintain familiar strategies in practice, regardless of their efficacy.

This demanding environment has stimulated educators at the tertiary level and beyond to seek ways of teaching both the knowledge and thinking skills needed to practise successfully, with a variety of techniques and processes currently being used to encourage and develop reflective capacity in undergraduate, postgraduate and continuing education contexts (Redmond 2004; Fook 2004b; McDrury and Alterio 2003; Labonte and Feather 1996; Johns 1995). Some approaches include the use of one or more of: workshops, small-group discussion, field practicums with supervision and university-based 'integrative' seminars, problem-based learning tasks, professional supervision and mentoring, and learning journals. Morrison (1996), for instance, is a strong proponent of learning journals, in particular, and established a model for their use with students at the University of Durham, UK.

However, a number of educators have turned to narrative approaches, believing that exploration of narratives about professional work provides fertile ground for critical reflection and the potential for improved practice (McDrury and Alterio 2003; Bolton 2001; Kellett and Dalton 2001), and I have persistently used stories in recent years because they are engaging, worrying, replete with human foibles and struggles, and provocative. Stories reflect life as it has been lived and experienced – and as it might be lived and experienced by their audience. For me, stories provide a starting point from which to explore knowledge and theory, to develop our understanding of issues and people and, ultimately, to take action. They have the capacity to transform our thinking and future choices.

Clough (2002: 8) suggests that 'stories can provide a means by which those truths, which cannot otherwise be told, are uncovered' corroborating my experience that formal, theoretical literature has limitations when it comes to telling multiple versions of truth and maintaining the connections to a 'live' context. In addition, Moon (1999: 212) comments that 'tidied-up learning can reduce reflective ability and reduce the potential effectiveness of learning'. This suggests that learning can begin with the messiness and disturbance of lived experience and that, as professionals, we are able to build our knowledge and practice through reflective processes that connect with this 'ground'.

Brody et al. (1991) go further, suggesting that story and dialogue are at the heart of ethical and caring relationships, the implication being that we will not achieve such relationships without hearing and connecting to stories. Noddings (1991: 163) concurs, highlighting that 'interpersonal reasoning' is promoted by the use of narrative because it encourages attitudes of caring together with attention, flexibility, the effort to cultivate a relationship, and the search for an appropriate response. The idea that stories can provoke attention to moral and ethical decision-making was also a focus of the work of Tappan and Brown (1991).

By using stories we are able to tap into a spectrum of perspectives and possibilities which leads to dialogue within the learning context and the potential for change. Stories maintain their relevance because, as Introna (1997: 59) comments, the text does not stand still, rather its meaning changes 'as the historical, social, political, or moral context in which it is interpreted adapts and changes'. He also comments that stories are useful to explore our tacit knowledge, looking at both foreground and background ideas that are held within narrative. Introna (1997: 66) relates this to the hermeneutic cycle in which the reader

> uses her fore-understanding and prejudices to establish the initial meaning of the text; assuming it to be in some way coherent and understandable. She then relates this meaning to her current situation, tradition or form of life. She now possesses a new understanding of her context; this new understanding is projected onto the text which opens up new meanings to be projected back onto the context ... the hermeneutic cycle is, in a sense, the dialectic process of understanding.

It was the relationship between narrative and meaning-making, and the application of new understandings to organizational stories, that formed the basis of Reissner's (2004) work with stories as a tool for change. Her findings support the proposition that learning and change processes are embedded in storying, and that we are able to achieve new learnings and adaptation through sharing and exploring stories.

However, many of the narrative-based techniques assume learners have experience within the human services sector on which they can draw as they develop their reflective skills and their knowledge base. Further, it is assumed that participants in learning environments are able to 'story' their experience, making it available for analysis and review. For instance, McDrury and Alterio (2003) use 'story pathways' to achieve reflective learning using learners' storied experiences, while Redmond (2004) uses a model that assumes engagement in practice with clients.

While there is no doubt that practice-based narratives drawn from direct experience provide fertile ground for exploration and reflection, there is a range of reasons why learners' own stories can be problematic. For instance, in my work in rural contexts over many years I have found that some of the most interesting accounts drawn from contemporary experience cannot be used for teaching purposes because of the likelihood of individuals and agencies being readily identified. Other difficulties emerge when working with students who have not yet worked in the human services sector, or when learners feel unable to share their experiences within a group setting due to privacy or confidentiality issues. Sometimes practising professionals are not confident about disclosing their practice to others with whom they have professional or personal relationships outside the educational setting (Lehmann 2003b). It is also important to consider the impact an unexpected story may have on learners in the group context, especially when one participant's experience dominates the learning process, or has particularly traumatic content.

In an attempt to overcome some of the difficulties encountered, I have increasingly used fictionalized, practice-based stories (Lehmann 2003b); using this approach results in all participants in a group having the same starting point in terms of text with which to work. It also allows the learner to 'connect' with the characters in the narrative without concomitant risk of identifying real people. However, in all other respects the stories are 'real' and each person brings to bear their ideas and knowledge as they explore the narrative. It was the use of these stories in a range of educational settings that led to my interest in having a model for their analysis.

Using stories – fictionalized or 'live' – demands attention to processes of exploration and reflective skill development in order to achieve the reflective capacities considered essential to professional practice. In spite of some doubts and debates about precisely how to develop the desired reflective practice outcomes, a number of educators from a variety of disciplines have contributed to our knowledge of how to promote reflective learning. However, most approaches to the development of reflective practice rely on sets of questions that are designed to provoke professional and personal responses that are then available for closer scrutiny and discussion. It is assumed that learners are willing to share these responses and engage in dialogue which is likely to be challenging.

For instance, Morrison (1996) discusses the four-stage approaches of Habermas and Smythe that he has adapted for use with learning journals, the journalling being a vehicle for students to address a series of questions about personal development, professional development, academic development and evaluative development. Johns (1995: 227) has framed learning through reflection using Carper's (1978) fundamental ways of knowing – the empirical, ethical, personal, and aesthetic – developing 'cue questions' for each area and adding that of 'reflexivity'. Bolton (2001) also uses writing techniques together with questions and prompts. However, Bolton (2001: 47) notes that 'Tutors of reflective practice report very different levels of success', that not all people are naturally reflective, and that people develop reflective capacity at different times in their life and career. She suggests that 'reflective practice is most effective when undertaken with a discussion group (or pair) of peers' (Bolton 2001: 48).

My own work has extended beyond the development of fictionalized, practice-based narratives to the development and trial of a model for analysis and critically reflective learning using stories. The '345' model, as I have called it, has been trialled across the disciplines of social work, management and biographical studies and in Australian, UK and German teaching contexts with undergraduate, postgraduate and continuing education students. Using a story chosen either from *The Harveys and Other Stories* (Lehmann 2003c) or my story 'bank' to provide the content for exploration, the model was applied by students to guide their learning. The students' responses suggested that they not only engaged with the practice-based stories, but also quickly developed a sense of purpose for seeking knowledge, connecting understanding with meaning, and identifying opportunities for change. Student responses to using the stories, together with the model, have been predominantly positive with feedback that suggests significant learning occurred:

> We've never worked with stories before. It was a new and good experience and I think using them is a very good way to learn, and to learn to effect.
>
> Stories can help us to understand experiences people have had, they make us 'feel with' the character(s) of the story. It's important to listen to people, to the stories they have to tell and to reflect on your own feelings and thinking about these stories.
>
> If you read the story you think and feel and then you think 'why it was so?' and you search for solutions.
>
> They [stories] are very good to understand complicated connections. I think that the stories were very good for reflective learning because you have to think about the contexts in the story.

In developing the model a number of factors were important, including applicability to a range of disciplines and narratives, the latter ranging from published accounts and journal documents (e.g. learning journals) to the unfolding narratives of human service practitioners who are still 'living' their experiences. The model needed to be easy to remember and provide guidance, or steps, in exploring narratives. More importantly, I wanted it to tap the potential to create new understandings and a variety of perspectives for the learner to consider that would lead to transformative action.

The name of the model itself provides an in-built reminder of 3 ways in which reflective thinking can be focused, 4 processes at work as reflective thinking occurs, and 5 questions that stimulate reflective thinking. The research of a number of people has informed the development of the model, but primary links are to the work of Fook (2004b), Redmond (2004) and McDrury and Alterio (2003). Other writers whose ideas have contributed to the model are Moon (1999), Johns and Freshwater (1998), Labonte and Feather (1996) and Jalongo *et al.* (1995).

One of the difficulties with developing the '345' model, as with many models, is that in real life the development of reflective thinking does not take place in separate stages or activities. It is usual to experience a tangle of thoughts and emotions that meld together at some level of consciousness, bringing together established learning from many experiences. In untangling ideas and feelings, and identifying and naming them, we become aware of the blurring, the interconnectedness and multi-directional nature of thinking. However, for ease of understanding and using the model, I describe the steps in the process as discrete because this provides a starting point which can be adapted when a level of familiarity with reflective processes has been established. The core components of the '345' model are described below.

Three ways to reflect

When conscious of reflective thought it is usual to be aware of the topic, or the focus, of our attention and our thoughts may be directed towards an event or a person; or we may be mulling over information we have been given and how pieces of information fit together. Or perhaps our thinking is primarily directed towards how to act using information and understanding. For convenience, I have referred to these three different targets or foci of reflective thought as 'reflection on content', 'reflection on meaning' and 'critical reflection' (see Figure 14.1).

Reflection on content is the thinking that essentially concerns information and knowledge (or theories) presented and immediately accessible in the narrative. Every story contains apparently factual material, as well as assuming knowledge or familiarity with theories. For instance, the story may provide

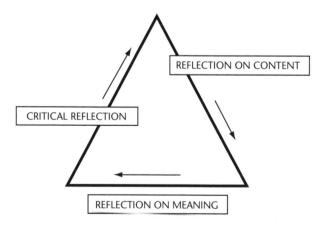

Figure 14.1 Three ways to reflect

information about the characteristics of people or the location and time during which certain events take place. It is assumed this information is relevant and in some way familiar to the listener or reader; and that it makes sense. As we think about this information we synthesize, or integrate, the material so that it is coherent. Having grasped the content of the story, it is then possible to analyse it – to investigate it further and reflect upon it.

Reflection on meaning is the second focus of attention that follows the reception of information or content of a story. We are, in a sense, working at a deeper level with the information by considering what it means to us. How the information is understood will determine whether we decide to agree with the storyteller's perspective, or to take an alternative point of view. At this level of reflection assumptions and values are accessed together with a review of attitudes and beliefs. We begin to notice aspects of the story that surprise us, make us laugh or feel uncomfortable. Reflecting on meaning means that we have to bring ourselves into the equation. It is somewhat like having a private, unseen dialogue with the storyteller or with another of our 'selves'.

Critical reflection is the reflective thinking that takes as its focus action and transformation. Inherent in reflection on change is the need to consider power, so at this stage reflection includes an analysis of the dynamics of power expressed in the story. Self-reflection is also needed in order to address issues of personal change that usually sit alongside any potential to alter a situation. Stories usually hold within their structures the possibility of other outcomes, and these can be identified together with the power dynamics that prevent or promote change. In our everyday practice as professionals we need to make decisions about action that affects others (and ourselves) so the ability to critically reflect completes the cycle of reflection. Most stories lend themselves to critically reflective analysis as well as being opportunities for rehearsal of transformative processes.

Four processes in reflective thinking

It is impossible to reflect without some level of curiosity – without some aspect of investigation taking place. Often the knowledge, theory, or information available falls short in some way, so in order to get a more thorough grasp of the story further exploration is needed. For instance, if one of the characters in a story seems concerned about the culture of a human service organization, knowledge about the concept of organizational culture is required prior to understanding its implications within the narrative and beyond – and for our own narratives, present and future. Once the areas of knowledge have been identified it is usually not difficult to locate information and espoused theory about specific issues. When stories are used in a formal educational setting this *investigation process* (see Figure 14.2) may include tapping the knowledge of

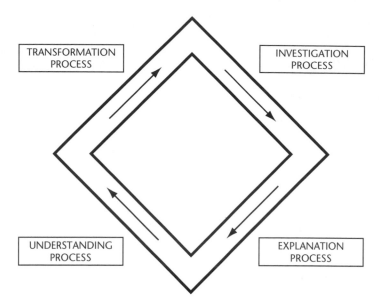

Figure 14.2 Four processes in reflective thinking

other students, of the staff, and from articles or books in a library. Seeking and finding knowledge leads to the second process – that of explanation.

The *explanation process* is really the reasoning and 'fitting together' that is done both in our heads and in dialogue with others. For instance, if organizational culture is the subject of our explorations it should be possible to form an explanation of why it might be difficult to change. Explanation is the making sense, and the connecting up, of information or knowledge with questions such as 'what happens next . . .?', or 'what will happen if . . .?'. This is only a small step to the next process – that of understanding.

Inherent in the *understanding process* is the introduction of 'I' and 'you' and 'other'. This is the moment when knowledge and explanation result in meaning by drawing on the values, attitudes, beliefs and assumptions that are brought to a story as well as embracing those embedded in the story itself. Understanding the reasons why a character in the story acted as she or he did and why this elicited the particular responses of other characters is useful, together with personal insights into our own reactions – feeling frustrated by the character's lack of action, for instance. This is an essential step for subsequent contemplation of the possibilities of change, for example developing an alternative outcome for the story, or formulating an alternative approach to use ourselves in the future.

The *transformation process* includes considering 'what ifs' and the shifts in relation to power dynamics that will allow for a different outcome to be achieved. Often the process of transformation takes place within ourselves, together with the development of awareness of what constrains or pushes us to feel and act in the way we do. Adjustments to beliefs or values may occur due to this new awareness. For instance, we may begin to feel differently about the character in a story because we have glimpsed our own difficulties when faced with this kind of situation. The transformation process includes the realization of multiple truths and perspectives for every situation and brings into consciousness the choices that are made in the process of interpreting lived experience. In acting on our choices, like the characters in the stories, we live out one of many possibilities and develop a sense of ownership for what lies within our repertoire of professional actions.

Five questions for reflective thinking

There are an infinite number of questions that encourage reflective thinking. However, the five questions as outlined in Figure 14.3 are fundamental in providing the logical steps from contemplation to transformation.

Figure 14.3   Five questions for reflective thinking

The first question, *What is this about?*, seeks to access the information contained within the story itself. This is not so simple as first anticipated because people often give quite different answers, having studied the same narrative. For example, a 'life histories' class in London using the '345' model and a practice-based story titled 'Neat and Tidy' (Lehmann 2003d) gave the following responses:

Someone who cleans an office.

It's about restructuring in an organization and its impacts on people.

I think the story is about change, different sorts of changes that happen at work.

I think it's about loss too. This man gradually loses parts of his job until finally he loses the job and goes to another one.

But somewhere in there is the issue of how changes are being managed.

The greatest benefit in asking this first question is to access all the initial ideas about the subject and 'facts' of the story.

The question 'What is this about?' establishes the 'ground' from which to decide what is important to explore. For example, a narrative might appear to be about changing work practices, but it might also be about the impact of organizational restructuring. If the concepts and knowledge of organizational restructuring are unfamiliar territory then an investigation of that topic might be necessary.

As knowledge is collected, a process of synthesis occurs that is a response to the question *How do I understand this?* The process may be an individual or group task, but when working with a group it is often reflected in the 'comparing of notes' that frequently takes place. It also tends to lead to values and attitudes being expressed. Debates concerning emphasis given to aspects of the story and the importance placed on specific knowledge and actions of characters are common.

There is usually a natural progression to the fourth question, *What other perspectives are there? What else?* as a wider range of alternatives for understanding is pursued. I have found it useful to proceed steadily through this phase as it represents the last scanning for omissions before coming to ask *How could this be different?*

This fifth question assists the often difficult process of identifying personal changes that are needed in the formation of new perspectives and ways of tackling issues. A shift in values, attitudes and beliefs is often the forerunner to making changes in how a situation is tackled, or deciding to do things differently next time. Applying this question to a story enables an expansion in repertoire – the range of possibilities that could be applied to lived experience at some later point. One valuable aspect of 'How could this be different?' is that responses can be personalized. We all have different skills and experience, differing levels of confidence and different personal attributes that combine to produce our individual style. These differences can be celebrated within the group learning context as part of reflective practice. Even the insight that 'I am not yet ready to change' is a change!

Conclusion

While most models benefit from refinement through use, the results of applying the '345' model (see Figure 14.4) to both fictionalized and 'live' narratives have been promising. Undergraduate and postgraduate students, and professional practitioners in continuing education workshops, have reported finding the model straightforward in its structure and easy to remember. Having five core questions is reported to be useful – more would be hard to memorize. The risk of using question 'sets' is that they are abandoned for the purposes of day-to-day practice. In addition, having a model with a starting and finishing point

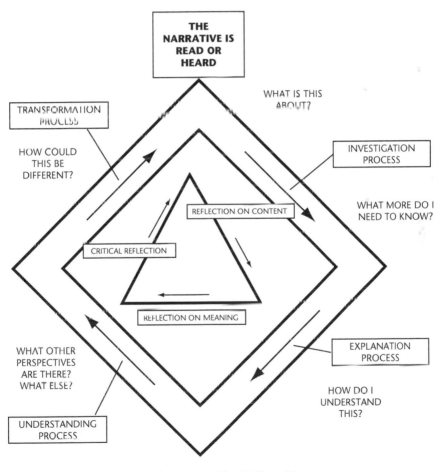

Figure 14.4 The '345' model

is useful to some people, while others have said they preferred to focus on a process that has applicability across contexts and situations.

The 'life histories' and business management students in UK and Australia, respectively, were not familiar with the idea of reflective learning, so I began those seminars with the five questions. Following lively discussions I explained the model to them, and their sense of having achieved a new and interesting way of reflective investigation was evident. This suggests the model might be usefully applied as a '543' approach for those who are unfamiliar with learning based on reflective processes. Disciplines other than those associated with human service delivery may find the model applicable where understanding of personal interactions is an important factor. However, those learners already attracted to, or familiar with, reflective learning seem to prefer beginning with the three ways to reflect as a means of making sense of the learning process about to unfold.

In addition, it is my impression, from using the model in mentoring sessions and supervision contexts, that this approach to thinking about accounts of practice in context can assist exploration and dialogue. Where both people are committed to considering a range of information, understandings and perspectives, and share the effort and energy needed to confront difficulties, there is the potential for establishing a commitment to reflective learning as a positive experience. This is especially significant in the current human services context in which anecdotal evidence suggests many practitioners feel they lack support, are under scrutiny, and report anxiety about adverse practice outcomes that may result in stressful processes which reinforce adherence to protocols and administrative practices rather than encouraging creative solutions. This atmosphere, where it exists, is not conducive to reflective learning or genuine practice improvement so practitioners must rely on other ways to sustain themselves. Perhaps the '345' model will go some way to contributing to establishing a sense of confidence and the reflective capacity needed by those who continue to meet the challenges of being a professional in this complex world.

15 Starting as we mean to go on: introducing beginning social work students to reflective practice

Bairbre Redmond

This chapter looks at a reflective teaching model designed to meet the learning needs of beginning social work students in their first six weeks on a master's in social work programme. Based on reflective pedagogy, this model allows students to draw on their previous work experiences, however limited, and to critically reflect on their attitudes and perspectives towards service users. This opportunity to experience a supported, small-group reflective environment exposes beginning students to the practice of perspective transformation at a very early stage in their professional development. The case examples discussed in this chapter are based on research into the efficacy of the model carried out by me with first-year students on the master's in social work programme (2005–7) at University College Dublin (UCD). In this research all my reflective sessions with the students were taped and transcribed and follow-up questionnaires were completed by the students, recording their reactions to the teaching model.

Background

Since the mid-1990s in Ireland changes in personal social service provision and health-care legislation have led to a significant increase in the number of social work posts, particularly in the area of child protection and welfare. The National Social Work Qualifications Board (2002) noted that 150 existing social work posts were unfilled in Ireland in 1999 (a 10.8% vacancy rate); by 2001 the number of vacant posts had increased to 307 (a 15.4% vacancy rate). Although no more recent data exists, it is generally accepted that this situation has not improved since then. Measures have been taken to address the problem, including the recruitment of social workers from other countries

(National Social Work Qualifications Board 2001) and the expansion of places on professional training programmes. By 2006 this will have resulted in a doubling of places on master's in social work programmes, by far the most common form of professional social work training in Ireland. The master's in social work programme at UCD now has 50 students in each of its two years, representing an increase of 60% in student numbers since 2000. This increase has also impacted on the level of students' pre-training work experience and, in the 2004 intake of students on to the UCD programme, 34% of students came directly from their relevant degree or higher diploma. This compares with 22% of direct entry students in 1998. Although many students now come directly from a degree programme, all of them will have gained some relevant work experience, either paid or voluntary.

This change in the profile of beginning social work students has had an impact on learning needs, particularly in the first 12 weeks of the course, before students undertake their first fieldwork placement. There is a concern that direct entry students might expect the transmission of social work knowledge to be one-directional, from teacher to student, where they are 'taught' how to be a social worker. This can lead to a perception that professional education can be reduced to a set of competencies, thus ignoring the creativity and artistry that professionals must bring to their job (Yelloly 1995: 61). The teaching and learning model described in this chapter was developed to engage these beginning students in a reflective dialogue which would help them recognize their previous experiences, attitudes and perspectives. By doing so, they also have the opportunity to appreciate their growing abilities to be creative in their practice.

Theoretical roots of the teaching and learning approach

Cowan (1998: 47) describes teaching as 'the purposeful creating of situations from which motivated learners should not be able to escape without learning or developing'. This teaching method for beginning social workers consists of interlinked teaching approaches that combine to offer students a comprehensive learning environment that encourages critical reflection within the first six weeks of their training. Taken in isolation, these approaches are not unusual ways of teaching social work theory and practice. What is particular about this overall method is that it is designed and co-ordinated to offer a specific reflective experience that can elicit the maximum levels of critical reflective learning in these beginning students. Within professional training for health and social care professionals other creative new curricula have been created (Taylor 1997; Taylor et al. 1999; Burgess et al. 1999; Redmond 2004) that incorporate such a reflective structure.

In the training of social workers and other professionals there is a dilemma of how to blend the delivery of lecture courses and of reflective teaching environments. Taylor (1997: 39) notes that professional training and education have relied significantly on the development of a knowledge base and the beginning of professional courses is often characterized by offering students and introduction to 'knowledge-driven' theory. Eraut (1994) broke down the elements of professional education, proposing that there were three different kinds of knowledge necessary for professional education: propositional knowledge, personal knowledge and the interpretation of experience; and process knowledge. Eraut saw propositional knowledge as a necessary component of professional learning, but in itself it is limited and Bloom and co-workers (Bloom 1956) saw proposition knowledge as the lowest level of their cognitive domain.

In professional curricula, there is a temptation to offer knowledge-driven classes to beginning students because they 'need to know the facts first'. This can lead to the well-tried formula of a class with the first half devoted to the delivery of propositional knowledge and the second half given over to small-group discussion. The concept of creating small, post-lecture discussion subgroups is familiar but may be overused, particularly at the beginning stages of class formation. For many social work students the often-repeated request to 'get into small groups and discuss X' may be, at best, tedious and, at worst, detrimental to their learning. More seriously, many social work students at the beginning of their training may feel that they have no legitimate experiences to share, and Brookfield (1993: 27) cautions that for a teacher to ask a group of relative strangers to share insights and experiences may be unreasonable. One student on our master's in social work programme a number of years ago noted in her evaluation of the first term:

> being asked to break up into small groups again and again for discussion doesn't achieve anything; you're asked to discuss issues and until you've been on placement you don't really know if you know what the issues are.

This teaching model is based upon reflective teaching and learning principles and draws on the work of Argyris and Schön (1974), Schön (1983), Boud and Walker (1998), Mezirow (1991) and Brookfield (1995). The model has also been developed from my own previous experience of designing a reflective model for a multi-disciplinary group of health professionals (Redmond 2004). This earlier work has highlighted the need to appreciate reflection as a multi-faceted process where students can move to higher level of reflection through planned teaching environments: 'by partialising the teaching and learning experience in this way, [a] teaching model is responsive to individual differences in the students' progress with their reflective learning, so that subtle changes can be noted and fostered' (Redmond 2004: 140). This reflective model for beginning social workers also encompasses the postmodern theories of critical reflection in professional training as articulated by Fook (2002), Taylor (1997) and Eraut (1994). It recognizes that beginning students need to experience a teaching environment that helps them see their professional development as a continuum of learning and that they need to be able to link their previous experiences and their attitudes to those experiences with their new role as beginning social workers. 'Learning is always related, in one way or another, to what has gone before. There is never a clean slate on which to begin: unless new ideas and new experiences link to previous experiences, they exist as abstractions, isolated and without meaning' (Boud *et al.* 1993: 8).

The reflective model in practice

Dewey (1974: 181) outlined the factors necessary for studying the sophisticated and subtle nuances of reflective practice. These were the causal conditions of learning – the accuracy of observation needed to assess progress and the candour and sincerity necessary to keep track of failures. This pedagogical model for beginning students consists of a number of interrelated reflective teaching and learning approaches. These combine to offer students opportunities to explore their past experiences and to provide a safe practicum where students can be helped to analyse these experiences in a reflective manner. Within these settings students are also introduced to the theoretical basis and the practical application of specific aspects of social work practice. These include the preparation of a process recording, the application and interpretation of a genogram and an introduction to the application of a family systems approach to a particular case. These stages of the model are backed up by the students' ongoing social work theory programme that provides them with a background to areas such as solution-focused theory and systems theory – this teaching occurs in parallel with my reflective work. All these approaches are designed and delivered through a reflective lens, with the primary focus being on allowing the students to experience as much perspective transformation as possible about their own attitudes to their work.

Beginning the reflective process

The first week of the programme is devoted to a number of reflective sessions with the students in which I ask them to focus on what strengths they bring to the programme – experientially, educationally and personally. This is to help them to appreciate that they do not come to training, in Boud *et al.*'s (1993) terms, as 'clean slates', but bring substantial experience and strengths to their learning and professional development. Boud and Knights (1996: 27) note that the capacity for reflective learning is grounded in the 'experiences that have shaped the person and helped create the person he or she is now and their intent that gives a particular focus to the learning'.

The first of these reflective sessions is designed to introduce students to the concept of reflective learning and to demonstrate some of the reflective teaching and learning tools used on the social work programme. These include reflective learning journals, planned reflective questions and process recordings. This session also starts to look at the first phase of the students' beginning strengths – their previous experience. Care need to be taken at this point to emphasize that all students bring relevant experience to the group and to avoid situations where some very vocal students can overemphasize their previous work in a way that intimidates other students. Such 'showboating' can create a misleading experiential hierarchy in the class, leading to an unhelpful class dynamic. Boud and Walker (1993: 80–1) identify such presuppositions about one's own and other's levels of knowledge as significant internal barriers to learning. The value of all students' previous experiences is developed further by their skills teachers in small groups where they are further helped to identify the practice skills they already have at the start of the course. Emphasis is placed on helping students appreciate their own occupational strengths and on minimizing student anxiety brought about by meeting each other and comparing previous work experience situations. The students' responses to a given set of reflective questions are also used as a basis for group discussion.

The second reflective session with the class focuses on their academic strengths. Using a learning assessment package (Soloman and Felder 1999), this session allows students to assess and appreciate their own learning styles. Students are helped to understand different approaches to learning and how they can maximize their own individual learning style by use of note-taking, visual aids, class discussion, etc. Again, the emphasis in this session is on helping students to identify their learning strengths.

The last reflective session of the first week brings students to the third main area, their own personal and family background. This session introduces students to genograms and demonstrates, through class exercises, the use of the genogram to identify patterns and strengths in families. At this point the students also asked to prepare a genogram of their family of origin. As Hildebrand (1995: 176–7) notes, this exercise helps students to think systematically and to make links between their private and professional worlds. These personal genograms are not shared with the class but students are asked, by means of written reflective questions, to begin to explore their own personal value base in preparation for the subsequent small-group skills sessions.

Preparing a process recording

The preparation and examination of a process recording is a pivotal entity in the entire teaching and learning approach used with these beginning students. In reflective terms, the process recording remains one of the most powerful teaching and learning tools in social work education (Papell and Skolnick 1992; Walsh 2002). As a reflective teaching method its usefulness goes beyond the social work arena and has also been used in nursing (Clarke 1998), medicine (McIlvain *et al.* 1998) and the training of health professionals (Turzynski 2001). Argyris and Schön (1992: xxii) also asked professionals to use the process recording format when they studied the written cases from over five thousand professionals in order to evaluate their theories of action. Argyris and Schön (1974: 39) found the process recording system to be more readily acceptable by those who used it than role-play, video- or audiotaping. They also found the process recording system to be useful in generating data on levels of reflection.

As part of their strengths audit in the first week of term I ask students to write a process recording; this sets down a clear marker that I have a conviction that they all bring a level of relevant personal experience to the programme. It also signals that my teaching will be based on a fundamental principle of transformative learning through critical reflection – moving beyond knowledge acquisition to an exploration of the learner's meaning perspectives (Mezirow 1991: 359–60). The instructions for the process recording ask students to identify a challenging intervention or issue that they have encountered with a client or a co-worker in either a paid or voluntary setting. At this stage help is given to students, particularly those who may have more limited experience, to choose a suitable incident upon which to base their process recording. There are no limits to the subject selected, except that it should relate to a problem or issue which was central to their relationship with this person. The recording is to be a simple exercise of remembered conversation in one column, while the student's internal thoughts are recoded in parallel in the second column. The written instructions for this exercise stress that students should try and focus on issues in the interaction that confused or perplexed them. They are specifically asked to choose an incident where their original plan of action ceased to be productive or created surprising or unnerving results. The importance of encouraging the students to focus on such an issue is of central importance to the levels of reflection they can hope to gain from the exercise. The successful creation of critical reflection is brought about by the impetus of what Mezirow (1991: 168) calls a 'distorting dilemma'.

At this early level of their training it would be neither fair nor productive to ask students to prepare their process recording without modelling significant aspects of the exercise for them. Along with the basic instruction for completing the process recording, I also give the students a copy of a process recording of my own work which, in Schönian terms, reveals a good deal of technically rational, unreflective practice that leads, not surprisingly, to an impasse with a client. Pinsky and Irby (1997) studied how reflection on failed approaches in medicine could be successfully used as a tool for experiential learning. Brookfield (1995: 254) also proposes that recognition and admission of failure are more productive in prompting new learning than reviewing successful pieces of work. The use of my own unsuccessful work as a model is important at this juncture as it demonstrates to students that it is not only permissible, but also potentially useful to acknowledge, record and reflect upon 'failure' in practice.

The opening reflective sessions on appreciating previous experience have laid emphasis on acknowledging and validating previous work incidences as being relevant for this exercise. Boud *et al.* (1993: 8) point out that learning can only occur if the experience of the learner is engaged. Beginning students who go into a teaching situation perceiving themselves as being devoid of the minimum experience needed for that environment are in serious danger of feeling isolated and excluded from the learning process.

Reflective case analysis

The next stage of the reflective teaching approach allows students to focus on the case upon which they have prepared their process recording, particularly to help them analyse what led up to the incident described therein. This exercise is designed to help them recognize their 'theory of action' – the approach or plan for their work with which they enter the interaction. Argyris and Schön (1974: 6–8) reported that there is frequently a lack of congruence between what many professionals say they intend to do (their espoused theory) and what they end up doing in practice (their theory-in-use). Espoused theories are frequently affected by workers' individual belief systems, by their assumption about their client's abilities and problems and by the organizational pressures under which they practise. Many of these factors strongly influence the direction of a professional's work, yet frequently they remain tacit and unacknowledged. The work of helping the students to recognize their theories of action takes place in 'reflective case analysis workshops', two-hour, small-groups settings where a number of the cases are presented and discussed within a reflective teaching framework. These workshops are held from the second to the sixth week of the first term with a maximum of 17 students in each group.

In discussion with the students we agree a number of cases to be worked on at each session and I provide photocopies of the appropriate process recordings for each case. Unfortunately, with 50 students in the class, it is not possible to work on each student's case, but cases are chosen that are as representative as possible of the types of cases being presented by the class. I also suggest cases where the process recording indicates that the student has had an involvement with the individual or family for a period of time. This factor is important as such knowledge about the background to a case gives the students who work on their cases in class a greater sense of confidence and knowledge about the process. The difference in the experiences for students who present their cases and those who do not is discussed at the end of this chapter.

At the start of the class I explain to the students that we will explore the case up to the point chronicled in the process recording. We begin with one of the students giving background information to their case and, as the student talks, I start to construct a genogram, or family tree, on the board charting the main individuals in the interaction, using McGoldrick and Gerson's (1985) protocol for genograms. I also note on the board any significant descriptive phrases that are being used and ask students to look out for emerging systems in the genogram. The use of the genogram is an essential element to the teaching approach. Fook (2002: 41) reminds us that a postmodern and critical approach to social work allows for a deconstruction of knowledge and an unearthing of multiple constructions on practice. Genograms, by their nature, are founded on constructivist principles, allowing for the generation of hypotheses to describe dynamic relationships (McIlvain *et al.* 1998). The visual nature of the genogram is also important in helping students to 'see' the family complexities and patterns developing in each particular case. The learning style assessment (Felder and Silverman 1988) administered to the students by me at the beginning of term revealed that over 65% of the 2004 cohort of students (those involved in this research) are primarily visual rather than verbal learners. This notion of 'seeing' and then 'reseeing' is central to the concept of reflection. For Mezirow (1991: 119–23), perspective transformation (reseeing) cannot occur before individuals recognize and challenge the distorted assumptions of their existing perspectives (seeing). The following is an example of a case presented by Denise, one of the students. Names and details of this student and the individuals involved in the case have been changed to protect their anonymity.

Reflection in action

Denise presents the case of a family living in a refuge for women experiencing family violence. Denise has been working in the refuge as a key worker with Nicky, a 25-year-old woman with two small children. In her process recording she has detailed an interview with Nicky who, in the previous week (while Denise was on holiday), had left the refuge with her children and was now living in a hostel for the homeless. This move caused a good deal of concern for Denise, who feared that Nicky's two children would be removed into care.

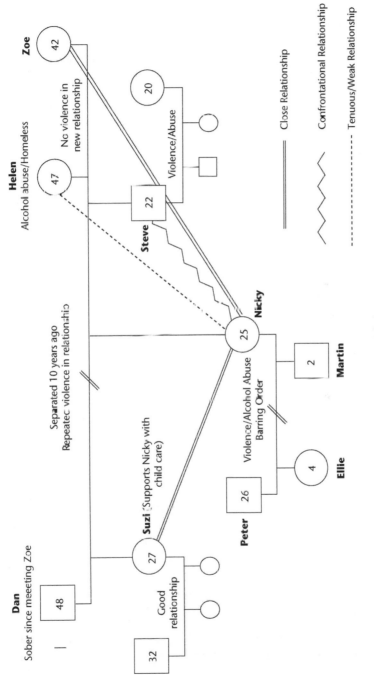

Dan
Sober since meeting Zoe

Zoe

Helen
Alcohol abuse/Homeless

No violence in
new relationship

Separated 10 years ago
Repeated violence in relationship

Steve

Violence/Abuse

Suzi (Supports Nicky with
child care)

Good
relationship

Nicky

Peter

Violence/Alcohol Abuse
Barring Order

Ellie

Martin

Close Relationship

Confrontational Relationship

Tenuous/Weak Relationship

Figure 15.1 Nicky's genogram

The process recording charts a fruitless argument between Denise and Nicky in which Denise repeatedly informs Nicky of the problems associated with her leaving the refuge and Nicky retorts that the refuge was too strict and too cold for her and that she is tired of people judging her and watching. No resolution is reached and Denise cannot persuade her to return to the refuge. Both Denise and Nicky emerge from the interaction frustrated and angry.

Nicky's genogram (see Figure 15.1) shows her to be one of three children. Her mother and father separated 10 years ago and her father is now living with a new partner. Nicky's parents' relationship was affected by both violence and alcoholism; her mother is currently living in a hostel and has an alcohol addiction. Nicky's father no longer drinks and his current relationship is stable and violence-free. Nicky's brother is a drug addict with a history of violence towards his partner; her sister is married with children and her marriage seems stable and free of violence. Nicky has been living with Peter for 5 years. The couple have had a turbulent relationship, marked by violence and alcohol misuse. Two years ago, after the birth of her second child, Nicky's children were taken into care. Nicky subsequently gave up drink and regained custody of her children; she has been sober ever since. Peter is currently living about 50 miles away from Nicky and their children since Nicky had a barring order taken out against him for a violent assault on her 6 months ago. Interestingly for the case, Sue, another student in the class, has also worked with Nicky, but primarily in relation to child protection issues in the family. Although it is primarily Denise who presents the case, Sue also contributes to the discussion.

The first issues that emerge when the case chart was drawn up related to the recurrence of patterns in the family, primarily violence and addiction. McGoldrick and Gerson (1985: 76) note that patterns of functioning, whether adaptive or maladaptive, can occur across generations of families. They advise that a recognition of pattern repetition makes it easier to understand and effect change in the family's current adaptation to their situation. The students saw the negative patterns with ease, one commenting 'so violence isn't such a big deal. I mean it's still dreadful, but it's become normal and kind of bad normal.' However, there is also a risk in presenting family patterns as a given, in effect proposing an inescapable destiny from which individuals can never escape. Reflective social work theorists and those who advocate a constructivist or anti-oppressive view in social work all caution about the need to adopt alternative perspectives on the client's reality – the need to reframe unhelpful notions about clients and their circumstances (McPhee and Bronstein 2002: 655). Berg (1994) and de Shazer's (1988) brief solution focused approaches seek for exceptions to presenting problems and the possibilities for positive change. Such a solution-focused view is useful in finding alternative perspectives to family patterns, and an exception question yielded an interesting reply in this case from Denise:

Teacher: Do you see any exceptions to the patterns that you've identified?

Denise: I can see that violence is normal for Nicky, but she was also very clear that she didn't want violence for herself. She was instrumental in getting the barring order taken out and she identifies with members of her family, particularly women, who don't put up with violence – like her sister and her father's new partner.

Denise's reframing of the family's patterns also represents a reseeing of the family from a perspective of their strengths rather than weaknesses. Fook's work on the deconstructive process in social work (2002: 92) highlights the need to critically question dominant discourses, those 'taken-for-granted' and often unproven assumptions about clients. Through a reflective lens Denise has, in Fook's terms, deconstructed Nicky's situation and has searched for a new perspective and interpretation on Nicky's past. At another point in the discussion Denise also resees Nicky's addiction patterns and her dealings with social workers to get her children back from care.

Teacher: How did she do it, how did she get the children back?

Denise: She got sober herself, cold turkey, and she never drank again. that's two years ago. She also worked with social workers as a means to an end – she did what she had to do to get her kids back. She turned up in court every week, sober, and fought for them, she fought very hard. Actually she fights for everything.

Having completed the genogram Denise then revisits her process recording and it is read out loud by the class to see, in retrospect, what has happened in the interaction. Denise admits that she saw the interview as a failure when she could not get Nicky to return to the refuge. She also notes from the process recording that she has asked Nicky no questions in the interaction – she primarily restated the reasons why Nicky should come back with her. The lack of questions in an interaction can be a good indication that the professional has adopted an unreflective expert stance with a client and is determined to persuade the client of the superiority of that professional view (Redmond 2004: 116–17). Denise's wry observation concurs with this hypothesis:

I didn't have any questions because I was on a mission that day. I was with her for two hours and I wanted to get her back and also I knew the agency wanted her to come back and I knew that my supervisor wanted her back, there was no reason to ask questions!

The class then reviewed the case and the intervention as described in the process recording and offered an analysis of what had transpired and how the case could be handled differently. They suggested that Denise's theory-in-use – to keep trying to persuade Nicky to return to the refuge – did not allow her to fully hear Nicky's reasons for leaving or to confirm her possible strengths. Sue, who knew the case from a child protection perspective, noted:

> In retrospect I see a lot more positives in this mother – more hope. I don't think anybody in the case saw those positives. They saw her as making mistakes before and [being] likely to make them again.

The positives identified in the class relate to Nicky's past successes to 'escape' her family patterns, her efforts to avoid violence and her admiration for women who had had successful non-violent relationships. Nicky's long-term sobriety and her determination to keep her children were also seen as strengths to be worked with. The overall analysis reached by the class reiterated Nicky's capacity for 'fighting', and the students discussed with Denise that Nicky's move could also be seen as her taking more control over her own future. They also noted the different systems that have become clear in the case. The bigger system, which Denise recognized, was the one that encompassed the wider dimensions to Nicky's life (including her strengths). The smaller system, primarily seen by the child protection team, tended only to recognize Nicky's abilities and weaknesses as a mother. Sue said:

> For me it's made me realize that it's very easy to focus on individual aspects of the case instead of looking at the bigger picture and I think that a lot of people who worked with her [in child protection] only saw it that way.

Student evaluations of the model

Written student evaluation at the end of the workshops showed a positive response to the combined teaching techniques. The students in the class found that the model provided them with a good (58%) or very good (42%) learning experience; many commented on enjoying hearing other people's work experiences. A number of students also noted that they liked the 'real life' nature of the cases discussed in the workshop:

> I liked the openness of the class, seeing cases that were real, working through the case and seeing the situation in a new light.

The other very popular aspect of the approach was the chance of seeing genograms used in practice. Some noted that they would now feel more confident in using the genogram as an analytic tool for themselves in understanding their cases:

> I went back to a couple of old cases and did genograms . . . it helps to get an overview of the case and create an viewpoint where the case can be seen more objectively.

Above all, the students note that the workshops helped them to see cases in a broader perspective:

> I recognize the need to think more 'out of the box' – realize the importance of looking at the whole picture, not just taking a narrow view.

Interestingly there was no difference in levels of satisfaction between students who presented cases and those who did not. Those who did present found it useful to have revisited a case, and a number of these students noted that they had found the experience confidence-building:

> in some ways I feel that the workshops have validated and given language to my prior practice . . . [I] feel more confident.

One student found the experience

> nerve-wracking at first – I settled down though, and as all I knew about the client emerged I was quite surprised. It had been a difficult case at the time and it was good to get other points of view on it.

This reference to being pleasantly surprised at the amount of information they were capable of presenting does highlight an issue of concern for the confidence of those students who did not get to present a case. The questionnaire asked students how they felt about this. The majority of the group who did not present said that they would have liked the opportunity to do so, but a number of these added that they learned a lot listening to others and some stated that they had used the process themselves to go over past cases. Two students mentioned that they felt more relaxed not presenting and three students said that they did not feel their case was of a sufficiently substantial weight to be discussed. All of the students felt that they would feel more confident presenting cases after their first field placement.

Conclusion

This chapter has explored how a number of planned and co-ordinated teaching and learning approaches can contribute to the achievement of levels of critical refection for beginning students. It demonstrates the need to resist the temptation to burden these new students with substantial amounts of knowledge, rather to consider the patterns of their learning and their wider learning needs. By doing so it is possible to create higher learning opportunities that lead them to experience a reflective perspective in their practice. Aspects of the teaching approach still need to be developed, and the issue of not having time to give every student the opportunity of analysing their work remains problematic. Indeed, pressure on the time within the social work curriculum remains a threat to reflective teaching models such as this that may not be perceived as 'teaching' a specific subject or competency.

The model presented here is not limited to the training of social workers and could be easily adapted and used for any group of health and social service professionals in a teaching or training situation. My previous reflective work has demonstrated that a reflective environment can be effectively used with a number of different professional groups, either singly or together. As Taylor (1997: 4) noted in her work on professional education, there are common interests and dilemmas in the development of reflective education that transcend professional boundaries.

The ability to reframe and resee one's work in a new light is the basis of perspective transformation in critical refection. Arguably, it is also a fundamental ability that social workers must have if they are to practise intelligently and creatively in professional practice. This puts the onus back to social work teachers and trainers to think of innovative and creative ways to allow beginning social workers to appreciate and experience reflective learning environments from the start of their training. To do this we have to see ourselves less as transmitters of expert knowledge and more as facilitators of critical learning and perspective transformation. As Boud *et al.* (1993: 9) state, 'while we commonly assume that teaching leads to learning, it is the experiences which teaching helps create that prompt learning, not primarily the acts of the teacher'.

Acknowledgement

My thanks to the MSocSc (Social Work) class (2005–7) at University College Dublin for their participation in this research and for the openness and honesty that they have brought to their reflective work.

16 Critical reflection: possibilities for developing effectiveness in conditions of uncertainty

Fiona Gardner, Jan Fook and Sue White

Open-mindedness [is] an attitude of mind which actively welcomes suggestions and relevant information from all sides . . . The worst thing about stub-
bornness of mind, about prejudices, is that they arrest development; they shut
off the mind from new stimuli. Open-mindedness means retention of the
childlike attitude . . . Open-mindedness is not the same as empty-mindedness.
To hang out a sign saying 'Come right in; there is no one at home' . . . But
there is a kind of passivity, willingness to let experiences accumulate and sink
in and ripen . . .

(Dewey 1916: 174–5)

In this book, we have presented the work of a range of scholars, with a view
to encouraging an 'open-mindedness' in which new ideas can gestate and
ripen. But our task as editors cannot be entirely passive. We hope the works we
have showcased demonstrate how critical reflection can illuminate practice,
research and teaching, prompting awareness of the importance of language,
the value of reflexive processes and the relevance of social context. The processes used can apply across professional domains, providing a connection, for
example, between research and direct practice. The wide selection of methods
and processes suggested by contributors are often focused on creating 'open-
mindedness' and new possibilities for practice, research or teaching. These
include the use of critical incidents, discourse analysis and the use of stories or
narratives.

The richness and diversity of the field constitute both its value and vul-
nerability. As we outlined in Chapter 1, there are many definitions of critical
reflection, which themselves reflect differing theoretical perspectives. These
diverse approaches may be celebrated in the way Dewey suggests above, but
they also mean that diligence is required on the part of a reader, to determine
which approach each writer is taking, and what are the implications for their
expectations of the process, and their choice of method or process. In this

chapter we aim to identify some of the strengths of the field at present, as well as challenges for the future development of critical reflection.

The value of critical reflection – shared experience

We start by looking at the common themes that emerge in this book about critical reflection and its value. We have divided these into three areas: identifying what critical reflection is, how people learn to be critically reflective, and the outcomes of critical reflection.

What is 'critical reflection'?

In spite of the variety of backgrounds of the practitioners and theoretical frameworks used, there seems to be a surprising degree of consensus about why some kind of critically reflective practice is important. The differences are of emphasis or focus; some writers imply certain expectations, whilst others are more explicit.

In broad terms, there seems to be agreement about the following aspects of critical reflection:

Developing the capacity for awareness of underlying assumptions
All the writers identify the importance of the ability to articulate previously taken-for-granted, hidden or tacit assumptions at both personal and social levels. This is often represented in terms of disjunctures between espoused knowledge and knowledge in action – the gap between what we say or think we do and what we do in practice. Articulating assumptions and values often helps explore this gap. There is variation in what assumptions are explored, reflecting the particular setting or example that is being discussed. Naudi, for example, particularly focuses on the example of a student negotiating a discussion about a parent's sexuality; students in Whitmore and Stuart's research class are questioning their assumptions about the research process. Bilson advocates the use research findings to 'trigger a conversation that enables participants to try out new assumptions if they wish'.

The value of learning and/or knowledge making from experience
All of the writers value using direct experience of practice as a means of learning. This is implicit in the use of processes that start with examples from direct experience for students, practitioners and researchers. The experience combined with critical reflection – including reflection using theoretical frameworks – can then lead to new forms of knowledge-making. For example, Frost uses two stories or experiences – one of a nurse, the other of a consumer of health services – to illustrate how reflection on experience can be illuminating.

This focus on experience and everyday practices means we need to rethink and broaden ideas about what constitutes valuable 'evidence' for the improvement of practice (White and Stancombe 2003).

The capacity to see how we are reflexive

Writers articulate this in different ways; some would name this as reflexivity, others talk more about subjectivity or an interpretive or constructivist approach. Bilson, for example, talks about 'living in conversations', Taylor about the narratives or stories through which we express our lives. Essentially, though, all agree that critical reflection means having awareness of what we bring to any interaction in terms of our knowledge, values, past experiences and our social and cultural selves

Understanding that there is no one version of 'truth' or 'reality'

This connects for most writers with a view that there are always multiple versions of a particular story or approach. This is an important part of student learning; for example, Riemann's use of fieldnotes in class enabled students to see that a situation had many perspectives and possible readings. Fook and Askeland document results of working with experienced allied health and human service workers who were able to develop 'openness' to other views and perspectives, 'reconstructing a more flexible and complex frame of choices'. One of Crawford's research students commented that research had 'created a space . . . where ideas may be useful but can't be accepted as universal truth'.

An understanding of how dominant thinking becomes internalized and embedded in culture, particularly as expressed in language

This is expressed in some form by nearly all the writers in the book, some more explicitly than others. This may reflect a major difference in theoretical orientation, with those using critical theory more likely to be explicit. Fook and Askeland, for example, articulate the theoretical background in the development of critical theory. Others focus more on how dominant discourses can be deconstructed: for example, Taylor and Naudi both use discourse analysis to focus on how language reinforces a particular dominant perspective.

An awareness of the social and/or political context and its influence on practice

All the writers seem to acknowledge how the broader social context impacts on individuals and organizations, whether it is in terms of problem definition (Bilson, Gardner) or professional intervention (Whitmore and Stuart). White gives examples of how current socially and politically acceptable 'vocabularies' can stifle debate and lively discussion, leading to decisions that fit the current context but are narrowing and undermining of creative and responsive practice.

Understanding of the complexities of power
Most writers are explicit about the need to understand the dynamics of power in relation to change and the maintenance of dominant discourses. Some contributors make passing references to this, whilst others provide a more focused analysis. Fook and Askeland, for example, explore Foucault's understanding of power and how it is useful for professionals in developing a critical awareness of practice. In their experience of using critical incidents in working with professionals they found that participants developed a more empowered sense of self, 'moving from seeing themselves as relatively powerless or as marginal individuals, able to see themselves as reflexive social agents with an ability to act and influence a situation'.

An expectation that awareness will lead to change, at least at a personal level, and for some at an organizational or societal level
This is perhaps the least consistent feature of the chapters. There is a clear implicit expectation that change will result from critical reflection, at least at the level of the individual, in terms of 'transformative learning' (Redmond) or having more capacity for reflection (Taylor). This might mean awareness of new perspectives or being able to see multiple possibilities rather than operating with simplistic, mutually exclusive binaries. Some writers clearly expect organizational or practice change (Bilson, Sung-Chan and Yuen-Tsang). Some demonstrate organizational change in terms of new subject development (Crawford, Whitmore and Stuart). Perhaps half the writers are explicit about seeing 'socially just' change as a goal, but it is often unclear what is meant by this or what is their view about how such change would be achieved.

How do people learn to be critically reflective?

A common theme in the book is an interest in how people learn to be critically reflective in direct practice, in professional development and in research. Writers suggest the following are significant:

The methods and processes used to aid critical reflection
Most of the writers in this book have affirmed the value of using some kind of specific method or process, which they articulate and justify for their particular context. These have been clearly outlined so that readers can see how they might be used or adapted.

We have divided these into three main areas – exploring through discussion, exploring through written material and exploring through research. Inevitably, while these categories are useful heuristic devices, such a division is ultimately artificial and, in practice, the approaches will often overlap.

Exploring through discussion   There are essentially two kinds of methods used here. Fook and Askeland ask members of small groups to bring what they call 'critical incidents' to the small group for discussion; Redmond asks students in a social work class to bring examples from experience of a problem or issue with a client focusing on the aspects that 'confused or perplexed them'. In both examples the group works with the person bringing the practice example to explore meanings. The emphasis is on an incident that has not worked. Redmond uses the word 'failure', suggesting that part of the aim is to change the culture, so that a perceived failure can be an opportunity for change. Similarly, Riemann uses what he calls 'field notes': students write up their observations and thoughts about an aspect of practice such as working with a family over time. These are then used as the basis of class discussion at a week-long seminar.

Lehmann uses stories she has written about practice experiences, in group work with students. She suggests this provides helpful distance – students are not expected to reveal their own experience, but are expected to explore their reactions.

Both Fook and Askeland and Lehmann have a series of questions that can be used as prompts or to direct the process, although Lehmann would suggest that such questions be kept to a minimum. All value the spontaneity of the group process, working with what arises, rather than having a prescriptive agenda.

Exploring through writing   Again there are a variety of methods suggested here.

1   Discourse analysis – focusing on how language is used in a particular situation, often using recordings of interviews to deconstruct what is or is not being said and what this might mean. Naudi's chapter is a particularly detailed example of this. She explores a student's reactions to homosexuality, noticing that the student 'switches codes' or uses a different language when she is talking about more culturally sensitive matters. White uses discourse analysis to consider how a nurse's expression of his identify changes as he move across 'boundaries', or between parts of his organization with different cultures.

2   Use of narratives. Several writers use written or spoken stories or narratives to encourage critical reflection. Often stories are written as part of a journal or research notes. The aim is similar to discourse analysis – to explore the underlying meaning(s) of what is expressed. Given that narratives are created by their writers, the authors' values, beliefs and assumptions are embedded in them. Taylor suggests that stories always need to be seen in context; they are told with a particular purpose in mind. Frost uses two examples of narratives, one from a nurse and one from a patient; these can be seen as performance (to a particular audience), conversation (to developed shared meaning),

a social process and a way of developing collective stories to provide legitimacy for political action.

3   Journals/learning diaries. These are often used as a means of encouraging student and practitioner reflection. Whitmore and Stuart, for example, require students to use reflexive journals in a research class to explore their reactions to the research process.

4   Process recording. Redmond suggests that this can also be used in a reflective fashion: she asks students to write about a conversation with a client about a problem or issue central to their relationship. The conversation is written in the left-hand column, the student's thoughts on the right.

These tools may also be used as part of group discussion or in one-to-one sessions with a supervisor or a peer or, indeed, in personal reflection.

Exploring through research   Several of the chapters in the book suggest that using specific research approaches can be a way of developing and/or refining a critically reflective approach to practice. These are generally research methods that are congruent with the values of critical reflection such as ethnographic (Riemann) or participatory action research approaches (Froggett). Alternatively, critical reflection may be used as part of research to create a more reflective culture for practice (Gardner) or research results may be used to generate reflection on practice (Bilson). A critically reflective approach can also be used in the teaching of research (Whitmore and Stuart, Crawford).

What is the role of emotion?

Paying attention to emotion is recognized as important in learning to be critically reflective, particularly given the current performance management orientation in health and welfare contexts internationally. Critical reflection can be a difficult process, involving students and practitioners struggling with clarification of assumptions and values. Often the process of critical reflection begins with a sense of discomfort about an event or action. The continuing process of reflecting can cause further distress (Palmer *et al.* 1994) until either a sense of deeper understanding is reached or, as White suggests, we learn to live in 'a less comfortable place', accepting the need to live with – and value – ambiguity rather than 'right' answers.

What emerges from critical reflection cannot be reliably predicted; sometimes practitioners and students make unexpected connections to experiences that are deeply emotional – positively or negatively. How do groups or classes using critical reflection deal with incidents that are traumatic and need more time and attention than can be given in these settings? Some literature exists which traces the sorts of emotions which are raised during a critical reflection process (Wong *et al.* 2001). The influence of culture may also be important here – some cultures are likely to see expressing emotion at work or study as more appropriate than others (Trompenaars and Hampden-Turner 1998). Because of this uncertainty, it would be useful to articulate more clearly the place of emotions. Is it necessary to have some degree of emotional engagement for reflective learning? How does emotion inform the process? What degree of emotion, if any, is unhelpful for critical reflection and why? How can discomfort or anxiety be reframed to used as opportunities for learning? How can emotional experience be harnessed for learning in professional practice?

Often, references to emotion are implicit in the chapters. The issue of emotion is raised more explicitly by some: Lehmann, for example, suggests that using fictionalized stories can provide some distance, so that participants are less anxious about exploring an issue, while still being able to access their emotional reactions. Redmond, on the other hand, talks about the value of naming 'failure' so that it can become part of learning, which is another way of dealing with anxiety. Gardner talks about how the feelings of frustration for workers about the research process need to be expressed in order for them to progress.

Bilson (as the presenter of research data) and Froggett are perhaps the most explicit about the place of emotion. Bilson asserts that he is 'passionate to convey my emotions about what I have seen, and at the same time open to change through attending to the views and emotions of participants'. He finds that his recognition and articulation of the emotional helps generate questioning of assumptions and a more creative attitude to change. Froggett, in evaluating an arts and storytelling community organization, suggests that critical reflection or deep learning is more likely to happen when the 'whole self is brought to bear on the task, including emotions or perceptions'. She also links this to 'embodiment' – arguing that the body 'expresses inner states while inner states contain bodily representations'. Relating at a feeling level enables participants to make connections not possible at a purely academic level. Finally, Fook and Askeland, in evaluating what participants in critical reflection groups learnt from the experience, identified a movement to a 'more complex sense of professional self . . . which can include their own emotions'. This suggests that the expression of emotions, perhaps even the reconstruction of emotion as an integral part of professional learning, is important in the process.

Building a climate for critical reflection

Another common theme is the need to build a culture in which learning critical reflection can be possible and effective. Given that the process generally requires exploring practice in an open and exploratory way, it is important to generate an atmosphere that is respectful and non-judgemental but also challenging, opening up new possibilities.

Given the limitations of space, writers have often simply said that climate and atmosphere are important, rather than explaining how these might be generated. Fook and Askeland, for example, say 'A collegiate and trusting climate was established in order to facilitate openness to learning'. Riemann expresses the value of a particular atmosphere: 'It was important that all of this was part of a friendly and egalitarian discourse and that no one expected the student writer to don sackcloth and ashes because he had revealed that he had not been sufficiently "enlightened" '. White talks about the need to create spaces in professional domains where there is safety for 'boundary-crossing activities'.

The issue of safety is also raised by Froggett who talks about the importance of a 'holding space', where it is possible to explore without being pressured to take a particular view – or, using the analogy of the artistic process, not shaping an image or recognizable space too quickly. This highlights the importance of the dynamic of the reflective process, allowing respectful time and emotional and mental space for 'boundary-crossing'. Froggett also articulates the importance of the physical geography and space of the organization. The environment of the organization she is evaluating is welcoming, aesthetic and replete with symbolism all of which can encourage a receptivity to reflection.

Redmond describes in more detail how a class participates in a range of exercises to develop readiness for critical reflection. This includes sessions where students identify relevant strengths – experientially, educationally and personally – which reinforces that all students have useful experience and knowledge to share. She is explicit about the value of critical reflection, including naming and reflecting on 'failure'. As part of establishing that this is a useful way to learn, she uses an 'unsuccessful' example from her own practice first, then examples from other class members. However, building a sufficiently accepting climate is not always possible. Whitmore and Stuart found that, given the power dynamics of the classroom and the grading system, not all students felt able to be 'fully candid' either in class or in their reflective journals.

Sensitivity to social and cultural differences

Learning to be critically reflective enables participants to articulate assumptions and values about social and cultural difference and to see that multiple realities are possible. Writers about critical reflection have tended to assume that as a process it is flexible enough to work across social and cultural differences, but this in itself is an assumption that needs to be interrogated. Writers here, for example, represent a reasonable range of cultural difference from Western countries, but only one chapter is written from a non-Western experience. Two chapters particularly have raised cultural and social differences and these both broach further questions about how people learn to be critically reflective.

In Sung-Chan and Yuen-Tsang's experience of teaching social work in China, their first group of students accepted the use of critical reflection, but some members of the second group were reluctant. Exploring why this might be so deepened the authors' understanding of different perceptions of reflection related to historical, cultural and social context. From this experience, they suggest that those using Western theories such as critical reflection need to be culturally sensitive, inviting participants to explore first their own definitions of reflection.

What are the outcomes of critical reflection?

All the chapters of this book affirm that there are positive outcomes for students and practitioners using critical reflection. Critically reflective practitioners tend to be less comfortable with talking about outcomes, having had experience of the limiting effects of too much focus on narrowly defined measures. However, there clearly are outcomes from critical reflection and if practitioners are to be able to justify using this approach, we need to find ways of identifying these. Organizations are showing interest in critical reflection, but want to know that there will be benefits.

The researchers in this book have tended to use evaluations from students, observation, participant action research and ethnography. There are many illuminating examples of positive change in behaviour, shifts in understanding and new awareness of options. However, there is little systematic gathering of evidence about what happens as a result of learning how to reflect critically in a form that is likely to be convincing to sceptics. Fook and Askeland's chapter analyses results from a significant-sized sample of practitioners who identified such changes as:

- changes in construction of themselves – a broader and more reflexive and empowered sense of themselves as professionals;
- having a greater sense of mastery, control and self-actualization;
- greater sense of new choices created;
- connection between the personal and social.

A candidate research agenda

The review of the literature in Chapter 1 highlights how under-researched critical reflection is. Generally speaking, the existing research focuses on the researcher's own area of practice. There is very little that explores in a systematic way what are the processes of critical reflection or what changes as a result. E.W. Taylor's (2000) comments about transformational learning could well apply here. He analysed the literature on transformational learning and found that it tended to be either theoretical critique, or limited to conceptual doctoral work, with very little from an empirical perspective. Because of this, he emphasizes the need for more research on articulating how change happens, including in-depth component analysis, strategies for fostering change and use of more varied methods of data collection.

While it generates much common understanding, this book also raises many possible areas for research. These include:

Research about what critical reflection is and what it is aiming to do

We were interested in the high degree of commonality about what critical reflection is. We wondered what would happen if the writers here were able to spend time exploring their approaches more deeply. Would we reinforce the view that we come to a similar place through different routes or find that, as we explore what we seem to have in common, the differences are greater than they appear on the surface? Of course, we should ask whether the diversity of the field matters. Should we not simply celebrate the wide range of ways in which critical reflection is expressed?

It seems important at least that we each understand what the other means by critical reflection. Perhaps most clarity is needed about what kinds of change we see as desirable – we could ask what we mean by 'transformative' or why we want practitioners to be critically reflective at all. Naudi, for example, is explicit about seeing critical reflection as a means of achieving broader social change, but for others this is not so explicit. It is interesting to compare this with Brookfield's use of critical theory which makes explicit what he expects from critical reflection: 'critical theory can be deemed effective to the extent that it keeps alive the hope that the world can be changed to make it fairer and more compassionate' (Brookfield 2005: 9). It may be that many writers eschew prescriptions for social change because it is so difficult to identify exactly what this might mean in a given context. Moreover, as White notes in this volume, reforming zeal can create new dominant orthodoxies and limit creativity and debate. This connects to questions about what kind of change we are seeking through critical reflection in terms of outcomes for practitioners, students and service users.

Research about outcomes

Clearly, from the evaluations undertaken by most of the writers in this book, students and practitioners find critical reflection useful at many levels. However, while this may well be accurate, we think there is a need for more systematic research to validate critical reflection across different contexts, professions and cultures. Critical reflection is not without its sceptics. It may, for example, be seen as a rather self-indulgent distraction from the proper business of health and welfare organizations, particular in an era of performance management. There are legitimate questions about how and when critical reflection should be used. Is it simply the latest fashion or an enduring development? How does it make practitioners or students more effective in their practice? What benefits does it have for individuals and organizations? Do these last over time, and if so, are there ways to ensure this happens?

Research about different methods

Given the range of methods and processes identified in this book and elsewhere, there are many questions that could be usefully explored about their use. We could ask how people learn to be reflective and the role of specific tools in the process. Writers agree that people need to learn from experience in some way. Does this need to be their *own* experience of practice? Can people learn equally from other people's experiences?

In Chapter 1, a number of frameworks were identified for thinking about stages of developing reflective practice. These imply a linear progression, but in practice the development of critical reflection is more complex. Nevertheless, these stages of development could usefully be explored in relation to the selection of appropriate tools. Are there particular methods and processes that seem more effective at earlier levels? Can we, and would we want to, refine our use of specific tools to suit particular students or student groups or practitioners at varying levels of experience or exposure to critical reflection? Are some tools more suited to some personalities (Cranton 1991), specific purposes or contexts?

There is some agreement that some people are more readily reflective than others, but it is not clear in what ways, or why. One variable here may be the familiarity of the language that is used (Palmer *et al.* 1994). The idea of being reflective is new for some, particularly those from educational backgrounds that emphasize a positivist approach. It may be that those who have already been exposed to a variety of frameworks or approaches can more easily use a critical reflection process. They have already experienced that there are many perspectives or, as White puts it, 'many vocabularies'. Whitmore and Stuart note that being reflexive in journals takes 'time, training and an ability and willingness to engage in a process of examining one's own most deeply held beliefs and actions – not an easy process'.

There are clearly dangers in being prescriptive – looking for a 'one size fits all' approach is likely to be counterproductive. A class, for example, will have a range of students likely to have different preferences. It may be more helpful to think about how tools can be used in flexible and creative ways to increase their appeal to participants – recall White's use of the metaphor of the trickster who 'nurtures the liveliness of ideas' using humour and playfulness to question whatever is being taken for granted. Brookfield (1995) suggests that because critically reflective teachers 'know that every class has its own dynamic, they cease to rely only on methods and activities that have worked well in the past. Their practice is infused with a sense of excitement and purpose.' However, there would be value in having some guidelines, for example, about what is likely to work better where.

Research on climate for critical reflection
We also need to be able to articulate what constitutes a supportive and enabling climate, in appropriate emotional, physical and organizational spaces. The need for people to be safe when taking the risk of reflecting and revealing personal vulnerabilities is important. And clearly, developing culturally relevant approaches is crucial to the effectiveness of critical reflection in widely differing contexts.

Role of facilitator/researcher
It would be useful to know more about the role of the facilitator, rarely addressed explicitly in this book Implied in most accounts is a relationship of trust and respect related to the facilitator's knowledge and skills, but again it is not clear what specific skills are needed and how these are developed. In addition, the need to keep group processes spontaneous and relatively unprescriptive implies a need for flexible and open facilitation, but it is difficult to identify exactly what this involves.

Conclusion

Finally, we want to emphasize that this book demonstrates the value of critical reflection and its utility across many settings. We have identified a significant amount of common understanding in the variety of approaches. A high degree of creativity is evident in how it is practised in teaching, research and direct practice. The specific methods and processes for aiding critical reflection are varied and often flexible, able to be used in various contexts.

We are also left with a series of questions that need to be more thoroughly considered through further research and evaluation. These include:

- Theory development and the connection between theory and practice. What are the similarities and differences in theoretical approaches; and what seems to make a difference? How important is a particular way of theorizing and understanding experience to the actual changes that take place?
- The use of specific methods and processes. Do some work more effectively in particular contexts and/or for particular individuals?
- Establishing the climate for critical reflection. How are the appropriate climates established, especially given that many organizational contexts do not encourage reflection?

- Outcomes from critical reflection. What are the outcomes for practitioners and organizations, and are there changes over time? What are the implications for organizations?
- Role of the facilitator. How much is the effectiveness of the critical reflection process dependent on the role of the facilitator, what are the features of effective facilitation and how are these developed?
- Influence of cultural difference. What are the implications of using critical reflection across cultures, both interprofessionally and internationally?

It seems, then, that we are concluding with many questions as well as a sense of significant respect for the diverse theoretical approaches to, and processes of, critical reflection. These questions provide timely opportunities to deepen and extend our knowledge of critical reflection and its processes. The challenge for the future is to keep the exploration of critical reflection lively and creative, while attending to rigour and effectiveness. There is a paradox at the heart of the notion of *critical* reflection – the need to maintain a sense of constant learning and openness, which is part of practising in uncertainty, whilst working towards the essentially normative mission of improved professional practices in occupations where people can be hurt or helped. We hope this book will go some way towards keeping language lively and helping professionals to practise, educators to educate and researchers to research with imagination, compassion and hope.

References

Aamodt, L.G. (1997) *Den Gode Relasjonen – Støtte, Omsorg eller Anerkjennelse?* Oslo: Ad Notam Gyldendal.

Abela, A.M. (1994a) *Shifting Family Values in Malta – A Western European Perspective.* Blata I-Bajda, Malta: Media Centre for DISCERN.

Abela, A.M. (1994b) Values for Malta's future: Social change, values and social policy. In R. Sultana and G. Baldacchino (eds) *Maltese Society: A Sociological Inquiry*, pp. 253–270. Msido, Malta: Mireva.

Abela, A.M. (1994c) Young people, religion and social development in Malta. In C. Cini (ed.) *Young People in Europe – Malta 1994.* Sliema, Malta: Polisportive Giovanili Salesiani.

Abela, A.M. (1998) *Secularised Sexuality: Youth Values in a City-Island.* Valletta: Social Values Studies.

Abela, A.M. (2000) *Values of Women and Men in the Maltese Islands – A Comparative European Perspective.* Valletta: Commission for the Advancement of Women, Ministry for Social Policy.

Adams, R. (2002) Developing critical practice in social work. In R, Adams, L. Dominelli, and M. Payne, *Critical Practice in Social Work.* Basingstoke: Palgrave.

Agger, B. (1998) *Critical Social Theories. An Introduction.* Boulder, CO: Westview Press.

Antonacopoulou, E. (2004) The dynamics of reflexive practice: The relationship between learning and changing. In M. Reynolds and R. Vince (eds) *Organising Reflection.* Aldershot: Ashgate.

Argyris, C. and Schön, D. A. (1974) *Theory in Practice: Increasing Professional Effectiveness.* San Francisco: Jossey-Bass.

Argyris, C., and Schön, D.A. (1978) *Organisational Learning: A Theory of Action Perspective.* Reading, MA: Addison-Wesley.

Argyris, C. and Schön, D.A. (1992) Introduction to the Classic Paperback. In C. Argyris and D.A. Schön, *Theory in Practice: Increasing Personal Effectiveness*, pp. xi–xxvi. San Francisco: Jossey-Bass.

Argyris, C., and Schön, D. (1996) *Organisational learning II: Theory, Method and Practice.* Reading, MA: Addison-Wesley.

Argyris, C., Putnam, R. and McLain Smith, D. (1985) *Action Science: Concepts, Methods, and Skills for Research and Intervention.* San Francisco: Jossey-Bass.

Askeland, G. A. (2006) Kritisk reflekterende – mer enn å reflektere og kritisere. *Nordisk Sosialt Arbeid*, 26(2): 123–134.

Atkinson, B.J. and Heath, A.W. (1987) Beyond objectivism and relativism: implications for family therapy research. *Journal of Strategic and Systemic Therapies*, 1: 8–17.

Atkinson, P. (1990) *The Ethnographic Imagination: Textual Constructions of Reality*. London: Routledge.

Atkinson, P. and Coffey, P. (1997) Documentary realities. In D. Silverman (ed.) *Qualitative Research: Theory, Method and Practice*. London: Sage.

Auer, P. (1998) Introduction: Bilingual conversation revisited. In P. Auer (ed.) *Code-Switching in Conversation: Language, Interaction and Identity*. London: Routledge.

Australian Association of Social Workers (1999) *The Code of Ethics*. Canberra: AASW.

Australian Association of Social Workers (2003) *Practice Standards for Social Workers*. Canberra: AASW.

Babuscio, J. (1988) *We Speak for Ourselves: The Experiences of Gay Men and Lesbians*, (2nd edn). London: SPCK.

Bakhtin, M. M. (1986) Speech Genres and Other Late Essays. C. Emerson and M. Holquist (Eds), V. W. McGee (Trans.). Austin, TX: University of Texas Press.

Baldwin, M. (2004) Critical reflection: Opportunities and threats to professional learning and service development in social work organizations. In N. Gould and M. Baldwin (eds) *Social Work, Critical Reflection and the Learning Organization*. Aldershot: Ashgate.

Bamberger, J. and Schön, D. A. (1991) Learning as reflective conversation with materials. In F. Steier (Ed.), *Research and Reflexivity*, pp. 186–209. London: Sage.

Barthes, R. (1977) The death of the author. In *Image-Music-Text*. Glasgow: Fontana/Collins.

Bassnett, S. (1991) *Translation Studies* (rev. edn). London: Routledge.

Bassnett, S. and Trivedi, H. (eds) (1999) *Post-colonial Translation: Theory and Practice*. London: Routledge.

Bateson G. (1980) *Mind and Nature – A Necessary Unity*. London: Fontana.

Bean, T.W. and Stevens, L.P. (2002) Scaffolding reflection for pre-service and in service teachers. *Reflective Practice*, 3(2): 205–218.

Beck, U. (1992) *Risk Society: Towards a New Modernity*. London: Sage.

Becker, H.S. (1967) Whose side are we on? *Social Problems*, 14(Winter): 239–247.

Bell, M. (1990) How primordial is narrative? In C. Nash (ed.) *Narrative in Culture: The Uses of Storytelling in the Sciences, Philosophy, and Literature*. London: Routledge.

Benner, P. (1984) *From Novice To Expert: Excellence and Power in Clinical Nursing Practice*. Menlo Park, CA: Addison-Wesley.

Benner P. (ed.) (1994) *Interpretive Phenomenology; Embodiment, Caring and Ethics in Health and Illness* London: Sage.

Benner, P. and Wrubel, J. (1989) *The Primacy of Caring*. Menlo Park, CA: Addison-Wesley.

Benner, P., Hooper-Kyriadis, P. and Stannard, D. (1999) *Clinical Wisdom and*

Interventions in Critical Care: A Thinking-in-Action Approach. Philadelphia: W.B. Saunders.

Berg, I.K. (1994) *Family-Based Services: A Solution-Focused Approach.* New York: W.W. Norton.

Berger, P. and Luckmann, T. (1966) *The Social Construction of Reality.* New York: Doubleday.

Bernstein, R.J. (1983) *Beyond Objectivism and Relativism: Science Hermeneutics and Praxis.* Philadelphia: University of Pennsylvania Press.

Bettelheim, B. (1976) *The Uses of Enchantment. The Meaning and Importance of Fairy Tales.* New York: Knopf.

Betts, J. (2004) Theology, therapy or picket line? What's the 'good' of reflective practice in management education? *Reflective Practice,* 5(2): 239–251.

Bilson, A. (1995a) Facts, figures and fantasy: A constructivist approach to professional training in the use of client information systems. In B. Kolleck and J. Rafferty (eds) *Both Sides: Technology and Human Services.* Berlin: Alice-Saloman-Fachhochschule.

Bilson, A. (1995b) Systems monitoring: A constructivist approach. Paper presented at Systems Monitoring in the Human Services 2, Lancaster University.

Bilson, A. (1997) Guidelines for a constructivist approach: Steps towards the adaptation of ideas from family therapy for use in organizations. *Systems Practice,* 10(2): 153–178.

Bilson, A. (2002) Family support: messages from research. *Representing Children,* 15(1): 10–20.

Bilson, A. (2004) Escaping from intrinsically unstable and untrustful relations: Implications of a constitutive ontology for responding to issues of power, *Journal of Cybernetics and Human Knowing.* 11(2): 21–35.

Bilson, A. (ed.) (2005) *Evidence Based Practice in Social Work: International Research and Policy Perspectives.* London: Whiting and Birch.

Bilson, A. (forthcoming) Not just another gadget: Bateson and whole system problems in health and social work. *Kybernetes.*

Bilson, A. and Barker, R. (1998) Looked after children and contact: Reassessing the social work task. *Research, Policy and Planning,* 16(1): 20–27.

Bilson, A. and Markova, G. (2005) "Но вы должны увидеть нх роднтелей!" Казахской Академии труда и социальных отнощений. Almaty.

Bilson, A. and Ross, S. (1999) *Social Work Management and Practice: Systems Principles* (2nd edn). London: Jessica Kingsley.

Bilson, A. and Thorpe D.H. (1988) *Child Care Careers and Their Management – A Systems Perspective.* Glenrothes: Fife Regional Council.

Bilson, A. and White, S. (2004) The limits of governance? Interrogating the tacit dimensions of clinical practice. In A. Gray and S. Harrison (eds) *Governing Medicine.* Maidenhead: Open University Press.

Bion, W. (1967) *Second Thoughts: Selected Papers on Psychoanalysis.* London: Karnac.

Bion, W. (1970) *Attention and Interpretation*. London: Tavistock.

Blagg, H., Hughes, J.A. and Wattam, C. (1989) Introduction: Discovering a child centred approach. In H. Blagg, J.A. Hughes and C. Wattam (eds) *Child Sexual Abuse: Listening, Hearing and Validating the Experiences of Children*, pp. 1–11. U.K.: Longman.

Bleakley, A. (1999) From reflective practice to holistic reflexivity. *Studies in Higher Education*, 24(3): 315–30.

Bloom, B.S. (ed.) (1956) *Taxonomy of Educational Objectives, Vol. 1: Cognitive Domain*. New York: D. McKay.

Bloor, M. (1976) Bishop Berkeley and the adeno-tonsillectomy enigma: an exploration of variation in the social construction of medical disposal. *Sociology*, 10: 43–61.

Bogdewic, S.P. (1992) Participant observation. In B.F. Crabtree and W.L. Miller (eds) *Doing Qualitative Research*, Vol. 3, pp. 45–69. Newbury Park, CA: Sage

Bollas, C. (1987) *The Shadow of the Object*. London: Free Association Books.

Bolton, G. (2001) *Reflective Practice: Writing and Professional Development*. London: Paul Chapman.

Borton, T. (1970) *Reach, Touch and Teach*. London: Hutchinson.

Boud, D. and Garrick, J. (eds) (1999) *Understanding Learning at Work*. London: Routledge.

Boud, D. and Knights, S. (1996) Course design for reflective practice. In N. Gould and I. Taylor (eds) *Reflective Learning for Social Work*. Aldershot: Arena.

Boud, D. and Walker, D. (1993) Barriers to reflection on experience. In D. Boud, R. Cohen and D. Walker (eds) *Using Experience for Learning*, pp. 73–86. Buckingham: SRHE and Open University Press.

Boud, D. and Walker, D. (1998) Promoting reflection in professionals courses: the challenge of context. *Studies in Higher Education*, 23(2): 191–206.

Boud, D., Keogh, R. and Walker, D. (eds) (1984) *Reflection: Turning Experience into Learning*. London: Kogan Page/New York: Nichols.

Boud, D., Cohen, R. and Walker, D. (1993) Introduction: Understanding learning from experience. In D. Boud, R. Cohen and D. Walker (eds.) *Using Experience for Learning*, pp. 1–18. Buckingham: SRHE and Open University Press.

Bourdieu, P. (1977) *Outline of a Theory of Practice*. Cambridge: Cambridge University Press.

Boyd, E.M. and Fales, A.W. (1983) Reflective learning: Key to learning from experience. *Journal of Humanistic Psychology*, 23(2): 99–117.

Bradbury, H. (2004) Doing work that matters despite the obstacles: An interview with Riane Eisler. *Action Research*, 2(2): 209–27.

Bradbury, H. and Reason, P. (2003) Action research: An opportunity for revitalising research purpose and practice. *Qualitative Social Work*, 2(2): 155–75.

Brockbank, A. and McGill, I. (1998) *Facilitating Reflective Learning in Higher Education*. Buckingham: Open University Press.

Brockbank, A., McGill, I. and Beech, N. (eds) (2002) *Reflective Learning in Practice*. Aldershot: Gower.

Brody, C. and Witherell, C. with Donald, K. and Lundblad, R. (1991) Story and voice in the education of professionals. In C. Witherell and N. Noddings (eds) *Stories Lives Tell: Narrative and Dialogue in Education*, pp. 257–78. New York: Teachers College Press.

Brookfield, S. (1991) On ideology, pillage, language and risk: Critical thinking and the tensions of critical practice. *Studies in Continuing Education*, 13(1): 1–14.

Brookfield, S. (1993) Through the lens of learning: How the visceral experience of learning reframes teaching. In D. Boud, R. Cohen and D. Walker (eds) *Using Experience for Learning*, pp. 21–32. Buckingham: SRHE and Open University Press.

Brookfield, S. (1994) Tales from the darkside: A phenomenography of adult critical reflection. *International Journal of Lifelong Learning*, 13(3): 203–16.

Brookfield, S. (1995) *Becoming a Critically Reflective Teacher*. San Francisco: Jossey-Bass.

Brookfield, S. (2000) Transformative learning as ideology critique. In J. Mezirow and associates, *Learning as Transformation: Critical Perspectives on a Theory in Progress*, pp. 125–48. San Francisco: Jossey-Bass.

Brookfield, S. (2001a) Repositioning ideology critique in a critical theory of adult learning. *Adult Education Quarterly*, 52(1): 7–22.

Brookfield, S. (2001b) Unmasking power: Foucault and adult learning. *Canadian Journal for the Study of Adult Education*, 15(1): 1–23.

Brookfield, S. (2005) *The Power of Critical Theory: Liberating Adult Learning and Teaching*. San Francisco: Jossey-Bass.

Buckner, S. (2005) Taking the debate on reflexivity further: psychodynamic team analysis of a BNIM interview. *Journal of Social Work Practice*, 19(1): 59–72.

Burgess, H., Baldwin, M., Dalrymple, J. and Thomas, J (1999) Developing self-assessment in social work education. *Social Work Education*, 18(2): 133–46.

Butler, J. (1990) *Gender Trouble: Feminism and the Subversion of Identity*. London: Routledge.

Cameron, H. (2003) Educating the social work practitioner. *Australian Journal of Adult Learning*, 43(3): 361–79.

Canadian Institutes of Health Research, Natural Sciences and Engineering Research Council of Canada, and Social Sciences and Humanities Research Council of Canada (2005) *Tri-Council Policy Statement: Ethical Conduct for Research Involving Humans.Ottawa: Interagency Secretariat on Research Ethics*. http://www.pre. ethics.gc.ca/english/policystatement/policystatement.cfm (accessed 30 January 2006).

Carper, B.A. (1978) Fundamental patterns of knowing in nursing. *Advances in Nursing Science*, 1: 13–23.

Carr, W. and Kemmis, S. (1986) *Becoming Critical. Education, Knowledge and Action Research* (2nd edn). Geelong, Vic.: Deakin University.

Catterall, M., Maclaran, P. and Stevens, L. (2002) Critical reflection in the marketing curriculum. *Journal of Marketing Education*, 24(3): 184–92.

Chafe, W. (1990) Some things that narrative tells us about the mind. In B.K. Britton and A.D. Pellegrini (eds) *Narrative Thought and Narrative Language*. Hillsdale, NJ: Erlbaum.

Chamberlayne, P., Bornat, J. and Apitzsch, U. (eds) (2004) *Biographical Methods and Professional Practice*. Bristol: Policy Press.

Chambon, A.C., Irving, A. and Epstein, L. (eds) (1999) *Reading Foucault for Social Work*. New York: Columbia University Press.

Chatman, S. (1981) What novels can do that films can't (and vice versa). In W.J. Mitchell (ed.) *On Narrative*. Chicago: University of Chicago Press.

Cherry, N. (1999) *Action Research: A Pathway to Action, Knowledge and Learning*. Melbourne: RMIT Publishing.

Clarke, D.J. (1998) Process recording: of what value is examining nursing interaction through assignment work? *Nurse Education Today*, 18: 138–43.

Clifford, J. and Marcus, G.E. (eds) (1986) *Writing Culture: The Poetics and Politics of Ethnography*. Berkeley: University of California Press.

Clough, P. (2002) *Narratives and Fictions in Educational Research*. Buckingham: Open University Press.

Cole, M. (1994) Outsiders. In R. Sultana and G. Baldacchino (eds) *Maltese Society: A Sociological Inquiry*, pp. 595–616. Msida, Malta: Mireva.

Cordes, C. (1998) Community-based projects help scholars build public support. *Chronicle of Higher Education*, 45: A37. Posted on the LOKA website, www.loka.org.

Cortazzi, M. (1993) *Narrative Analysis*. London: Falmer Press.

Cousins, J.B. and Earl, L.M. (1992) The case for participatory evaluation. *Educational Evaluation and Policy Analysis*, 14(4): 397–418.

Cranton, P. (2000) Individual differences and transformative learning. In J. Mezirow and associates, *Learning as Transformation: Critical Perspectives on a Theory in Progress*. San Francisco: Jossey-Bass.

Cowan, J. (1998) *On Becoming an Innovative University Teacher: Reflection in Action*. Buckingham: SRHE and Open University Press.

Crawford, F. (1976) The story of Looma. Unpublished MSW dissertation, University of Western Australia.

Crawford, F. (1989) *Jalinardi Ways: Whitefellas Working in Aboriginal Communities*. Perth: Curtin.

Crawford, F. and Gacik, Z. (1998) *The Art of Researching with People*. Perth: Curtin University Media Productions.

Crawford, F., Leitmann, S. and Dickinson, J. (2002) Mirroring meaning making: Narrative ways of reflecting on practice for action. *Qualitative Social Work*, 1(2): 170–89.

Cross, V., Liles, C., Conduit, J., and Price, J. (2004) Linking reflective practice to evidence of competence: A workshop for allied health professionals. *Reflective Practice*, 5(1): 3–31.

Cunliffe, A. and Easterby-Smith, M. (2004) From experiential learning to practical reflexivity: experiential learning as lived experience. In M. Reynolds and R. Vince (eds) *Organizing Reflection*. Aldershot: Ashgate.

de Shazer, S. (1988) *Clues: Investigating Solutions in Brief Therapy*. New York: W.W. Norton.

Denzin, N. (1989) *Interpretive Interactionism*. Newbury Park, CA: Sage.

Dewey, J. (1910) *How We Think*. Lexington, MA: D.C. Heath.

Dewey, J. (1916) *Democracy and Education: An Introduction to the Philosophy of Education*, The Free Press

Dewey, J. (1933) *How We Think: A Restatement of the Relation of Reflective Thinking to the Educative Process*. Boston: Heath.

Dewey, J. (1974) *John Dewey on Education: Selected Writings* (R.D. Archambault, ed.). Chicago: University of Chicago Press.

Dingwall, R. (1977) 'Atrocity stories' and professional relationships. *Sociology of Work and Occupations*, 4: 371–96.

Dolitsky, M. and Bensimon-Choukroun, G. (2000) Introduction: Special issue on codeswitching. *Journal of Pragmatics*, 32: 1255–7.

Dominelli, L. 1991, 'What's in a name?' A comment on 'Puritans and Paradigms'. *Social Work and Social Sciences Review*, 2(3): 231–5.

Donnelly, T.T. (2002) Representing 'others': Avoiding the reproduction of unequal social relations in research. *Nurse Researcher*, 9(3): 57–67.

Eade, D. (1997) *Capacity-Building: An Approach to People-Centred Development*. Oxford: Oxfam.

Edwards, D. (1997) *Discourse and Cognition*. London: Sage.

Edwards, R., Ranson, S. and Strain, M. (2002) Reflexivity: towards a theory of lifelong learning. *International Journal of Lifelong Education*, 21(6): 525–36.

Ehrenzweig, A. (1967) *The Hidden Order of Art*. London: Weidenfeld and Nicolson.

Ellermann, A. (1998) Can discourse analysis enable reflective social work practice? *Social Work Education*, 17(1): 36–44.

Emerson, R.M., Fretz, R.I. and Shaw, L.L. (1995) *Writing Ethnographic Fieldnotes*. Chicago: University of Chicago Press.

Ennis, R. (1991) Critical thinking: A streamlined conception. *Teaching Philosophy*, 14(1): 5–25.

Eraut, M. (1994) *Developing Professional Knowledge and Competence*. London: Falmer Press.

Everett, A., Hardiker, P., Littlewood, J. and Mullender, A. (1992) *Applied Research for Better Practice*. London: Macmillan.

Fahlberg, V. (1994) *A Child's Journey Through Placement*. London: British Agencies for Adoption and Fostering.

Fawcett, B., Featherstone, B., Fook, J. and Rossiter, A. (eds) (2000) *Practice and Research in Social Work: Postmodern Feminist Perspectives*. London: Routledge

Fay, B. (1977) How people change themselves: the relationship between critical theory and its audience. In T. Ball (ed.) *Political Theory and Praxis*, pp. 200–69. Minneapolis: University of Minnesota Press.

Featherstone, B. (2005) Feminism, child welfare and child protection: a critical analysis and review. Unpublished PhD thesis, University of Huddersfield.

Featherstone, B. and Trinder, L. (1997) Familiar subjects? Domestic violence and child welfare. *Child and Family Social Work*, 2(3) 147–61.

Felder, R.M. and Silverman L.K. (1988) Learning and teaching styles in engineering education. *Journal of Engineering Education*, 78(7): 674–81.

Ferguson, H. (2001) Social work, individualization and life politics. *British Journal of Social Work*, 31: 41–55.

Fetterman, D.M. (2000) *Foundations of Empowerment Evaluation*. Thousand Oaks, CA: Sage.

Fine, E. and Speer, J. (1977) A new look at performance. *Communication Monographs*, 44: 374–389.

Fleck, L. (1979) *Genesis and Development of a Scientific Fact*. Chicago: University of Chicago Press. First published in 1935.

Fook, J. (ed.) (1996) *The Reflective Researcher: Social Workers' Theories of Practice Research*. Sydney: Allen & Unwin.

Fook, J. (1999a) Critical reflectivity in education and practice. In B. Pease and J. Fook (eds) *Transforming Social Work Practice: Postmodern Critical Perspectives*, pp. 195–208. London: Routledge.

Fook, J. (1999b) Reflexivity as method. In J. Daly, A. Kellehear and E. Willis (eds). *Annual Review of Health Social Sciences*, 9: 11–20.

Fook, J. (2002) *Social Work: Critical Theory and Practice*. London: Sage.

Fook, J. (2003) Critical social work: the current issues. *Qualitative Social Work*, 2: 123–30.

Fook, J. (2004a) Critical reflection and organizational learning and change: A case study. In N. Gould and M. Baldwin (eds) *Social Work, Critical Reflection and the Learning Organization*. Aldershot: Ashgate.

Fook, J. (2004b) Critical reflection and transformative possibilities. In L. Davies and P. Leonard (eds) *Scepticism/Emancipation: Social Work in a Corporate Era*. Avebury: Ashgate.

Fook, J. (forthcoming) Reflective practice and critical reflective. In J. Lishman (ed.) *Handbook of Theory for Practice Teachers* (2nd edn). London: Jessica Kingsley.

Fook, J., Ryan, M., and Hawkins, L. (2000) *Professional Expertise: Practice, Theory and Education for Working in Uncertainty*. London: Whiting and Birch.

Foucault, M. (1972) *The Archaeology of Knowledge*. New York: Harper & Row.

Foucault, M. (1980) *Power/Knowledge: Selected Interviews and Other Writings 1972–1977* (ed. C. Gordon). Hemel Hempstead: Harvester Wheatsheaf.

Foucault, M. (1981) Questions of method. *Ideology and Consciousness*, 8: 13–14.

Foucault, M. (1983) Structuralism and poststructuralism: An interview with Gerard Raulet. *Telos: A Quarterly Journal of Critical Thoughts*, 55(Spring): 195–211.

Foucault, M. (1990) *The History of Sexuality, Vol. 1: An Introduction*. New York: Random House.

Foucault, M. (1994) An interview with Simon Riggins. In P. Rabinow (ed.) *Michel Foucault: Ethics: The Essential Works*. London: Penguin.

Foucault, M. (1997) *Madness And Civilization: A History of Insanity in the Age of Reason*. London: Routledge.

Foucault, M. (1999) Social work, social control, and normalization: Roundtable discussion with Michael Foucault. In A.C. Chambon, A. Irving and L. Epstein (eds) *Reading Foucault for Social Work*. New York: Columbia University Press.

Fox, N. (1999) *Beyond Health: Postmodernism and Embodiment*. London: Free Association Books.

Fox, R. (1991) *The Inner Sea – The Mediterranean and its People*. London: Quality Paperbacks Direct.

Frank, A. (1995) *The Wounded Storyteller: Body, Illness and Ethics*. Chicago: University of Chicago Press.

Freire, P. (1970) *Pedagogy of the Oppressed*. New York: Seabury.

Freire, P. (1972) *Pedagogy of the Oppressed*. London: Penguin.

Freshwater, D. (2002) *Therapeutic Nursing: Improving Patient Care Through Self-awareness and Reflection*. London: Sage.

Froggett, L. (2005) Social work, art and the politics of recognition. *Social Work and Social Science Review*, 11(3): 29–51.

Froggett, L. and Chamberlayne, P. (2004) Narratives of Social Enterprise: from biography to practice and policy critique. *Qualitative Social Work*, 3(1): 61–77.

Froggett, L. and Wengraf, T. (2004) Interpreting interviews in the light of research team dynamics: a study of Nila's biographic narrative. *Critical Psychology*, 10: 94–122.

Froggett, L., Chamberlayne, P., Buckner, S, Wengraf, T. (2005) The Bromley by Bow Centre research and evaluation project: integrated working, focus on older people. University of Central Lancashire. http://www.uclan.ac.uk/facs/health/-socialwork/bromleybybow/index.htm

Frost, S. and Cliff, D. (2003) Narrative approaches to research in community nursing. *British Journal of Community Nursing* 9(4). 172–8.

Frost S and Horrocks C (2004) Developing cultural sensitivity by mediating the 'casting' and 'recasting' in health. Paper presented to the Tenth Annual Qualitative Health Rsearch Conference, 30 April–4 May, Banff, Alberta, Canada.

Gardner Chloro, P., Reeva C. and Cheshire, J. (2000) Parallel patterns? A comparison of monolingual speech and bilingual codeswitching discourse. *Journal of Pragmatics*, 32: 1305–41.

Garfinkel, H. (1967) *Studies in Ethnomethodology*, Cambridge: Polity.

Garfinkel, H. (1984) *Studies in Ethnomethodology*. Malden, MA: Polity Press/Blackwell Publishing.

Geertz, C. (1973) *The Interpretation of Cultures*. New York: Basic Books.

George, E., Iveson, C. and Ratner, H. (1999) *Problems to Solutions* (rev. edn). London: Brief Therapy Press.

Gergen, K. (1985) The social constructionist movement in modern psychology. *American Psychologist*, 40: 266–75.

Gergen, K. (1991) *The Saturated Self: Dilemmas of Identity in Contemporary Life*. New York: Basic Books.

Ghaye, T. (2004) Editorial: Reflection for spritual practice? *Reflective Practice*, 5(3): 291–5.

Ghaye, T. (2005) *Developing the Reflective Health Care Organisation*. Oxford: Blackwell.

Ghaye, T. and Lillyman, S. (1997) *Learning Journals and Critical Incidents: Reflective Practice for Health Care Professionals*. Dinton: Quay Books.

Ghaye, T. and Lillyman, S. (2000a) *Reflection: Principles and Practice for Healthcare Professionals*. Dinton: Quay Books.

Ghaye, T. and Lillyman, S. (eds) (2000b) *Caring Moments: The Discourse of Reflective Practice*. Dinton: Quay Books.

Ghaye, T. and Lillyman, S. (eds) (2000c) *Effective Clinical Supervision: The Role of Reflection*. Dinton: Quay Books.

Gherardi, S. and Nicolini, D. (2003) To transfer is to transform: The circulation of safety knowledge. In D. Nicolini, S. Gherardi and D. Yanow (eds) *Knowing in Organizations: A Practice-Based Approach*, pp 204–24. Armonk, NY: M.E. Sharpe.

Gherardi, S., Nicolini, D. and Odella, F. (1998) Towards a social understanding of how people learn in organizations. *Management Learning*, 29(3): 273–97.

Gibbs, G.R. (2003) *How to Produce Data by Ethnography and Observational Research* London: Sage.

Giddens, A. (1991) *Modernity and Self-Identity*. Cambridge: Polity.

Giddens, A. (1992) *The Transformation of Intimacy*. Cambridge: Polity.

Gilbert, G.N. and Mulkay, M.J. (1984) *Opening Pandora's Box: A Sociological Analysis of Scientists' Discourse*. Cambridge: Cambridge University Press.

Giorgi, A. (1985) Sketch of a psychological methods. In A. Georgi (ed,) *Phenomenology and Psychological Research*, pp 8–22. Pittsburgh: Duquesne University Press.

Glaser, B. and Strauss, A. (1967) *The Discovery of Grounded Theory. Strategies for Qualitative Research*. Chicago: Aldine.

Goodman, N. (1978) *Ways of Worldmaking*. Indianapolis: Hackett.

Gould, N. (2004) Introduction: The learning organisation and reflective practice – the emergence of a concept. In N. Gould and M. Baldwin (eds) *Social Work, Critical Reflection and the Learning Organization*, pp. 1–9. Aldershot: Ashgate.

Gould, N., and Baldwin, M. (eds) (2004a) *Social Work, Critical Reflection and the Learning Organization*. Aldershot: Ashgate.

Gould, N. and Baldwin, M. (eds) (2004b) *The Learning Organization and Reflective Practice – the Emergence of a Concept*. Aldershot: Ashgate.

Gould, N. and Taylor, I. (eds) (1996) *Reflective Learning for Social Work*. Aldershot: Arena Ashgate.

Grace, A.P. (1997) Where critical postmodern theory meets practice: Working in the intersection of instrumental, social, and cultural education. *Studies in Continuing Education*, 19(1): 51–70.

Griffen, M.L. (2003) Using critical incidents to promote and assess reflective thinking in pre-service teachers. *Reflective Practice*, 4(2): 207–20.

Gubrium, J.F. and Holstein, J.A. (1997) *The New Language of Qualitative Research*. New York: Oxford University Press.

Gumperz, J. (ed.) (1982a) *Language and Social Identity*. Cambridge: Cambridge University Press

Gumperz, J. (1982b) *Discourse Strategies*. Cambridge: Cambridge University Press.

Habermass, J. (1981) *Theorie de kommunikataven Handlens*, Bd. 1–2. Frankfurt-a-M: Suhrkamp Verlag.

Hacking, I. (1999) *The Social Construction of What?* Cambridge, MA: Harvard University Press.

Hall, B. (1992) From margins to center? The development and purpose of participatory research. *American Sociologist*, 23(4): 15–28.

Hall, C. (1997) *Social Work as Narrative: Storytelling and Persuasion in Professional Texts*. Aldershot: Ashgate

Hall, C. and White, S. (2005) Looking inside professional practice: Discourse, narrative and ethnographic approaches to social work and counselling. *Qualitative Social Work*, 4: 379–390.

Hall, M.H., Phillips, S.D., Meillat, C. and Pickering, D. (2003) *Assessing Performance: Evaluation Practices and Perspectives in Canada's Voluntary Sector*. Toronto: Canadian Centre for Philanthropy; and Ottawa: Centre for Voluntary Sector Research and Development.

Hall, S. (1992) Cultural studies and its theoretical legacies. In L. Grossberg, C. Nelson and P. Treichler (eds) *Cultural Studies*, pp. 277–94. London: Routledge.

Hamlin, K.D. (2004) Beginning the journey: Supporting reflection in early field experiences. *Journal of Reflective Practice*, 5(2). 167–179.

Hammersley, M. and Atkinson, P. (1995) *Ethnography: Principles in Practice* (2nd edn). London: Routledge.

Hargreaves, A. (1981) Contrastive rhetoric and extremist talk: teachers, hegemony and the educationalist context. In L. Barton and S. Walker (eds) *Schools, Teachers and Teaching*. Lewes: Falmer Press.

Hargreaves, J. (2004) So how do you feel about that? Assessing reflective practice. *Nurse Education Today*, 24(3): 196–201.

Harré, R. (1990) Some narrative conventions in scientific discourse. In C. Nash (ed.) *Narrative in Culture: The Uses of Storytelling in the Sciences, Philosophy, and Literature*. London: Routledge.

Hart, M.V. (1990) Liberation through consciousness raising. In J. Mezirow and associates, *Fostering Critical Reflection in Adulthood: A Guide to Transformative and Emancipatory Learning*. San Francisco: Jossey-Bass.

Hartman, A. (1990) Many ways of knowing. *Social Work*, 35(1): 3–4.

Hassard, J. and Parker, M. (eds) (1993) *Postmodernism and Organizations*. London: Sage.

Hatton, N. and Smith, D. (1995) Reflection in teacher education: Toward definition and implementation. *Teaching and Teacher Education*, 11: 33–49.

Hawke, S. and Gallagher, M. (1989) *Noonkanbah: Whose Land, Whose Law?* Fremantle: Fremantle Arts Centre Press.

Heron, B. (2005) Self-reflection in critical social work practice: Subjectivity and the possibilities of resistance. *Journal of Reflective Practice*, 6(3).

Heron, J. (ed.) (1985) *The Role of Reflection in Co-operative Inquiry*. London: Kogan Page.

Heron, J. (1996) *Co-operative Inquiry Research into the Human Condition*. London: Sage.

Heron, J. and Reason, P. (1997) A participatory inquiry paradigm. *Qualitative Inquiry*, 3(3): 274–94.

Heron, J. and Reason, P. (2001) The practice of co-operative inquiry. In P. Reason and H. Bradbury (eds), *Handbook of Action Research*, pp. 179–99. London: Sage.

Hess, P.McC. and Mullen, E.J. (eds) (1995) *Practitioner–Researcher Partnerships: Building Knowledge from, in, and for Practice*. Washington, DC: NASW Press.

Hilderbrand, J. (1995) Learning through supervision. In M. Yelloly and M. Henkel (eds) *Learning and Teaching in Social Work*, pp. 172–88. London: Jessica Kingsley.

Hillier, Y. (2002) *Reflective Teaching in Further and Adult Education*. London: Continuum.

Houston, S. (2001) Beyond social constructionism: Critical realism and social work. *British Journal of Social Work*, 31: 845–61.

How, A. (2003) *Critical Theory*. Basingstoke: Palgrave.

Howe, D. (1987) *An Introduction to Social Work Theory*. Aldershot: Wildwood House.

Howe, D. (1994a) *An Introduction To Social Work Theory*. Aldershot: Arena.

Howe, D. (1994b) Modernity, postmodernity and social work. *British Journal of Social Work*, 24(5): 513–32.

Hughes, E.C. (1984) The humble and the proud: The comparative study of occupations. In E.C. Hughes, *The Sociological Eye*, pp. 417–27. New Brunswick, NJ: Transaction Books.

Hughes, L. and Pengelly, P. (1997) *Staff Supervision in a Turbulent Environment: Managing Process and Task in Front-Line Services*. London: Jessica Kingsley.

Hunt, C. (2001) Shifting shadows: Metaphors and maps for facilitating reflective practice. *Reflective Practice*, 3(1): 275–87.

Huotari, R. (2003) A perspective on ethical reflection in multiprofessional care. *Reflective Practice*, 4(2): 121–38.

Hyde, L. (1998) *Trickster Makes This World: Mischief, Myth and Art*. New York: North Point Press.

Issitt, M. (1999) Towards the development of anti-oppressive reflective practice: The challenge for multi-disciplinary working. *Journal of Practice Teaching*, 2(2): 21–36.

Issitt, M. (2000) Critical professional and reflective practice. In J. Batsleer and B. Humphries (eds), *Welfare, Exclusion and Political Agency*, pp. 116–33. London: Routledge.

Ixer, G. (1999) There's no such thing as reflection. *British Journal of Social Work*, 29(4): 513–27.

Ixer, G. (2000) Assessing reflective practice: New research findings. *Journal of Practice Teaching in Health and Social Work*, 2(3): 19–27.

Jalongo, M. and Isenberg, J. with Gerbracht, G. (1995) *Teachers' Stories: From Personal Narrative to Professional Insight*. San Francisco: Jossey-Bass.

Jasper, M. (2003) *Beginning Reflective Practice*. Cheltenham: Nelson Thornes.

Jennings, L. (1992) Workplace trainers as reflective practitioners: Changing mind-sets. Paper presented at the 'What Future for Technical and Vocational Education and Training?' conference, Melbourne.

Johns, C. (1995) Framing learning through reflection within Carper's fundamental ways of knowing in nursing. *Journal of Advanced Nursing*, 22: 226–34.

Johns, C. (1998) *Transforming Nursing through Reflective Practice*. Oxford: Blackwell.

Johns. C. (2000) *Becoming a Reflective Practitioner: A Reflective and Holistic Approach to Clinical Nursing, Practice Development and Clinical Supervision*. Oxford: Blackwell.

Johns, C. (2002) *Guided Reflection: Advancing Practice*. Oxford: Blackwell Science.

Johns, C. (2004) *Becoming a Reflective Practitioner* (2nd edn). Oxford: Blackwell.

Johns, C. (2005) Balancing the winds. *Reflective Practice*, 6(1): 67–84.

Johns, C. and Freshwater, D. (eds) (1998) *Transforming Nursing Through Reflective Practice*. Oxford: Blackwell Science.

Kearney, R. (2002) *On Stories*. London: Routledge.

Keating, E. (2001) The ethnography of communication. In P. Atkinson, A. Coffey, S. Delamont, J. Lofland and L. Lofland (eds) *Handbook of Ethnography*, pp. 285–301. London: Sage.

Keeney, B. (2004) Tricksters of the world, unite! How going crazy will help save America, *Utne*, May/June. http://utne.com/pub/2004_123/features/11185-1.html (accessed 18 January 2006).

Kellett, P. and Dalton, D. (2001) *Managing Conflict in a Negotiated World*. Thousand Oaks, CA: Sage.

Kember, D. (2001) *Reflective Teaching and Learning in the Health Professions*. Oxford: Blackwell.

Kemmis, S. (1998) System and lifeworld, and the conditions of learning in late modernity. *Curriculum Studies*, 6(3): 269–305.

Kemmis, S. (2001) Exploring the relevance of critical theory for action research: Emancipatory action research in the footsteps of Jürgen Habermas. In P.A. Reason and H. Bradbury (eds) *Handbook of Action Research: Participative Inquiry and Practice*, pp. 91–102. London: Sage.

Kenny, M.A. (2004) Looking at you looking at me looking at you: Learning through reflection in a law school clinic. *E LAW – Murdoch University Electronic Journal of Law*, 11(1).

King, P.M. and Kitchener, K.S. (1994) *Developing Reflective Judgment*. San Francisco: Jossey-Bass.

Kinsella, E.A. (2001) Reflections on reflective practice. *Canadian Journal of Occupational Therapy*, 68(3).

Kirby, S. and McKenna, K. (1989) *Experience, Research, Social Change: Methods from the Margins*. Toronto: Garamond Press.

Knorr-Cetina, K. (1981) *The Manufacture of Knowledge*. Oxford: Pergamon.

Kolb, D. (1984) *Experiential Learning: Experience as a Source of Learning and Development*. Englewood Cliffs, NJ: Prentice Hall.

Kondrat, M.E. (1999) Who is the 'self' in self-aware: Professional self-awareness from a critical theory perspective. *Social Service Review*, 3: 451–77.

Ku, H.B. and Yau, Y.L. (1997) Study of the life histories of Hong Kong middle-aged women and employment policy: Problems and implications. *Taiwan Sociological Research*, 26: 168–207 (in Chinese).

Kuhn, T.S. (1962) *The Structure of Scientific Revolution*. Chicago: University of Chicago Press.

Kuhn, T.S. (1970) *The Structure of Scientific Revolutions* (2nd edn). Chicago: University of Chicago Press.

Kvale, S. (1996) *Interviews: An Introduction to Qualitative Research Interviewing*. London: Sage.

Labonte, R. and Feather, J. (1996) *Handbook on Using Stories in Health Promotion Practice*. Ottawa: Health Canada.

Langellier, K. (1989) Personal narratives: Perspectives on theory and research. *Text and Performance Quarterly*, 9(4): 243–76.

Langer, A.M. (2002) Reflecting on practice: Using learning journals in higher and continuing education. *Teaching in Higher Education*, 7(3): 337–51.

Latimer, J. (2000) The *Conduct of Care: Understanding Nursing Practice*. Oxford: Blackwell.

Latour, B. (1987) *Science in Action*. Milton Keynes: Open University Press.

Latour, B. and Woolgar, S. (1986) *Laboratory Life: The Construction of Social Facts*. Princeton, NJ: Princeton University Press.

Lauvås, P. and Handal, G. (2000) *Veiledning og praktisk yrkesteori*. Oslo: J.W. Cappelens Forlag.

Lave, J. and Wenger, E. (1991) *Situated Learning: Legitimate Peripheral Participation*. Cambridge: Cambridge University Press.

Lawler, J. and Bilson, A (2004) Towards a more reflexive research aware practice:

The influence and potential of professional and team culture. *Social Work and Social Science Review*, 11(1): 52–69.

Lawson, S. and Sachdev, I. (2000) Codeswitching in Tunisia: Attitudinal and behavioural dimensions. *Journal of Pragmatics*, 32: 1343–61.

Lee, S.K.F. and Loughran, J. (2000) Fascilitating pre service teachers reflection through a school base teaching program. *Reflective Practice*, 1(1): 69–89.

Lehmann, J. (2003a) Managing organisational change in rural social and community services: The nature of the experience. PhD thesis, RMIT University, Melbourne.

Lehmann, J. (2003b) Practice-based stories: Tools for Teaching and Learning. *Children Australia*, 28(1): 29–33.

Lehmann, J. (2003c) *The Harveys and Other Stories*. Bendigo, Vic.: St Luke's Innovative Resources.

Lehmann, J. (2003d) Neat and tidy. Unpublished.

Lesnick, A. (2005) The mirror in motion: Redefining reflective practice in an undergraduate fieldwork seminar. *Reflective Practice*, 6(1): 33–48.

Leung, D.Y.P. and Kember, D. (2003) The relationship between approaches to learning and reflection upon practice. *Educational Psychology: An International Journal of Experimental Educational Psychology*, 23(1): 61–71.

Li, V.C. and Wang, S.X. (2001) Capacity building to improve women's health in rural China. *Social Science and Medicine*, 52(2): 279–92.

Lieblich, A., Tuval-Mashiach, R. and Zilber, T. (1998) *Narrative Research*. London: Sage.

Lincoln, Y. and Guba, E. (1985) *Naturalistic Inquiry*. Beverley Hills, CA: Sage.

Longenecker, R. (2002) The jotter wallet: Invoking reflective practice in a family practice residency program. *Reflective Practice*, 3(2): 219–24.

Loreman, T., Deppeler, J., and Harvey, D. (2005) *Inclusive Education: A Practical Guide to Supporting Diversity in the Classroom*. London: Routledge-Falmer.

Loughran, J.J. (2002) Effective reflective practice: In search of meaning in learning about teaching. *Journal of Teacher Education*, 53(1): 33–43.

Lovelock, R. and Powell, J. (2004) Habermas and Foucault for social work: Practice of critical reflection. In R. Lovelock, K. Lyons and J. Powell (eds) *Reflecting on Social Work: Discipline and Profession*, pp. 181–223. Aldershot: Ashgate.

Lowe, P. and Kerr, C. (1998) Learning by reflection: The effect on educational outcomes. *Journal of Advanced Nursing*, 27(5): 1030–3.

Malta Gay Rights Movement (2003) *Sexual Orientation Discrimination in Malta: A Report on Discrimination, Harassment, and Violence against Malta's Gay, Lesbian and Bisexual Community*. Mosta, Malta: Union Press.

Mamede, S. and Schmidt, H.G. (2004) The structure of reflective practice in medicine. *Medical Education*, 38(12): 1302–8.

Marsick, V. (1987) *Learning in the Workplace*. London: Croom Helm.

Marsick, V. (1990) Action learning and reflection in the workplace. In J. Mezirow and associates, *Fostering Critical Reflection in Adulthood: A Guide to Transformative and Emancipatory Learning*, pp. 23–46. San Francisco: Jossey-Bass.

Marton, F., Hounwell, D. and Entwhistle, N. (1997) *The Experience of Learning: Implications for Teaching and Studying in Higher Education*. Edinburgh: Scottish Academic Press.

Mattingly, C. (1998) *Healing Drama and Clinical Plots: The Narrative Structure of Experience*. Cambridge: Cambridge University Press.

Mattinson, J. (1975) *The Reflection Process in Case-Work Supervision*. London: Institute of Marital Studies.

Maturana, H.R. (1988) Reality: The search for objectivity or the quest for a compelling argument. *Irish Journal of Psychology*, 9: 25–82.

Maturana, H.R. (1980) Afterword. In H.R. Maturana and F.G. Varela, *Autopoiesis and Cognition: The Realization of the Living*. Dordecht: Reidel.

Maturana, H.R. and Varela, F.G. (1998) *The Tree of Knowledge: The Biological Roots of Human Understanding*: (rev. edn). Boston: Shambala.

Maturana, H.R. and Poerksen, B. (2004) *From Being to Doing: The Origins of the Biology of Cognition*. Heidelberg: Carl-Auer Verlag.

McCloskey, D.N. (1990) Storytelling in economics. In C. Nash (ed.) *Narrative in Culture: The Uses of Storytelling in the Sciences, Philosophy, and Literature*. London: Routledge.

McDermott, F. (2002) *Inside Groupwork*. Sydney: Allen & Unwin.

McDrury, J. and Alterio, M. (2003) *Learning through Storytelling in Higher Education*. London: Kogan Page.

McGill, I. and Beatty, L. (1992) *Action Learning*. London: Kogan Page.

McGoldrick, M. and Gerson, R. (1985) *Genograms in Family Assessment*. New York: W.W. Norton.

McIlvain, H., Crabtree, B., Medder, J., Strange, K.C. and Miller, W.L. (1998) Using practice genograms to understand and describe practice configurations. *Family Medicine*, 30(7): 490–6.

McMaster, T., Wastell, D. and Zinner Henrikson, H. (2005) Fooling around: The corporate jester as effective change agent for technological innovation. In R. Baskerville, L. Mathiassen, J. Pries-Heje and J. DeGross, *Business Agility and Information Technology Diffusion*. New York: Springer.

McPhee D.M. and Bronstein, L. (2002) Constructing meaning: strengthening the policy–practice link. *Social Work Education*, 21(6): 651–62.

Mead, M. (1968) Cybernetics of cybernetics. In H. von Foerster, J.D. White, L.J. Peterson and J.K. Russell (eds) *Purposive Systems: The First Annual Symposium of the American Society for Cybernetics*. New York: Spartan.

Melnyk, B and Fineout-Overholt, E (2005) *Evidence-Based Practice in Nursing and Health Care*. Philadelphia: Lippincott, Williams and Wilkins.

Mezirow, J. (1990) How critical reflection triggers transformative learning. In J. Mezirow and associates, *Fostering Critical Reflection in Adulthood: A Guide to Transformative and Emancipatory Learning*. San Francisco: Jossey-Bass.

Mezirow, J. (1991) *Transformative Dimensions of Adult Learning*. San Francisco: Jossey-Bass.

Mezirow, J. and associates (1990) *Fostering Critical Reflection in Adulthood: A Guide to Transformative and Emancipatory Learning*. San Francisco: Jossey-Bass.

Mezirow, J. and associates (2000) *Learning as Transformation: Critical Perspectives on a Theory in Progress*. San Francisco: Jossey-Bass.

Miller, G. (1994) Toward ethnographies of institutional discourse: proposal and suggestions. *Journal of Contemporary Ethnography*, 23(3): 280–306.

Milner, M. (1950) *On Not Being Able to Paint*. London: Heinemann.

Mills, C.W. (1959) *The Sociological Imagination*. London: Oxford University Press.

Moon, J. (1999) *Reflection in Learning and Professional Development: Theory and Practice*. London: Kogan Page.

Morrison, K. (1996) 'Developing reflective practice in higher degree students through a learning journal. *Studies in Higher Education*, 21(3): 317–32.

Moyer, A., Coristine, M., MacLean, L. and Meyer, M. (1999) A model for building collective capacity in community-based programs: The Elderly in Need Project. *Public Health Nursing*, 16(3): 205–14.

Napier, L. and Fook, J. (2000) Reflective practice in social work. In L. Napier and J. Fook (eds) *Breakthroughs in Practice: Theorising Critical Moments in Social Work*, pp. 1–15. London: Whiting and Birch.

National Social Work Qualifications Board (2001) *Annual Report 2001*. Dublin: NSWQB.

National Social Work Qualifications Board (2002) *Social Work Posts in Ireland*. Dublin: NSWQB.

Nelson, S. (2004) Expertise or performance? Questioning the rhetoric of contemporary narrative use in nursing. *Journal of Advanced Nursing*, 47(6): 631–8.

Noddings, N. (1991) Stories in dialogue. In C. Witherell and N. Noddings (eds) *Stories Lives Tell: Narrative and Dialogue in Education*, pp. 157–70. New York: Teachers College Press.

Nussbaum, M. (1997) *Cultivating Humanity: A Classical Defence of Reform in Liberal Education*. Cambridge, MA: Harvard University Press.

Nussbaum, M. (2001) *Upheavals of Thought: The Intelligence of Emotions*. Cambridge: Cambridge University Press.

Nussbaum, M. (2004) *Hiding from Humanity: Disgust, Shame and the Law*. Princeton, NJ: Princeton University Press.

O'Connor, A., Hyde, A. and Treacy, M. (2003) Nurse teachers' constructions of reflection and reflective practice. *Reflective Practice*, 4(2): 107–19.

Oevermann, U. (2001) Das Verstehen des Fremden als Scheideweg hermeneutischer Methoden in den Erfahrungswissenschaften. *Zeitschrift für qualitative Bildungs-, Beratungs- und Sozialforschung*, 2(1): 67–92.

O'Reilly Mizzi, S. (1994) Gossip: a means of social control. In R. Sultana and G. Baldacchino (eds) *Maltese Society: A Sociological Inquiry*, pp 369–82. Msida, Malta: Mireva.

Osmond, J. and Darlington, Y. (2005) Reflective analysis: Techniques for facilitating reflection. *Australian Social Work*, 58(1): 3–14.

Palmer, A., Burns, S. and Bulman, C. (1994) *Reflective Practice in Nursing: The Growth of the Professional Practitioner.* Oxford. Blackwell Scientific.

Papell, C. and Skolnik, L. (1992) The reflective practitioner: A contemporary paradigm's relevance for social work education. *Journal of Social Work Education*, 28(1): 18–25.

Parker, S. (1997) *Reflective Teaching in the Postmodern World.* Buckingham: Open University Press.

Pask, G. (1975) *Conversation, Cognition and Learning.* Amsterdam: Elsevier.

Payne, M. (2005) *Modern Social Work Theory* (3rd edn). Basingstoke: Palgrave.

Pedro, J.Y. (2005) Reflection in teacher education: Exploring pre-service teachers' meanings of reflective practice. *Reflective Practice*, 6(1): 49–66.

Pennycook, A. (1998) *English and the Discourses of Colonialism.* London: Routledge.

Perriton, L. (2004) A reflection of what exactly? Questioning the use of 'critical reflection' in management education contexts. In M. Reynolds and R. Vince (eds) *Organising Reflection.* Aldershot: Ashgate.

Pierson, C. (1998) *Beyond the Welfare State* (2nd edn) Cambridge: Polity Press.

Pinsky, L.E. and Irby, D.M. (1997) 'If at first you don't succeed': Using failure to improve teaching. *Academic Medicine*, 72(11): 973–6.

Pithouse, A. (1987) *Social Work: The Social Organisation of an Invisible Trade.* Aldershot: Avebury Gower.

Plath, D., English, B., Connors, L. and Beveridge, A. (1999) Evaluating the outcomes of intensive critical thinking instruction for social work students. *Social Work Education*, 18(2): 207–17.

Plummer, J. (2000) *Municipalities and Community Participation: A Sourcebook for Capacity Building.* London: Earthscan.

Plummer, K. (2001) *Documents of Life 2: An Invitation to Critical Humanism.* London: Sage.

Polanyi, L. (1985) *Telling the American Story: A Structural and Cultural Analysis of Conversational Storytelling.* Norwood, NJ: Ablex.

Polanyi, M. (1970) *The Tacit Dimension.* New York: Doubleday.

Polkinghorne, D.E. (1987) *Narrative Knowing and the Human Sciences,* Albany: State University of New York Press.

Pololi, L., Clay, M., Lipkin, M., Kaplan, C. and Frankel, R. (2001) Reflections on integrating theories of adult education into a medical school faculty development course. *Medical Teacher*, 23(3): 276–83.

Preskill, H. and Torres, R. (1999) Building capacity for organizational learning through evaluative inquiry. *Evaluation*, 5(1): 42–60.

Pyett, P. (2002) Towards reconciliation in indigenous health research: The responsibilities of the non-indigenous researcher. *Contemporary Nurse*, 14(1): 56–65.

Quicke, J. (1997) Reflexivity, community and education for the learning society. *Curriculum Studies*, 5(2): 139–61.

Radin, P. (1956) *The Trickster: A Study in American Indian Mythology*. New York: Schocken Books.

Reason, P. and Bradbury, H. (eds) (2001) *Handbook on Action Research*. London: Sage.

Redmond, B. (2004) *Reflection in Action: Developing Reflective Practice in Health and Social Services*. Aldershot: Ashgate

Rees, C., Shepherd, M., and Chamberlain, S. (2005) The utility of reflective portfolios as a method of assessing first year medical students' personal and professional development. *Reflective Practice*, 6(1): 3–14.

Reinharz, S. (1992) *Feminist Methods in Social Research*. New York: Oxford University Press.

Reissner, S. (2004) Learning by story-telling? Narratives in the study of work-based learning. *Journal of Adult and Continuing Education*, 10(2): 99–113.

Resnick, L.B. (1987) *Education and Learning to Think*. Washington, DC: National Academy Press.

Reynolds, M. (1998) Reflection and critical reflection in management learning. *Management Learning*, 29(2): 183–200.

Reynolds, M. and Vince, R. (eds) (2004) *Organising Reflection*. Aldershot: Ashgate.

Richardson, L. (1990) *Writing Strategies: Reaching Diverse Audiences*. Newbury Park, CA: Sage.

Richardson, L. (2000) Writing: A method of inquiry. In N. Denzin and Y. Lincoln (eds) *Handbook of Qualitative Research* (2nd edn). Thousand Oaks, CA: Sage.

Richens, B. (1995) *Beginning Journeys . . . Reflective Practice and Journalling: A Collection of Work, Volume 1*. Christchurch, NZ: Department of Nursing, Midwifery and Health Education.

Ricoeur, P. (1976) *Interpretation Theory: Discourse and the Surplus of Meaning*. Fort Worth: Texas Christian University Press.

Riemann, G. (2000) *Die Arbeit in der sozialpädagogischen Familienberatung. Interaktionsprozesse in einem Handlungsfeld der sozialen Arbeit*. Weinheim and Munich: Juventa.

Riemann, G. (2003) A joint project against the backdrop of a research tradition: An introduction to 'Doing Biographical Research'. *Forum Qualitative Sozialforschung*, 4(3). http://www.qualitative-research.net/fqs-texte/3-03/3-03hrsg-e.htm (accessed 27 September 2005).

Riemann, G. (2005a) Ethnographies of practice – practicing ethnography. Resources for self-reflective social work. *Journal of Social Work Practice*, 19(1): 87–101.

Riemann, G. (2005b) Zur Bedeutung ethnographischer und erzählanalytischer Arbeitsweisen für die (Selbst-)Reflexion professioneller Arbeit. Ein Erfahrungsbericht. In B. Völter, G. Dausien, H. Lutz and G. Rosenthal (eds) *Biographieforschung im Diskurs*, pp. 248–270. Wiesbaden: VS Verlag.

Riemann, G. (2005c) Zur Bedeutung von Forschungswerkstätten in der Tradition von Anselm Strauss. Paper presented to 1. Berliner Methodentreffen Qualitative Forschung, 24–25 June. http://www.berliner-methodentreffen.de/material/2005/riemann.pdf (accessed 12 September 2005).

Riemann, G. (2005d) Trying to make sense of cases: Features and problems of social workers' case discussions. *Qualitative Social Work*, 4(4): 405–22.

Riemann, G. and Schütze, F. (1987) Some notes on a student research workshop on biography analysis, interaction analysis, and analysis of social worlds. In E. Hoerning and W. Fischer (eds), *Newsletter of the International Sociological Association Research Committee*, 38: 54–70.

Riessman, C. (1993) *Narrative Analysis*. Newbury Park, CA: Sage.

Riessman, C.K. (2000) Stigma and everyday resistance practice: Childless women in South India. *Gender and Society*, 14(1): 111–135.

Risner, D. (2002) Motion and marking in reflective practice. *Reflective Practice*, 3(1): 5–19.

Roberts, A.E.K. (2002) Advancing practice through continuing professional education: The case for reflection. *British Journal of Occupational Therapy*, 65(5): 237–41.

Rolfe, G. (2000) *Research, Truth and Authority; Postmodern Perspectives on Nursing*. Basingstoke: Macmillan.

Rolfe, G. (2002) *Closing the Theory–Practice Gap: A New Paradigm for Nursing*. Oxford: Butterworth-Heinemann.

Rolfe, G., Freshwater, D. and Jasper, M. (2001) *Critical Reflection for Nursing and the Helping Professions: A User's Guide*. Basingstoke: Palgrave Macmillan.

Rorty, R. (1989) *Contingency, Irony, and Solidarity*. Cambridge: Cambridge University Press.

Rorty, R. (ed.) (1992) *The Linguistic Turn: Essays in Philosophical Method*. Chicago: University of Chicago Press.

Rosenwald, G.C. and Ochberg, R. (eds) (1992) Introduction: Life stories, cultural politics, and self-understanding. In G.C. Rosenwald and R. Ochberg (eds) *Storied Lives: The Cultural Politics of Self-Understanding*. New Haven, CT: Yale University Press.

Sacks, H. (1984) On doing being ordinary. In J.M. Atkinson and B. Heritage (eds) *Structures of Social Action: Studies in Conversation Analysis*. Cambridge: Cambridge University Press.

Sacks, O. (1986) *The Man who Mistook his Wife for a Hat*. London: Picador.

Saleesby, D. (1997) *The Strengths Perspective in Social Work Practice* (2nd edn). New York: Longman.

Sanjek, R. (ed.) (1990) *Fieldnotes. The Makings of Anthropology*. Ithaca, NY: Cornell University Press.

Schegloff, E. and Sacks, H. (1973) Opening up closings. *Semiotica*, 8: 289–327.

Schneider, J. and Wang, L. (2002) Telling true stories, writing fictions, doing ethnography at century's end: Stories of subjectivity and care from urban China.

In C. Barron, N. Bruce and D. Nunan (eds) *Knowledge and Discourse: Towards an Ecology of Language*. Harlow: Longman.

Schön, D.A. (1983) *The Reflective Practitioner: How Professionals Think in Action*. New York: Basic Books.

Schön, D. A. (1987) *Educating the Critically Reflective Practitioner: Toward a New Design for Teaching and Learning in the Professions*. San Francisco: Jossey-Bass.

Schön, D.A. (1991) *The Reflective Practitioner: How Professionals Think in Action* (2nd reprint). Avebury: Ashgate Publishing.

Schön, D. A. (1992) Designing as reflective conversation with the materials of a design situation. *Knowledge-Based Systems*, 5(1): 3–14.

Schön, D. A. (1994) Teaching artistry through reflection-in-action. In H. Tsoukas (ed.) *New Thinking in Organizational Behaviour*, pp. 235–49. Oxford: Butterworth-Heinemann.

Schön, D. (1995) Reflective inquiry in social work practice. In P.McC. Hess and E.J. Mullen (eds) *Practitioner–Researcher Partnerships: Building Knowledge from, in, and for practice*. Washington, DC: NASW Press.

Schön, D. A. and Rein, M. (1994) *Frame Reflection: Toward the Resolution of intractable Policy Controversies*. New York: Basic Books.

Schore, A. (1994) *Affect Regulation and the Origin of the Self*. Hove. Lawrence Erlbaum.

Schütze, F. (1992) Sozialarbeit als 'bescheidene' Profession. In B. Dewe, W. Ferchhoff and F.-O. Radtke (eds) *Erziehen als Profession. Zur Logik professionellen Handelns in pädagogischen Feldern*, pp. 132–70. Opladen: Leske und Budrich.

Schütze, F. (1994) Ethnographie und sozialwissenschaftliche Methoden der Feldforschung. Eine mögliche methodische Orientierung in der Ausbildung und Praxis der Sozialen Arbeit? In N. Groddeck and M. Schumann (eds) *Modernisierung Sozialer Arbeit durch Methodenentwicklung und -reflexion*, pp. 189–297. Freiburg: Lambertus.

Scott, J.W. (1992) Experience. In J Butler and J Scott (eds) *Feminists Theorize the Political*, pp. 22–40. New York: Routledge.

Seibert, K.W. and Daudelin, M.W. (1999) *The Role of Reflection in Managerial Learning: Theory, Research, and Practice*. Westport, CT: Quorum.

Shepherd, M. (2004) Reflections on developing a reflective journal as a management advisor. *Reflective Practice*, 5(2): 199–208.

Slim, H. and Thomson, P. (1995) *Listening for a change: Oral testimony and Community Development*. Philadelphia: New Society.

Smith, A. (1998) Learning about reflection. *Journal of Advanced Nursing*, 28(4): 891–8.

Smith, B.H. (1981) Narrative versions, narrative theories. In W.J. Mitchell (ed.) *On Narrative*. Chicago, University of Chicago Press

Smith, D. (1987) *The Everyday World as Problematic: A Feminist Sociology*. Boston: Northwestern University Press.

Smith, L.T. (2005) On tricky ground: Researching the native in the age of uncertainty. In N. Denzin and Y. Lincoln (eds) *The Handbook of Qualitiative Research* (3rd edn). Thousand Oaks, CA: Sage.

Smyth, J. (1988) Deliberating upon reflection in action as a critical form of professional education. *Studies in Continuing Education*, 10(2), 164–171.

Soloman, B.A. and Felder, R.M. (1999) *Index of Learning Style Questions*. http://www.ncsu.edu/felder-public/ILSdir/ilsweb.html (accessed 15 May 2005).

Stark, S.S., Stronach, I. and Cooke, P. (1999) Reflection and the gap between practice, education and research in nursing. *Journal of Practice Teaching*, 2(2): 6–20.

Steier, F. (1989) Towards a radical and ecological constructivist approach to family communication. *Journal of Applied Communication Research*, 17: 1–26.

Steier, F. (1991) Introduction: Research as a self-reflexivity, self-reflexivity as social process. In F. Steier (ed.) *Research and Reflexivity*, pp. 1–11. London: Sage.

Stein, D. (2000) Teaching critical reflection. *Myths and Realities*, 7. http://www.cete.org/acve/docgen.asp?tbl=mr&ID=98 (accessed 30 January 2006).

Stoecker, R. (2001) Community-based research: The next new thing. A Report to the Corella and Bertram F. Bonner Foundation and Campus Compact. http://comm-org.wisc.edu/papers99/hess.htm.

Stoecker, R. (2002) Community–university collaborations: future choices. The College of New Jersey Community-Engaged Learning Workshop. http://comm-org.wisc.edu/drafts/cbrutep2.htm.

Stoecker, R. (2003) Community-based research: From practice to theory and back again. *Michigan Journal of Community Service Learning*, 9(2): 35–46.

Strauss, A. (1987) *Qualitative Analysis for Social Scientists*. Cambridge: Cambridge University Press

Sultana, R. and Baldacchino, G. (1994) Sociology and Maltese society: The field and its context. In R. Sultana and G. Baldacchino (eds) *Maltese Society: A Sociological Inquiry*, pp 1–21. Msida, Malta: Mireva.

Sunday Circle (2002) Therese Vella interviews Professor Oliver Friggieri: 'No Time for Simplifications'. *Sunday Circle*, March: 47–8.

Sung-Chan, P.L. (2000a) Learning from an action experiment: Putting Schön's reciprocal-reflection theory into practice. *Cybernetics and Human Knowing*, 7 (2–3): 17–30.

Sung-Chan P.L. (2000b) A collaborative-action research into the teaching and learning of systemic family practice to school social work in Hong Kong. Unpublished doctoral dissertation, Graduate School of Sociology and Social Policy, University of Nottingham.

Sung-Chan, P.L., Yuen-Tsang, W.K.A. and Dou, Z.Y. (2003) Women struggling in the margins: identity crises of unemployed women in Beijing. In H.B. Ku, and M.K. Lee (eds) *Social Exclusion and Marginality in Chinese Societies*, pp. 145–66. Hong Kong: Social Policy Studies Centre, Hong Kong Polytechnic University.

Swoyer, C. (2003) Relativism. In *Stanford Encyclopedia of Philosophy* http://plato.stanford.edu/entries/relativism/ (accessed 1 April 2005)

Tabone, C. (1995) *Maltese Families in Transition – A Sociological Investigation.* Sta Venera, Malta: Ministry for Social Development.

Tappan, M. and Brown, L. (1991) Stories told and lessons learned. In C. Witherell and N. Noddings (eds) *Stories Lives Tell: Narrative and Dialogue in Education,* pp. 171–92. New York: Teachers College Press.

Task Force on Social Work Research (1991) *Building Social Work Knowledge for Effective Services and Policies: A Plan for Research Development.* Austin: University of Texas at Austin School of Social Work.

Taylor, B.J. (2000) *Reflective Practice: A Guide for Nurses and Midwives.* Buckingham: Open University Press.

Taylor, C. (2003) Narrating practice: Reflective accounts and the textual construction of reality. *Journal of Advanced Nursing,* 42(3): 244–51.

Taylor, C. (2006) Narrating significant experience: reflective accounts and the production of (self) knowledge. *British Journal of Social Work,* 36(2): 189–206.

Taylor, C. and White, S. (2000) *Practising Reflexivity in Health and Welfare. Making Knowledge.* Buckingham: Open University Press.

Taylor, C. and White, S. (2001) Knowledge, truth and reflexivity: the problem of judgement in social work. *Journal of Social Work,* 1(1): 37–59.

Taylor C. and White, S. (2005) Knowledge and reasoning in social work: Educating for humane judgement. *British Journal of Social Work,* 35. 1–10.

Taylor, E.W. (2000) Analysing research on transformative learning theory. In J. Mezirow and associates, *Learning as Transformation: Critical Perspectives on a Theory in Progress.* San Francisco: Jossey-Bass.

Taylor E.W. (2001) Transformative learning theory: a neurobiological perspective of the role of emotions and unconscious ways of knowing. *International Journal of Lifelong Education,* 20(3): 218–36.

Taylor, I. (1997) *Developing Learning in Professional Education: Partnerships for Practice.* Buckingham: SRHE and Open University Press.

Taylor, I., Thomas, J. and Sage, H. (1999) Portfolios for learning and assessment: Laying the foundations for continuing professional education. *Social Work Education,* 8(2): 147–60.

ten Have, P. (1999) *Doing Conversation Analysis. A Practical Guide.* London: Sage.

Thagard, P. (2000) *How Scientists Explain Disease.* Princeton, NJ: Princeton University Press.

Thorpe, K. (2004) Reflective learning journals from concept to practice. *Reflective Practice,* 5(3): 327–43.

Trompenaars, F.A. and Hampden-Turner, C.A. (1998) *Riding the Waves of Culture: Understanding Cultural Diversity in Global Business.* New York, McGraw-Hill.

Tsang, W.K. (2003) Journaling from internship to practice teaching. *Reflective Practice,* 4(2): 221–40.

Turzynski, K. (2001) Process recording: a student's perspective. *Journal of Child Health Care,* 5(1): 30–4.

Varela, F.J. (1999) *Ethical Know-How: Action, Wisdom and Cognition*. Stanford, CA: Stanford University Press.

van Dijk, T.A. (1997) The Study of Discourse. In T.A. van Dijk (ed.) *Discourse as Structure and Process*, pp. 1–34. London: Sage.

van Maanen, J. (1988) *Tales of the Field: On Writing Ethnography*. Chicago: University of Chicago Press.

von Foerster, H. (ed.) (1974) *Cybernetics if Cybernetics*. Urbana: University of Illinois, Biological Computer Laboratory.

von Glasersfeld, E. (1997) Distinguishing the Observer: An Attempt at Interpreting Maturana. http://www.oikos.org/vonobserv.htm (accessed 30 January 2006).

Vygotsky, L. (1978) *Mind in Society*. Cambridge, MA: Harvard University Press.

Wadsworth, Y (1992) *Everyday Evaluation on the Run*. Melbourne: Action Research Issues Association.

Wadsworth, Y. (1998) 'Coming to the table': Some conditions for achieving consumer-focused evaluation of human services by service providers and service users. *Evaluation Journal of Australasia*, 10(1–2): 11–29.

Walker, K. (2000) Nursing, narrative and research. Towards a poetics and politics of orality. In G. Rolfe (ed.) *Research, Truth and Authority: Post-modern Perspectives on Nursing*, pp. 87–102. Basingstoke: Macmillan.

Walker, T. (1988) Whose discourse? In S. Woolgar (ed.) *New Frontiers in the Sociology of Knowledge*, pp. 55–79. London: Sage.

Walsh, T.C. (2002) Structured process recording: a comprehensive model that incorporated the strengths perspective. *Social Work Education*, 21(1): 23–34.

Wattam, C. (1989) Investigating child sexual abuse – a question of relevance. In H. Blagg, J.A. Hughes and C. Wattam (eds) *Child Sexual Abuse: Listening, Hearing and Validating the Experiences of Children*, pp. 27–43. Harlow: Longman.

Webb, D. (1990) Puritans and paradigms: a speculation on the form of new moralities in social work. *Social Work and Social Sciences Review*, 2(2): 146–9.

Wenger, E. (1998) *Communities of Practice: Learning, Meaning, Identity*. Cambridge: Cambridge University Press.

Whipp, J.L. (2003) Scaffolding critical reflection in online discussions: Helping prospective teachers think deeply about field experiences in urban schools. *Journal of Teacher Education*, 54(4): 321–33.

White, H. (1989) The rhetoric of interpretation. In P. Hernadi (ed.) *The Rhetoric of Interpretation and the Interpretation of Rhetoric*, pp. 1–22. Durham, NC: Duke University Press.

White, M. and Epston, D. (1990) *Narrative Means to Therapeutic Ends*. New York: W.W. Norton.

White, S. (1997) Performing social work: An ethnographic study of talk and text in a metropolitan social services department. Unpublished PhD thesis, University of Salford.

White, S. (1998) Examining the artfulness of risk talk. In A. Jokinen, K. Juhila and T. Poso, *Constructing Social Work Practices*, Aldershot: Ashgate.

White, S. (2001) Auto-ethnography as reflexive inquiry: The research act as self surveillance. In I. Shaw and N. Gould (eds) *Qualitative Social Work Research: Method and Content*. London: Sage.

White, S. (2002) Accomplishing the case in paediatrics and child health: medicine and morality in inter-professional talk. *Sociology of Health and Illness*, 24(4): 409–35.

White, S. and Featherstone, B. (2005) Communicating misunderstandings: multi-agency work as social practice. *Child and Family Social Work*, 10: 207–16.

White, S. and Stancombe, J. (2003) *Clinical Judgement in the Health and Welfare Professions: Extending the Evidence Base*. Maidenhead: Open University Press.

Whitmore, E. and Stuart, C. (2001) Problematizing partnerships: Negotiating community based research and evaluation in the classroom. Paper presented at the annual conference of the American Evaluation Association, St Louis, MO.

Winnicott, D.W. (1965) *The Maturational Process and the Facilitating Environment: Studies in the Theory of Emotional Development*. London: Hogarth Press.

Winnicott, D.W. (1971) *Playing and Reality*. London: Tavistock.

Winter, R. (1987) *Action-Research and the Nature of Social Inquiry. Professional Innovation and Educational Work*. Aldershot: Avebury.

Winter, R. and Munn-Giddings, C. (2001) *A Handbook for Action Research in Health and Social Care*. London: Routledge.

Wisløff, E.M.S. (1998) *Det handler om å lære. Om ansvar, kreativitet, frigjøring og reflekterende fortellinger*. Oslo: Tano Aschehoug.

Wittgenstein, L. (1961) *Tractatus Logico-philosophicus*. London: Routledge & Kegan Paul

Wong, M., Kember, D., Wong, F. and Loke, A. (2001) The affective dimensions of reflection. In D. Kember with A. Jones, A. Loke, J. McKay, K. Sinclair, H. Tse, C. Webb, F. Wong, M. Wong, and E. Yeung, *Reflective Teaching and Learning in the Health Professions*. Oxford: Blackwell.

Woolgar, S. (1988) Reflexivity is the ethnographer of the text. In S. Woolgar (ed.) *New Frontiers in the Sociology of Knowledge*, pp. 14–34. London: Sage.

Yelloly, M. (1995) Professional competence and higher education. In M. Yelloly and M. Henkel (eds) *Learning and Teaching in Social Work*, pp. 51–66. London: Jessica Kingsley.

Yeung, F., Kember, D., Jones, A., Loke, A., McKay, J., Sinclair, K., Tse, H., Webb, C., Wong, F. and Wong, M. (1999) Determining the level of reflective thinking from students' written journals using a coding system based on the work of Mezirow. *International Journal of Lifelong Education*, 18(1): 18–30.

Yuen-Tsang, W.K.A. (1997) *Towards a Chinese Conception of Social Support: A Study on the Social Support Networks of Chinese Working Mothers in Beijing*. London: Ashgate.

Yuen-Tsang W.K.A., and Sung-Chan, P.L. (2002) Capacity building through networking: Integrating professional knowledge with indigenous practice. In N.T. Tan and I. Dodds (eds) *Social Work around the World II*, pp. 111–22. Bern: International Federation of Social Workers.

Index

Locators shown in *italics* refer to diagrams and illustrations.

Related books from Open University Press

Purchase from www.openup.co.uk or order through your local bookseller

---

PRACTISING REFLEXIVITY IN HEALTH AND WELFARE
MAKING KNOWLEDGE

Carolyn Taylor and Susan White

This promises to be a very important and influential book . . . The authors write well and deal with difficult and complex ideas in an accessible way and in a way that makes their implications for practice available to practitioners . . . There has been much discussion in recent years of the notion of the reflexive practitioner but as yet there are few texts available to help practitioners both understand the concept and integrate it directly into their practice. This is thus likely to be a core text for some years to come.

Professor Nigel Parton, University of Huddersfield

In recent years, professional practice in health and welfare has come under increasing scrutiny. The dominant response to this has been technical and procedural, as epitomized by the evidence based practice movement. This book offers an alternative, and equally rigorous approach to helping trainers and professionals to understand and analyse their practice. Drawing on a hitherto under-utilized literature about argument and persuasion, originating in qualitative research, ethnomethodology, conversation analysis and discursive psychology, the book provides a new and original perspective on the concept of professional reflexivity. It explores, not only how knowledge is used in professional practice, but how it is made and generated in everyday encounters. It will be a valuable resource for practitioners in health and welfare as well as students in health and social science disciplines.

Contents
Introduction – **Part I: Developing a theoretical framework** – *Arguing and thinking: Implications for professional practice* – *Knowledge, truth and reflexive practice* – *Analysing talk and text: Building a conceptual framework* – *Conversational strategies: Lessons from everyday talk* – **Part II: Analysing talk and text in health and welfare** – *'The appropriate client': Service users constructing their case* – *Doing professional authority: Practitioners constructing accounts* – *Arguing the case: Professionals talking together* – *Analysing written text: Documents, records and reports* – *Making knowledge: The Louise Woodward case* – *Practising reflexivity: Beyond objectivity and subjectivity* – *Glossary* – *Bibliography* – *Index.*

256pp   0 335 20518 6 (Paperback)

REFLECTIVE PRACTICE
A GUIDE FOR NURSES AND MIDWIVES
SECOND EDITION

Bev Taylor

- What is reflective practice?
- How can nurses and midwives improve their practice through reflection?
- How can nurses and midwives maintain reflective practices?

This book provides a practical guide to help nurses and midwives improve their work practices constantly. The new edition includes expanded sections on the nature of reflection and practice, preparing for reflection, and types of reflection, plus a new chapter on the 'Taylor Model of Reflection' and reflective practice in research and scholarship.

The writing style is accessible to any nurse or midwife interested in reflecting on her or his practice and the practice stories are of relevance to both new and experienced clinicians.

Reflective Practice is essential reading for nurses and midwives who are being introduced to reflective processes in their education and practice, and also for renewing interest and enthusiasm for health workers and practitioners who use reflective practices in their day-to-day work.

Contents
Introduction – The nature of reflection and practice – Preparing for reflection – The Taylor model of reflection – Types of reflection – Technical reflection – Practical reflection – Emancipatory reflection – Reflective practice in research and scholarship – Reflection as a lifelong process – References – Index.

0 335 21742 7 (Paperback)   0 335 21743 5 (Hardback)

SOCIAL WORK SKILLS
A PRACTICE HANDBOOK
SECOND EDITION

Pamela Trevithick

Written by an experienced academic-practitioner, the new edition of this best-selling text is updated to include the current educational, policy and practice context of social work.

The new edition contains additional material on social work methods and approaches, and revised sections on the importance of psychological and sociological theories, as well as more information on multi-disciplinary working, communication with children, and the use of language and jargon in social work.

The main focus of the book is on how skills can be perfected and made transferable across different contexts, service user groups and countries. The handbook is essential reading for all social work students and a valuable reference tool for practicing social workers and human service professionals.

Contents
Introduction – The importance of communication skills within social work – Creative listening – Observing and analysing non-verbal forms of communication – Using theory and research to enhance practice skills – Evidence-based practice: the importance of assessment, effective decision-making and evaluation skills – Basic interviewing skills – Providing help, guidance and direction – Enabling, empowerment and partnership skills – Dealing with conflict and defining professional boundaries and accountability – Conclusion – Notes – Bibliography – Index.

c.240pp   0 335 21499 1 (Paperback)   0 335 21500 9 (Hardback)